Power and Privilege
at an African University

Power and Privilege at an African University

Pierre L. van den Berghe

with the assistance of
Paul Alabi
Catherine M. Nuttney
Peter Olori
A. K. Sonaike

SCHENKMAN PUBLISHING COMPANY, INC.
CAMBRIDGE, MASSACHUSETTS

Distributed by General Learning Press

Schenkman books are distributed by

GENERAL LEARNING PRESS
250 JAMES STREET
MORRISTOWN, NEW JERSEY

CONTENTS

CHARTS

TABLES

To Yakubu Gowon, who showed that power does not necessarily corrupt.

ACKNOWLEDGMENTS

My first and most obvious debt is to the entire university community at Ilosho who not only made my research an extremely interesting venture, but contributed greatly through their warmth and hospitality to making my stay in Nigeria one of the happiest periods of my life. The climate of unhampered intellectual freedom which I found at Ilosho was all the more remarkable as the country was in the midst of a civil war. There are many people whom I should like to mention by name in recognition of their generous and wholehearted cooperation. However, the special nature of this work might expose them to embarrassment *vis à vis* their colleagues, so I must reluctantly leave most names unmentioned. The graciousness and patience with which they put up with an inquisitive sociologist, and a foreigner at that, are moving proofs of trust and friendship. If, as is alas inevitable, some of what I say about the University irritates them, I hope they will accept my gratitude and assurance that I tried to write with malice towards none, and according to the canons of my discipline.

To the University authorities, especially Senate and the Vice-Chancellor, I am grateful for their permission to conduct the study, and for their active cooperation in it. I hope that my findings will be of use to the institution and will thus vindicate their trust in me.

The title page of the book is meant to give to my four assistants the recognition they deserve. They were not simply collectors of facts but active participants in a research team. They helped formulate the research strategy, and had a hand in most of the phases of the field work. I can only hope that they learned as much from me as I did from them.

To my colleagues in the Sociology Department, and indeed in other departments as well, I owe many hours of stimulating discussion, and a very congenial academic atmosphere. The Acting Head of the Department in particular relieved me of a most unwelcome job to which I find myself more than averagely allergic, and thus allowed me to enjoy all the privileges and few of the responsibilities of my professorship. Among my colleagues who gave the manuscript the benefit of their criticisms, I should like to mention Jacob Ajayi, David Brokensha, William Chambliss, Philip Foster, Robert

Gavin, Richard Schermerhorn and David Spain. For capable and cheerful clerical assistance in Ilosho I am indebted to Mr. Ahanor, and in Seattle to Mrs. Beulah Reddaway who efficiently converted my scribblings into a neat typescript, a task which requires considerable graphological as well as typographical skills. My wife, Irmgard, contributed, as usual, to the logistics of an impeccably run household, and provided me with an invaluable sounding board for ideas and research problems.

Finally, I should like to thank the Rockefeller Foundation without whose financial support I should probably never have come to Nigeria at all. Not only did the Foundation sponsor my visiting professorship at Ilosho, but it also gave me a generous research grant to conduct the present study. Because of the large amount of support which the Foundation has given to the University of Ilosho, however, it is doubly important to stress that my research was a totally independent undertaking, and most assuredly *not* an "evaluation study" done on behalf of the Foundation. The Foundation is, as anybody else, free to draw the conclusions it chooses from my study, but it is not in any way accountable for the views contained therein. Nor am I, of course, accountable for the actions or policies of the Foundation. The entire study was undertaken with a clear understanding that I would be acting as an independent scholar *vis à vis* the University, the Foundation, the Nigerian and American governments, and indeed any other agency. Those are the only terms on which I would have undertaken the study in the first place. I am thus quite prepared to assume entire intellectual responsibility for the contents of this book.

Introduction

To the best of my knowledge, this study, conducted from July, 1968 to June, 1969, is the first comprehensive sociological survey of an African university. In many ways, it is surprising that this should be so. Several African universities are residential in the sense that both teaching staff and students live for the most part on campus; hence these universities are nicely self-contained communities, ideally suited for a study such as this one.[1]

To assert that this study is comprehensive is somewhat of an overstatement, because, obviously, this monograph stresses some topics much more heavily than others, and indeed omits a number of them altogether. This study did not begin with a set of specific hypotheses to be tested, nor does my research include everything of conceivable relevance to the University of Ilosho (U.I.). Instead, the focus is on the political structure of U.I., on social stratification and mobility, and on problems of ethnicity. These closely interrelated problems are of great importance to the development of Nigeria, where U.I. is located. In all of these areas, then, the attempt is to understand not only the micro-system of the University, but the latter's place in the larger multi-national state of Nigeria. For example, the concern is not solely with the academic community, but with the interplay between University and "national" politics, with the role of the University in the emergence of Nigeria's new stratification system, and with the vast network of kinship, locality and ethnicity ties which links U.I. with larger communities outside the ivory tower. In short, beyond endeavoring to understand the basic structure of the University, the study raises the problems of integration or lack of it between the University and the larger society. The present monograph is principally a case study of structure and process at a University in a post-colonial, multi-national state. The nature of the University is incomprehensible without constant reference to the larger society, a topic to which Chapter Two is specifically devoted, but the importance of which shall already become obvious in the historical Chapter One.

1

Rapport

Several conditions are instrumental for the successful completion of the present type of research. Ideally, the researcher should be both an insider, and indeed a high-status one, and an outsider, to the University. As a Visiting Professor, my academic rank was high enough to give me access to virtually all sources of information and to several important committees and corporate bodies of the University. Even when I could not personally attend meetings, e.g. of the Council, I had little difficulty in discovering what had taken place by interviewing committee members. Yet my short tenure of one year and the fact that I was not a Nigerian put me clearly in the category of an outsider without permanent stake in either the country or the University.

This is not to say that my role was always easy. For one thing, my Rockefeller Foundation sponsorship and my citizenship identified me with the second largest expatriate "tribe," one which was widely resented by both Nigerian and English staff for a variety of reasons. For another, the fact that I was a 24-hour-a-day participant observer imposed a certain uneasiness on relations with some colleagues who were conscious of being "guinea pigs." I was, of course, completely candid about my aims, and it was fairly common knowledge on campus that I was doing research on the University. In fact, my research was even the subject of a Senate debate.

Nevertheless, the vast majority of the people were extremely cooperative and willing informants. Nearly all my colleagues on the teaching staff, both Nigerian and foreign, were sufficiently acquainted with the norms of scientific research to accept the legitimacy and the value of the study, and a great many of them, being individualistic scholars actively engaged in academic politics, were quite willing to talk even about the most delicate and confidential of topics.

The Senior Administrative Staff and the Intermediate and Junior Staff were, on the whole, slightly more reluctant to talk freely. Not being academics, they did not have as clear an understanding of the study and hence they were sometimes suspicious. In addition, their positions were more vulnerable, and being part of the administration, they tended to take a less detached point of view than the academics. The defensiveness of some of the senior administrators was also heightened by a steady stream of press attacks and "probes" into the University. One of the senior administrators in particular was at first uncooperative and described my study as "useless" and "harmful to the University," but later when he saw some of my preliminary results his attitude became more positive. On the other hand, many of the Junior and Intermediate Staff were visibly flattered at the interest which a professor took in them, and were extremely kind and cooperative, perhaps sometimes in the hope that my research would result in an improvement of their living and work conditions. Students were on the whole quite willing to talk, except for some Student Union officials who had been under heavy fire for alleged misappropriation of funds and mismanagement of Union affairs.

Rapport, then, was not much of a problem. I lived on campus as did most of the Senior Staff, and I was accepted as a member of the university community. Even my transient status did not set me apart; the turnover of expatriate staff had always been relatively rapid, most foreigners spending between two and five years in Nigeria. In the racially tolerant atmosphere of West Africa, color was hardly an obstacle, and the supreme self-confidence of most Nigerian academics made human relations pleasantly free of the uneasiness which characterizes parts of the continent where the colonial legacy is still obtrusive.

Unlike many situations of field work where the researcher is a stranger to the society he studies, where he has to make concerted efforts to be accepted, and where he continues to be regarded as an outsider, my assistants and myself were regular members of the organization we studied. We had well defined roles which did not set us in any way apart from the rest of our peers in our respective status categories. Some degree of mutual discomfort sometimes was caused by my research role, especially among a few of my social science colleagues who were more aware of the nature of my investigations. A few went as far as to express doubts as to the value of the study, fears about its consequences to the University, or concern about invasion of privacy, but my research role was defined as fully legitimate according to the norms of the academic profession. Most colleagues felt that the subject, though unusual, was worthwhile and interesting.

The most common reaction was amusement at finding that I was training my research arsenal inwardly. This was felt to be a novel, incongruous and perhaps slightly embarrassing thing to do, but a "fair enough" one all the same. Some who held grudges against the administration, or a certain ethnic group, or a Department Head believed my study might "expose" what they felt to be wrong with the institution. Others, who enjoyed the game of university politics, took an intellectual interest in analyzing the situation with me. Others yet, mostly among the subordinate staff, perceived my study as part of the authorities' soul-searching attempts to bridge the gap between the living conditions of Junior and Senior Staff. (Simultaneously with my study, several *ad hoc* committees were investigating schools, health conditions and overcrowding in Junior Staff housing on campus, and many people saw me as just one other such investigator, presumably aiming to improve matters.)

I deliberately declined to accept any administrative responsibility in my department, and at Senate and other meetings I refrained from participating actively in controversial issues. In short, I attempted to play the role of a "minimally participating observer" in anything except my teaching responsibilities, and the recruitment of staff for my department. Even though my professorial status would normally have given me the departmental Headship, I requested not to assume this role.

Sources of Data

This study is based on four main types of data:

1) Voluminous existing records contained a great deal of information. With the exception of the confidential files about Senior Staff, I had access to almost all important documents. Frequently, the data were not in immediately usable form, and had to be laboriously collected and analyzed. This was especially true of the statistical information about students and staff. This work was done mostly by my four research assistants: Catherine M. Nuttney, a British post-graduate student worked on the student files, and my three Nigerian undergraduate assistants, Paul Alabi, Peter Olori and A. K. Sonaike, did most of the rest of the analysis. Other documents were in more directly usable form. The main written sources included published books, pamphlets and articles about the University, student publications, newspaper cuttings, the University Calendar, Gazette and Bulletin, the minutes and agenda of the Council, Senate and committees, student and personnel records, the files of various organizations such as the Association of University Teachers, and the University Workers' Union, results of student elections, speeches delivered at formal meetings, correspondence and openletters, memoranda, announcements on bulletin boards, examination papers, admission records, housing surveys, and the like.

Access to documents was inversely proportional to the status category of the persons to whom the documents referred. I was routinely granted access to the personnel records of the Intermediate and Subordinate Staff. It required a Senate debate to allow a post-graduate assistant to analyze the student files. As to the Senior Staff files, I was denied permission to work even on the summary data cards containing such non-sensitive items of information as name, age, sex, nationality, department, rank, date of appointment and the like. (Much of the information about Senior Staff was collected more laboriously through the University Calendar and through interviews.)

2) Supplementary written data, including life histories written by students, were collected specifically for this study. No questionnaires were used.

3) Interviews were a major source of information. Between 250 and 300

persons contributed verbal information to this study, and some thirty key informants were interviewed three or more times for periods of up to twelve hours each. These interviews varied in form and content. Some three-fourths of them were conducted by myself, and the remainder by my three Nigerian research assistants. For status reasons, I interviewed mostly Senior Staff, while my assistants concentrated on fellow students and Subordinate and Intermediate Staff. In a highly stratified and status-conscious society such as Nigeria, rapport is on the whole inversely proportional to the status gap between interviewer and respondent. However, I also interviewed some students and Junior Staff myself. The research assistants not only interviewed other persons, but they were extensively interviewed by myself, mostly about student affairs, and thus became themselves key informants in the study. Our weekly staff meetings, where we discussed the past week's work and planned that of the coming week, were especially valuable as these gave rise to lively discussions and disagreements between my assistants on the interpretation of campus events as well as on the substance of the issues at stake.

Interviews ranged from short and completely informal ones where a few questions were asked in the course of casual conversation, to fairly lengthy formal and structured ones where the person would be met by appointment and be asked a series of questions on definite topics about which he was especially conversant. In no cases were written interview schedules used. Our most common practice was to take cursory notes during the interview, unless the informant preferred not to have his words recorded in his presence. These sketchy notes were then written out in full as soon as possible after the interview. No tape recorders were used so as not to interfere with rapport, and also because the information was seldom of such a nature that the exact phrasing mattered. However, where relevant, key phrases were recorded verbatim during the interviews.

Informants were always assured of confidentiality, and were told that they would only be quoted with their express permission if at all. For most of the teaching staff, this was taken for granted, though a number of students and Junior Staff asked for specific reassurance on this point.

Virtually all interviews were conducted in English, a language in which all students and Senior Staff were fluent, and most of the Junior Staff conversant enough for interview purposes. Occasionally, however, the research assistants interviewed members of their own ethnic group in their mother tongue if the respondent showed preference for it over English.

Most interviews ranged from 45 minutes to one hour and a half, but the content of the interviews varied widely. Some people were interviewed mostly about their life history, especially the educational aspect of it. More commonly, key persons such as club or union officials, deans and heads of departments, members of committees, or persons involved in present or past controversies were questioned about the specific aspect of university life with which they were most directly concerned. Senior Staff were interviewed mostly in their own offices which were usually quiet, private and comfortable. For students and Junior Staff, when such conditions could not normally be met at their place of work, interviews often were held in my home or office, or in a quiet shady place outdoors.

In as heterogeneous and complex a community as the University of Ilosho, it was necessary to rely on a great number of informants. Indeed, the University is not only stratified into three estates, but segmented by nationality, "race," sex, religion, ethnicity, faculty, place of residence, and profession, to mention only the most salient lines of cleavage. Perhaps no more than three or four members of the University, mostly senior Nigerian staff of long standing, have anything like a general overview of the community. Most people's view of the system is extremely fragmentary. The choice of informants was thus primarily dictated by the need to cover all major segments of the University. In fact, even the choice of my assistants, apart from criteria of ability and prior research experience, was also dictated by considerations of sectional representation. (One was British, three Nigerians; two were men and two women; of the Nigerians, two were Yoruba and one a representative of the "minorities;" one was post-graduate and three undergraduates.)

As in most community studies, there was a class bias in the selection of the informants. Disproportionately many of the Senior Staff and especially professors were among the key informants. But, in the nature of the case, high status people are closer to the center of power, and thus have access to more crucial information and have a less fragmentary view of the system. Nevertheless, informants were drawn from every major section of the community, from market women to students, from labor union officials to senior administrators, and from secretaries to professors.

Of the ethnic groups that used to play an important role in University affairs until 1966, the Ibo are clearly under-represented because of their massive departure, especially at the Senior Staff level. This, however, reflects a traumatic change in the life of the University and the country, rather than a selective bias on my part. By default, most of my senior Nigerian informants were Yoruba, with a sprinkling of Edo, Ijaw, Ibibio and other Southern minorities. Nevertheless, this possible source of bias was remedied by interviewing expatriates, both on the Ilosho campus and on neighboring ones, who had been sympathetic to senior Ibo before the gathering of the storm in 1966–67.

4) Observation, almost all of it of a participant nature, was the last major source of data. Some forms of behavior such as language use were recorded

on pre-arranged schedules, but in most cases the data were recorded as narrative field notes written as soon as possible after the event. All three of my Nigerian assistants and myself attended a wide variety of events such as graduation ceremonies, student and staff dances, symposia, students' and workers' meetings and elections, statutory meetings of Senate, Faculty Boards and Committees, sport events, political demonstrations, public debates, theater performances, dinner and cocktail parties, religious services, charity bazaars, club gatherings, weddings, funerals, naming ceremonies, and so on.

Ethical Problems

Apart from the question of protecting the confidentiality of the source of information, there also arose the problem of maintaining as great a measure of anonymity about the actors as was consistent with an accurate description of the situation. At one extreme was the suggestion that even the name of the country be disguised. The very size, prominence and special character of Nigeria among African countries made it clear that it would be a silly charade to concoct fictitious ethnic and place names when the locale would be immediately recognizable to almost anybody. It would be like writing about the United States and hoping that readers would mistake it for Honduras or Paraguay. The next step was to use pseudonyms for the University itself and for individual actors when the analysis made it necessary to refer to specific persons. The arguments against disguising the name of the University were that this would prevent me from referring directly to the many printed sources about the University, and that anybody who knows anything about Nigeria would instantaneously recognize the University anyway. Despite these arguments, I decided to use a fictitious place name for the University. To my knowledge, there is no such place as Ilosho, and, while my Nigerian readers will be able to substitute the correct name for it, this disguise, thin as it is, might at least protect the University and its members from possible embarrassment abroad. In this connection, I must stress as strongly as I can that most of the implied or explicit criticisms which I make of Ilosho apply with minor variations to many other African and indeed non-African universities, and that therefore any step which might shift some of the burden of invidious exposure from the particular subject of my research was worth taking.

The rationale for disguising the names of persons was even stronger. Except for national political figures outside the University, and my assistants who play no role as actors in the book but whose work deserves recognition, all names in this monograph are fictitious. Insofar as was possible, the situation was analyzed without reference to specific persons at all, though in a few cases of prominent actors, especially Vice-Chancellors, this was impossible without distorting the account. Again, the use of pseudonyms will not prevent local readers from filling the cross-word puzzle with great ease, but at least they will be spared the embarrassment of seeing their name in print in a context which they might find distressing. Nearly all the events referring to specific persons are part of the public domain and have been extensively reported on in newspapers, pamphlets, books and other generally available printed sources. Thus, even when actors are easily recognizable despite the use of pseudonyms, there can be no question of breach of confidence. Finally, the Nigerian press in reporting many of these events has not been notable for its restraint and discretion, and has dropped names with great relish and frequency, often on the strength of the flimsiest rumors.

Here I have reported as fact only what could be confirmed from two or more independent (and often antagonistic) sources; beliefs and opinions are specifically labelled as such, and only reported insofar as they were symptomatic of the situation described. It is axiomatic in sociology that beliefs held by participants in a social situation are themselves an integral part of social reality, and thus cannot be disregarded. In sociology, we face not a sharp dichotomy between opinions and facts, but several different levels of reality which we must, however, keep clearly distinct in our analysis.

Our field work was conducted during a difficult period in both the University's and the country's history. The fact that Nigeria was in the throes of a civil war, and indeed of the most serious African war since the Algerian War of Independence, had, of course, an important bearing on this study. By the time this work began, the University had passed the climax of its own internal crisis in the second half of 1967. Nevertheless, the University was still in a state of extremely rapid change. It was by no means a "normal" period in the life of the institution, but, then the University of Ilosho has scarcely ever known any such thing as "normalcy."

Objectivity and Values

Ever since such eminent scholars as Gunnar Myrdal have sent the example, it has been regarded as good sociology to state one's biases instead of hiding them under a pretense of objectivity. As concerns the Nigerian Civil War itself, scarcely anybody who is not totally callous could be an indifferent witness to the carnage, devastation and suffering which it has caused. This is even less possible for somebody of African birth like myself. Here is not the place to review the merits of both sides of the conflict. That countless acts of brutality have taken place on both sides is incontrovertible. This is true of all wars; indeed, it is the definition of war. Nevertheless, the Ibo secession was an act of suicidal folly made partly understandable by the ghastly pogroms of 1966, but, in last analysis, an extremely ill-considered act, fraught with dire consequences for Nigeria, for the whole of Africa, but most tragically of all for the Ibo people themselves.

If the principle of national sovereignty (defined ethnically) were accepted, Africa would be reduced even more than it already is to a multiplicity of squabbling, tiny, client states of the "developed" countries. A successful "Biafran" secession would have been the first step in the disintegration of a large, viable state into a score or more of Togos, Gabons and Gambias.

The ultimate irony of Ibo secession, however, was that "Biafra" itself was not a nation-state but a multi-national state dominated by a large ethnic group, i.e. very much the same kind of state from which the Ibo tried to secede. This is, of course, not to say that the existing artificial frontiers which are the legacy of colonialism should be regarded as sacrosanct; but clearly the solution lies in the creation of larger federations, not in the fragmentation of existing ones.

In short, it is very difficult if not impossible to apportion blame to one side more than the other. All Nigerians, and especially the educated classes, must bear a share of responsibility for the Nigerian tragedy; and so, of course, must the British colonial government which brought the explosive mixture into existence, and wittingly or unwittingly sowed the seeds of present conflicts. No side is any more right or wrong in an ethical sense, but events have shown which side has made the ghastly error. One is reminded of Talleyrand's cynical comment about Napoleon's execution of the Duke of Enghien: "It is more than a crime; it is a mistake."

A few words must be said about my conception of what a university should be like, as these values are also clearly relevant to the present study. A university should be a place accessible to all that have the necessary natural endowment to profit by it, not an additional instrument whereby a ruling class can maintain itself in power, nor a nurturing ground for a new privileged elite. Also, a university, especially a public one, should be open to scrutiny by the public which contributes to its budget through taxation.

In "developing" countries where resources are scarce, and where universities are a disproportionately heavy drain on public finances, universities should be showpieces of monastic austerity, not architectural prestige projects in a lavish international display of conspicuous consumption. Furthermore, there should be a kind of "cost-accounting" in terms of returns on intellectual investments. By this, I do not mean that a narrowly applied and technological conception of the university should prevail, but that sterile scholasticism is a luxury which "developing" universities can ill afford. For example, it is the height of wastefulness for African universities to have departments of Classics devoted to the study of ancient Greek and Latin. Or before establishing an astrophysics observatory, one should ask whether it would not be better to develop economics, parasitology or soil chemistry.

Social scientists, physicians, lawyers, historians, geographers and indeed all scholars working in Africa should be concerned not only with the development of piecemeal solutions to local problems, and with superficial curriculum revisions to incorporate more African material, but should also make the much more fundamental effort of *rethinking their disciplines* and emancipating themselves from the Euro-centric perspective that still dominates many of these fields. The need is perhaps greatest and most obvious in the social sciences and humanities, but is not limited to them. For example in the medical field, the old conception of private practice and largely curative medicine should be abandoned in favor of public health with emphasis on preventive measures, family planning and a sociologically conscious medicine.

In my opinion, universities should also be lay, secular institutions. In so far as religion is taught there at all, it should be as a sociological specialty, not as theology in departments of religious studies. No public funds should be invested in building places of worship, and indeed none should exist on campus.

Finally universities should, by definition, be free of all forms of ascriptive discrimination based on such things as sex, religion, "race," ethnicity or social class. While most academics are agreed in principle on this point, universities are nevertheless rife with nepotism, favoritism, ethnic discrimination, anti-feminism, and other forms of behavior which negate or hinder the purposes of higher learning.

My only purpose for mentioning these points is to make the reader aware of what my position is, and how my values might have affected my study. Should the reader disagree with the substance of what I say, he shall have the satisfaction of finding evidence of bias.

Position of Expatriate Scholars in Africa

One last problem of wide import concerns the position of the "expatriate" scholar doing research in and about Africa, the so-called "Africanist." African scholars working in Africa wisely do not call themselves "Africanists" just as a European scholar working in Europe does not refer to himself as a "Europeanist." Someone aptly defined African Studies as the study of Africa by and for non-Africans. Here is not the place to review the close association of "Africanist" scholarship until the recent past with colonialism, and hence with a *Weltanschauung* which was at best very Euro-centric, and at worst downright racist.[2] "Africanists" have in the last ten years been under attack from many quarters, and justifiably so in many cases. They have been accused, mostly by Africans, by scholars from socialist countries, and by Afro-Americans, of distorting African realities, of propagating myths of savagery (noble and otherwise), of being racists, of serving wittingly or unwittingly the interests of colonialism and neo-colonialism, of exploiting the continent for their own selfish careerist aims without making any contribution in return, of having antiquarian interests unrelated to the needs of African countries, and of a multitude of other sins of omission or commission ranging from insensitivity to malevolence.

Consequently, European and American scholars working in Africa have become very sensitive and guilt-ridden in the last few years, and have tried to atone for either their own sins or those of their academic predecessors. I do not share these feelings of guilt, if only because I do not accept the principle of collective "racial" guilt on which these attitudes are largely based, even though many of the accusations made against the body of "Africanists" are valid. Personally, I do not regard myself as "white," and I resent all people who assume that the accident of skin pigmentation has any bearing on my behavior, scholarly or otherwise. Though an American by citizenship, and a francophone by native language, I am African by birth, and I like to think of myself as totally "detribalized," with a multiple affiliation in three continents: Africa, Europe and America.

The trouble with many of my colleagues' guilt feeling (and this is especially true in the United States where most academics are plagued with a domestic racial "hang-up" as well) is that it introduces new forms of biases in African scholarship which are perhaps even more insidious than the old ones because they are ostensibly benevolent. Basically, the desire to atone for the past has taken two forms among the "liberal" Euro-American scholarly establishment. At the conceptual level, it has led scholars to substitute for Euro-centrism not so much Afro-centrism (which would have been a healthy corrective), but rather a kind of neo-paternalistic double standard. This operates ostensibly "in favor" of Africa, but, in fact, it results in a new type of condescension which can have a devastating effect on Africa and Africans.

The neo-paternalism consists in not applying the same standards of criticism to phenomena in Africa as the scholars in question would use in reference to their own societies and fellow citizens. For fear of being branded racists or colonialists, Western (and Eastern) scholars have essentially suspended or watered down their standards of criticism *vis à vis* Africa and Africans. Corruption, inefficiency, militarism, bureaucratization, nepotism, ethnic particularism, oppression, exploitation, jingoism, and elitism which "liberals" stigmatize in no uncertain terms at home are explained away in the African context as "passing phenomena," "growing pains," "necessary evils," or simply the kind of thing to be expected in "developing countries." Thus, we are back, in a more insidious way, to the old stereotypes of lazy, backward, shiftless natives. A few foreign scholars like René Dumont (1966), Stanislav Andreski (1968), and Frantz Fanon (1963) have had the courage to apply their critical powers to Africa with no holds barred, but they have been a small minority.

The effects of this neo-paternalism on Africans, and especially on the intelligentsia, are quite damaging, and have contributed to maintaining Africa in its subordinate position on the world scene. Every "liberal" American or European professor who grants an undeserved Ph.D. to an African student, who abstains from criticizing the publications of his African colleagues, who warmly recommends a mediocrity to an African university on the assumption that the person cannot do much damage there and is good enough for a colonial university, is undermining the efforts of African countries to become intellectually independent, and thus indirectly preserving the quasi-proprietary rights of "Africanists" on their chosen field of scholarly activity. Nothing can be more intellectually castrating than this kind of condescension.

At a more practical level, the guilt feelings of many Western scholars lead them to respond to the demand for relevance by becoming handmaidens to the black mandarins who have become the successor-elites to the old colonial bureaucracies. By becoming policy advisers, experts, consultants, and the like to African governments, and by doing policy-oriented research, Western scholars are in effect providing the new ruling classes with the means to consolidate their power over the peasant masses. "Africanization" has meant the creation of a new cosmopolitan jet set of African bureaucrats and expatriate experts with a common interest in a mutually beneficial *status quo*. They share the same educational background, speak the same language, and espouse the same bureaucratic, technocratic and elitist values. This is the intellectual and cultural side of neocolonialism which, unlike the more obvious economic aspect of the phenomenon, has not received the attention it deserves.

There is indeed a need for "relevant" research in Africa, but there are two ways of defining relevance. The first one is the safe provision of technical answers to limited questions such as how to eradicate sleeping sickness, how to increase yam yields, how to control population growth, or how to provide adequate urban sanitation and housing. This conservative, technocratic definition is far and away the more common.

The second definition of relevance is much wider, more fundamental, and potentially much more radical and dangerous to vested interests. In the social sciences, it consists in studying the basic structure of society (which in last analysis means the differential distribution of privileges, power and wealth and all its concomitants) instead of concentrating on piecemeal and trivial aspects of social behavior. This should be our primary task as social scientists. Studying the basic structure of a society means, implicitly or explicitly, raising basic questions about the desirability and the mutability of the established order in terms of certain sets of goals or values. And there, of course, is where the dynamite comes in. That is why no established bureaucracy, military or civilian, capitalist or socialist, academic or commercial, wants that kind of relevance if it can help it. In the vast majority of African countries (and indeed in a great many non-African ones as well) that way of defining relevance is the quickest way for a national to find himself in jail or exile. It thus becomes doubly incumbent on the expatriate, who can engage in this kind of inquiry with relative impunity, to do so.

This is the sense in which I have tried to do relevant research here. My motivations for doing that kind of research are both intellectual and ideological. As a sociologist, the differential distribution of social rewards and the conflicts it engenders ranks high on my list of intellectually challenging problems. Although the specific constellation of factors described in the following chapters is, of course, unique to Nigeria, any one factor taken singly is universal or nearly so. Thus sociologically, what is true of Nigeria, is true, *mutatis mutandis,* of many other societies, especially the plural ones that have recently emerged from colonialism. And, at the most fundamental level of all, African reality is relevant to all societies. As a man interested in the human condition, I should like to contribute the little I can to the creation of a freer, more tolerant and more democratic order, both in the continent of my birth and in my country of adoption.

NOTES

[1] African universities have been extensively written about, notably by Sir Eric Ashby, Alexander Carr-Saunders, and Nduka Okafor, and the University of Ilosho alone has been the subject of two books written by former Principals of the institution, and is referred to in many other books (including novels), articles, and reports. But, to the best of my knowledge, no book-length sociological study of an African university has yet appeared in print.

[2] I have done so at greater length in the introduction to my *Africa, Social Problems of Change and Conflict* (1965).

CHAPTER ONE
Historical Background

The African academic tradition has two distinct historical sources. The first one, and by far the older, is the Islamic one represented by Al Azhar University in Cairo founded in the 10th century (some 300 years before Oxford and 650 years before Harvard), by Kairouine University in Fez, and by the defunct Sankore University which flourished in 16th century Timbuctoo until the Moroccan invasion of 1590. Sankore, unlike the other two great Koranic universities of North Africa, was not an Arab institution. Although Arabic was the language of learning (as was Latin in Medieval Europe), Sankore was a product of the black civilization of the Western Sudan which gave rise in succession to the great empires of Ghana, Mali and Songhai. Its importance as a center of learning may be judged by Leo Africanus' statement that the book trade in early 16th century Timbuctoo was one of the most profitable lines of business.[1] This is no mean statement considering that Timbuctoo was then the dominant commercial metropolis of the Western Sudan and one of the main Southern terminals of the trans-Saharan trade.

The second historical source of African universities, the Christian-European one, is of recent import and is still much more of an exotic product than Islamic learning which by now is thoroughly "africanized." The first European-style university appeared on African soil in 1827, when Fourah Bay College was established as a theological seminary in Sierra Leone. As far as most of tropical Africa is concerned, it was not until after the Second World War that university-level education really began. Of the universities of the new wave, now accounting for all but one of the tropical institutions, Ilosho is among the oldest, having been founded in 1948 along with what is now the University of Ghana. This head start has enabled Ilosho to establish itself as the "premier" university of Nigeria and one of the most distinguished in the whole of tropical Africa, a status of which it is very conscious. Now that racism and political oppression have reduced the South African

15

universities to mere shadows of their former selves, Ilosho has perhaps the best overall claim of any African university to international standing as a major center of original research and learning.

L. B. Macaulay, the first principal of University College, Ilosho (U.C.I.) records the selection of the site in the best tradition of European "exploration" of the impenetrable jungles of the "Dark Continent." He gives us in effect a colonial origin myth:

> At 5:30 p.m. on 28 December 1946 Sir William Hamilton Fife, Vice-Chancellor of the University of Aberdeen and leader of a delegation sent by the Inter-University Council for Higher Education in the Colonies, pushed his way through the undergrowth into the 'bush' a few miles north of the town of Ilosho in Nigeria until he reached a clearing where it was possible to see a few yards ahead. He planted his walking-stick firmly into the ground and said: 'Here shall be the University of Nigeria.' This book describes how his statement became a reality.[2]

What Sir William no doubt mistook for wild forest was in fact an intensively cultivated farmland full of palm trees, cocoa, oranges, kola, coffee, bananas, rubber, pawpaws, mangoes, peppers, yams and numerous other crops. A later survey showed that the 1600 acres first acquired as a site for the University College were occupied by 345 farmers and their families who had to be evicted (with compensation for their permanent crops, i.e. trees) before the construction of the campus began in early 1949. In 1955, the Government purchased an additional 1250 acres at a cost of £74,000 for the future extension of the University, but the University did not take physical possession of the new site until 1968. The site of the future university was on the outskirts of the largest city in tropical Africa, and indeed of a completely indigenous city that antedated the colonial period. It was located in the heartland of one of Africa's most impressive civilizations, among the then eight-million-strong Yoruba nation.

In 1947, L. B. Macaulay, a Cambridge-trained British entomologist with an applied interest in tropical medicine, was appointed Principal of the future University College, a post he held until 1953. By December 18, 1947, Macaulay had assembled an academic and senior administrative staff of twelve. Of the twelve foundation members of the Senior Staff, nine were British, with a strong representation of Cambridge graduates, one was a New Zealander and two were Nigerian. Macaulay notes that this proportion of one-sixth Nigerians among the Senior Staff was the highest which the University was to achieve for nearly ten years. Thus, it can be seen that U.C.I. was, until Nigerian Independence in 1960, an overwhelmingly British concern, with a powerful Cambridge influence on its academic and administrative make-up.

Three of the four non-Nigerian heads of the University and a disproportionate number of the academic staff have had ties with Cambridge, as
former students, staff, or administrators. The formal academic link between
the infant U.C.I. and Britain was, however, with the University of London.
Through a "Special Relationship" between the University of London and
the colonial institutions, U.C.I. students took London examinations and
received London degrees. That link continued until 1962 when U.C.I.
became the independent University of Ilosho (U.I.) and started giving
degrees of its own. The other colonial link of Ilosho, the Inter-University
Council, persists to this day, after a decade of political independence.

In January 1948, 104 students transferred from the Higher College of
Technology in Lagos to U.C.I., established residence in temporary quarters
in a former general hospital in the city of Ilosho, and started the University's
first academic session. Only three of the students were women. Nearly half
of the students were taking surveying and teachers' training courses which
did not lead to degrees, and only 55 of them were taking degree subjects in
arts, science and pre-medical studies. On February 2, U.C.I. was formally
opened by the Chief Commissioner of the Western Provinces of Nigeria with
all the pomp that the Principal could muster, but with, however, a slight
concession to local conditions. Macaulay writes:

> I felt that this was an occasion for all the colour and ceremony we could
> muster, and we wore academic dress. Academic gowns may be foreign to
> Nigeria, but a scarlet robe does help a Principal to compete a little in a coun-
> try where chiefs may be so colourfully apparelled. British convention demands
> that a gown should be worn over a black suit; this seemed unsuited to the
> tropics, so I devised our local adaptation for the occasion. I ruled that we
> should wear white under academic dress, and that a long-sleeved white shirt
> should suffice instead of a jacket. Those wearing scarlet gowns (only the
> Principal so far) were to wear white bow ties, and those wearing black gowns
> black ties.

Thus a combination of indigenous and exotic splendor set a precedent for
the lavish displays of academic pomp with which the University celebrates
its official functions.

Meanwhile, the permanent site of U.C.I. had been selected some four to
five miles north of the city, but construction had yet to begin. This called
for another ritual, performed by the Secretary of State for the Colonies on
November 17, 1948, and described by Macaulay:

> The ceremony went off quite well. The crowds were large and colourful. The
> Head of the Native Administration, the Oba of Ilosho, arrived on what could
> only be called 'a gaily caparisoned steed,' notwithstanding the fact that he was
> over eighty years old. Many other chiefs were present. The Governor, always

a good friend of the college, decided this time not to attend, not from any lack of interest, but because as he would have been the King's Representative he might have perforce found it difficult to see that the Secretary of State was the central figure. The academic procession was the first example of the sort that has been seen in Nigeria. Some of the robes had been hurriedly run up by local tailors from materials that the Universities represented might not have recognized, but the result competed well with the Native Rulers. Excellent speeches were made by the Secretary of State, the Emir of Abuja representing Northern Nigeria, Judge Nwoko representing the East (he incidentally also came from King's College, Cambridge), and Sir William Fyfe. The Secretary of State 'cut the sod.' Here we had some difficulty. The ground was very dry and powdery, and no discrete lump of turf could be removed. We therefore 'prefabricated' a sod, using some cement to hold it together, and we inserted the spade in the correct place for Mr. Creech-Jones to dig. The neatness of the result caused some comment! [3]

Four years later, enough buildings had been completed on the new site to make Foundation Day 1952 the formal opening of the new campus. By then, student enrollment had grown to 368, and 52 students had graduated. The Senior Staff was now composed of 117 members. Besides the three foundation faculties of Arts, Science, and Medicine, a Faculty of Agriculture had been added in 1950.

From the outset, the concern of the founders of the U.C.I. was to establish an institution which met the highest British academic standards. The Asquith Commission, Macaulay tells us, "had been very concerned to ensure that academic standards were maintained from the outset. They rejected proposals that the colleges should from the beginning give their own degrees, as these would not be likely to receive recognition. . . ." So concerned were the U.C.I. staff about "standards," that they even outdid the British universities. "At first many of those at Ilosho were over-anxious to preserve standards, and the London University examiners' duty was to suggest that a higher proportion of candidates should be allowed to pass."

Besides the *academic* emulation of the "best" British universities, U.C.I. authorities attempted from the first to reproduce the *social* conditions of Oxford and Cambridge as well. From the first, the intention was to create a West African intellectual and social elite patterned after the ideal of the Oxbridge gentleman-scholar. The University was residential, and students were assigned to halls of residence, which, though less autonomous than Oxford and Cambridge colleges, were, as far as the more limited resources allowed, modeled after them, complete with Master, high-tables, junior and senior common rooms, porter's lodges, formal dinners, and a vast servant meals.
staff to cater for the students' needs, sweep their rooms and wait on them at
In short, the conception of the Nigerian university was that, if it was to

be any good, it must replicate, with minor sartorial concessions to climate, the elite British pattern of Oxford and Cambridge, both in its conception of learning and in its social graces. "Nigeria's University" was Nigerian only by geographical location and in the composition of its student body. In every other respect, it was British. It should also be emphasized that the Oxbridge model used was not the more democratic version which was evolving during Britain's post-World-War-Two Labor Government days, but the Edwardian stereotype which the founders of U.C.I. remembered from their own student days. As usual, the colonies inherited the metropolitan pattern with a time-lag, and U.C.I. was thus a relatively low-cost colonial adaptation of an academic model which in Britain itself was already obsolete. In anticipation of the end of British political rule over Africa, the British were consciously creating a successor elite to themselves, an indigenous mandarinate in their own image.

It would be a serious mistake, however, to assume that this alien and elitist model of university education was imposed on Nigeria against the wishes of the Nigerians. The masses of the people, lacking both the experience of any kind of university and the channels to make their views known, did not in any significant way shape the formation of the University. At least in the South, they were probably in favor of establishing a university because it meant "progress" as well as more and better jobs. But they had little conception of what kind of institution it ought to be.

The elite in Nigeria was basically of two types. The "traditional" elite, which especially in the North meant a literate Muslim aristocracy, had, to be sure, an alternative model of scholarship, but one which was even more patently inappropriate to the needs of a developing country than the one proposed by the colonial masters. There remained the "modern" elite (overwhelmingly southern), i.e., the anglicized, Christian, mission-school educated class. In Yorubaland where U.C.I. was established, there emerged a small class of black Victorian gentlemen trained at British universities as far back as the second half of the 19th century. This anglicized intelligentsia produced Anglican bishops, barristers, physicians and politicians to whom "civilization" meant Britain, and who were strongly in favor of the importation of the British elitist pattern into Nigeria.[4] As a highly status-conscious group, the "modern" elite felt that any attempt by the British to create a more democratic, inexpensive and applied type of education better suited to Nigerian conditions would in fact be another device to introduce a cut-rate product "good enough for the colonies," and hence to keep the Nigerian elite as a whole in a subordinate position. Indeed, in a colonial context, any attempt to make university education more democratic would have made for invidious distinctions between the British-trained and the locally-trained elite.

To this factor must be added the extreme sensitivity of the Nigerian intelligentsia to the racism of their former colonial masters. While the pattern of racial discrimination was less blatant in colonial Nigeria than in Kenya or Rhodesia and did not much affect the average Nigerian who rarely came into contact with Europeans, British racial arrogance was acutely galling to the elite which did have the same qualifications as the colonial bureaucrats. Thus the Nigerian intelligentsia interpreted almost any attempt to deviate from the British model as a "lowering of standards" motivated by the alleged British belief that Africans were intellectually incapable of benefiting from the best that Britain had to offer. The modern Nigerian elite was thus quite adamant that the best was barely good enough for Nigeria, and the best meant Oxbridge, complete with its study of classical Greek and Latin.

With the exception of a few radicals, both Nigerians and expatriates, within U.C.I., the only significant voice which attacked U.C.I. for elitism and agitated for lower entrance requirements was the Nigerian press, which has been consistently hostile to the University. The press attacks on U.C.I. were, however, seriously undermined by the low regard of many Nigerian journalists for factual accuracy, and by the low caliber of their editorial polemics. Academics had an easy time dismissing badly presented but valid arguments as irresponsible.

The most vocal press attacks against the University were directed to charges of foreign control and racial discrimination. An "expatriation allowance" which gave non-Nigerians a total salary approximately one-third higher than that of Nigerians received such criticism that it was abolished in 1950, along with other differences in travel leave and fringe benefits. Nigerian staff were granted annual "home" leave to Britain on the same terms as the British, and the "expatriate allowance" was consolidated into a new higher "basic salary," given to all staff regardless of nationality. Interestingly, the salary differential between most Nigerians and most expatriates reappeared after independence when the British government decided to subsidize the salary of its nationals teaching overseas, and when most American teachers were supported by American foundations at an American salary level. Furthermore, in the interest of economy, O. P. Nwanneh, the first Nigerian Vice-Chancellor of the University, requested the Nigerian members of his staff voluntarily to relinquish their right to the paid annual leave to Britain in exchange for a lower local leave allowance and for a policy of more rapid promotions.

In addition to differences in terms of contract, University authorities were under fire for failure to africanize the staff fast enough, and for creating a climate which led Nigerians to leave U.C.I. shortly after arriving. Macaulay was sufficiently sensitive to such criticisms that he admits to discriminating *in favor of* Nigerians. For example, in 1950 Macaulay asked A. B. Akpe, a physician who falsely claimed having an advanced degree, to resign. Macaulay writes, "if he had been a European I would have seen that he was formally expelled and probably prosecuted into the bargain," and adds:

> There was later a comical sequel to this, for under the new Constitution adopted in 1954 Dr. Akpe returned to the college as a member of its Council, its supreme Governing Body, nominated by the Eastern Regional Governor-in-Council. By this time he had a D. Sc. degree, awarded as an 'Honorary Degree' by a negro university in America, so perhaps some of his colleagues thought everything was now all right! When Her Majesty the Queen visited the College in 1956 he was one of the eminent academic figures presented to her; one Nigerian lecturer told me that he considered this the most shameful episode in the history of the college.

In actual fact, "race" as such was seldom a salient issue or line of cleavage between members of the staff at U.C.I. Nevertheless, the colonial situation then existing put the University within a context of what in modern American usage could be called "institutional racism." Nigerians, and most especially intellectuals, were incensed at having to live under foreign rulers who, individually or collectively, latently or blatantly, *did* discriminate on racial grounds. The European staff reacted very sensitively to accusations of racism, and, in an attempt to absolve themselves of this charge, often discriminated in favor of Nigerians as Macaulay admitted.

From the start, "race" was more of an issue outside U.C.I., and in the relationship between U.C.I. and the general society, than within the University itself. Furthermore, after independence, "race" lost most of whatever importance it had in the early years of U.C.I. The same cannot be said of "tribalism" which generally became a sharper issue after independence.[5] Even in the early years, however, Macaulay reports isolated incidents of ethnic and religious tensions:

> Nigeria as a country is an artificial creation, and many people anticipated that differences which existed between those coming from different areas would give rise to trouble within the student body. There were from time to time quarrels which had a tribal or regional basis, but in my experience these were not common, and differences of opinion which appeared to reveal tribalism often had a political or religious origin. The small number of students from Northern Nigeria, particularly those who were Moslems, often felt that they were isolated. There were serious complaints that they were persecuted, and one student complained that he had been threatened with a beating up if he did not attend Christian chapel services. I think that in this case the man concerned had exaggerated what was intended as a joke, but in the circum-

stances it was a joke in bad taste and deplored by the vast majority of the students. I was glad to learn that the Students Christian Movement, which was one of our strongest undergraduate societies, took appropriate action to put an end to this situation. The most serious quarrel between Yoruba and Ibo students occurred in 1949 at the time when riots occurred at Enugu and many miners, mostly Ibos, were shot. Ibo students complained that Yorubas would not take part in sympathetic movements and I had to intervene when I found a Yoruba student besieged in his room with Ibos in the process of breaking down the door. Differences in the country as a whole were always mirrored inside the college, but on the whole the students got on well together as a group. There were occasions when they even set a good example to the Nigerian members of the staff, who sometimes allowed their actions and behaviour, inside as well as outside the college, to be governed by sectional rather than by Nigerian motives.

Concern for the display of ethnic particularism was shown by the deliberate policy of insuring that each hall of residence would approximate a random mixture of the ethnic groups. Notwithstanding these precautions, ethnicity became an ever more important line of cleavage at the University as the struggle for independence gave way to the struggle over the spoils of independence between the various ethnic segments of the elite. U.C.I. played a crucial role in this great tragedy which eventually led to the demise of the First Nigerian Republic, two military *coups d'état,* and two and one half years of bloody civil war.

University Authorities

A 1948 Ordinance, amended in 1954, vested ultimate authority in two statutory bodies with clearly differentiated areas of jurisdiction. A Senate (called Academic Board until 1954) was to make all academic decisions, subject, however, until 1962 to the University of London in matters of examination. It was composed of the Principal as *ex-officio* chairman and the more senior members of the teaching staff. Council, a smaller body which grew from an original nine members to twenty in 1969, was to have supreme authority on all matters other than academic. A third much larger and almost powerless body, Congregation, concerned itself primarily with questions affecting the material welfare of the Senior Staff.

In 1962, when the University of Ilosho Act of the now independent Nigerian Parliament transformed U.C.I. into the fully autonomous University of Ilosho (U.I.) granting its own degrees, the Principal became the Vice-Chancellor, the Vice-Principal became the Deputy Vice-Chancellor, and a fourth statutory body, Convocation, was established consisting in

effect of all members of Congregation and all graduates of the University who paid a nominal registration fee. Aside from being formally convened at the annual graduation exercise, the only effective function of Convocation has been to elect one member to Council.

The actual day-to-day conduct of University affairs was established under a dual system based on a distinction between policy-making and major decision-making on the one hand, and policy-implementation and routine decision-making on the other. The policy-making function was performed at the highest level by the Senate and Council, and at the operational level by their functionally specialized committees consisting principally of experienced senior academics. Thus, the major decision-making was in the hands of senior professors whose multiple memberships on key committees and bodies were the source of their power. This committee structure grew in complexity over time, but the oligarchic nature of the power structure remained fundamentally unchanged.

In addition to its committees structure, the Senate delegated some of its functions to its constituent Faculties, each of which met as Faculty Board (of Arts, Science, Medicine and so on). In contrast to the Senate, where membership was restricted to the more senior teachers, in the Faculty Board all teachers were members, and they all elected one of the Professors in their respective Faculty as Dean for one or two years. Below the Faculty level, each Department was headed by its single Professor, if the chair was occupied, or otherwise by a Senior Lecturer or Reader. The post of Professor and Head of Department was a permanent one, with the two functions almost co-terminous until the principle of multiple chairs per department was introduced in the 1960's.

The routine implementation of policy was vested in a cadre of full-time and professional university administrators who were not academics, nor even necessarily university graduates. The most senior of this administrative cadre was the Registrar whose status and area of competence became, as we shall see, matters of dispute in the history of the University. While lacking *de jure* almost all decision-making power, his intimate knowledge of the whole range of university affairs frequently put him in a strategic position where he could exercise considerable discretion in matters of importance. However, the definition of his role and that of his subordinates was clearly ancillary to the academics.

Relations to Government

In two major ways, the formative years of the University established practices and precedents which greatly contributed to its strength, independence,

FORMAL AUTHORITY STRUCTURE, UNIVERSITY OF ILOSHO

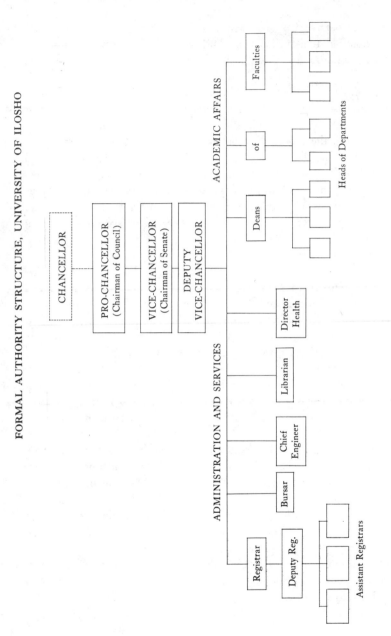

Note: Dotted lines indicate an honorific position. The structure is simplified for the sake of clarity.

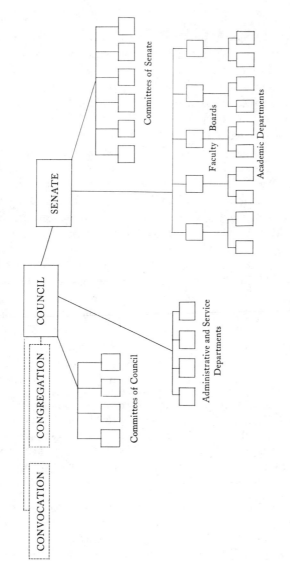

STRUCTURE OF STATUTORY BODIES AND DEPARTMENTS,
UNIVERSITY OF ILOSHO

Note: Dotted lines indicate bodies devoid of any substantial power. The structure is simplified for the sake of clarity.

and intellectual quality in later years, and which are probably in good part traceable to Macaulay's own stand on issues of university autonomy. First, U.C.I. remained relatively free of government pressures. Second, the internal control of university affairs remained solidly in the hands of academics, as distinguished from administrators. Independence from the government in the initial period resulted from the fact that U.C.I. was founded at a time when Britain was slowly preparing its political withdrawal from Nigeria. By 1954, Nigeria had internal self-government, and the tradition of non-interference in University affairs has, by and large, been respected since, with two or three notable exceptions in recent years. Certainly, compared to the pressures to which universities have been subjected since independence in countries like Ghana, Kenya, Senegal, Congo (Kinshasa), Ethiopia or Tanzania, Ilosho has been remarkably independent. Short of sedition, academics have been almost wholly free to criticize the government, even during the Civil War and the military regimes.

The tradition of academic dominance over university administrators was in good measure the product of Macaulay's anti-bureaucratic conception of the university. Macaulay's 1951 resignation from the chairmanship of the Council had the consequence of weakening the academic component of Council by establishing a precedent for the permanent dissociation of the chairmanship of Council from the Principalship, but it was certainly consistent with Macaulay's non-autocratic conception of his role. As to his attitude towards administrators, it was one of undisguised supercilliousness:

> Administration is inevitable. It should try to be efficient; it should make sure it is unobtrusive. Its job should be to see that the academic work of the college goes on as smoothly as possible, remembering that the college cannot live without the academic members however much their habits may irritate the administrators, whereas the academic staff at least imagine that they will get on quite well with no administrators.

But Macaulay's disdain for administration left a legacy of inefficiency from which the University never recovered. In an attempt to strengthen the administration of U.C.I., I. S. Simpson, a retired "Secretary General of the Faculties in the University of Cambridge," was appointed in 1953 as second Principal at Ilosho, a post he held for three years. A former colleague describes Simpson in the following terms:

> He was rigid, autocratic, inflexible and did not listen to anybody. He was much older than everybody else on the staff and was a 'grandfather type' who bullied his way through Academic Board and Committees. As a result he managed to unite the hitherto split Academic Board against his autocracy. Simpson was a dyed-in-the-wool administrator. He could only think in terms of the Cambridge model.

Simpson's book on U.C.I. shows a remarkable lack of sensitivity to the nature and needs of the society he was serving, and a lack of ability to adapt the Cambridge model to Ilosho. He devotes an entire chapter to "The Royal Visit" of 1956 when Queen Elizabeth and Prince Philip spent a day on campus and threw the college administration into a frenzy of protocolar anxiety: "no system of seniority or precedence had been evolved" and "the students were unaware of the time-honoured custom in the older universities of England of ignoring the students completely when there is a royal visit and using them to line the street as claquers." Elsewhere, Simpson hazards the guess that "local [Nigerian] languages may very soon disappear," [10] an astonishing prediction for anybody who has any knowledge of Nigeria.

Simpson took office just before Nigeria was granted internal self-government in preparation for complete independence six years later. Yet Simpson writes from the perspective of a Roman proconsul who fails to realize that the Empire has already crumbled from under him. His predecessor was sensitive to the political aspirations of the students, to their role as the intellectual vanguard of the independence movement, and to their difficult position of being caught between loyalty to a European-dominated university and devotion to their country's struggle for self-respect and self-determination. Under Simpson, relations between students and staff degenerated. From the outset, it became clear that the Oxbridge model of residential colleges was not going to work at Ilosho, and that the halls, originally patterned on that model, were gradually evolving toward American-style dormitories. Cultural barriers made it unattractive for the English staff to reside or eat in the halls. For one thing, the noise level in tropical countries where windows and doors are kept open for ventilation is always high, especially in a hall filled with young men. For another, the spicy Nigerian diet made eating in the halls an ordeal for most expatriate staff, as Macaulay describes: "Red pepper is a more important barrier to social intercourse between races than colour of skin! Most Nigerians eat food that is far hotter than the hottest South Indian curry; I learned to eat it, but I often saw colleagues groping for water with tears streaming down their faces at staff-student functions."

Among students, the paternalistic discipline of a British college was resented, especially having to be in between midnight and 6 a.m., and having to enter and leave through the porter's lodge. This often meant a detour of several hundred yards, and hence an inconvenience to the students. Students began to jump over the balustrade of the ground floor. In 1957, shortly after Simpson's term of office, the matter came to a head when wire-netting fences were erected on the ground floors of halls. Irate students tore down these fences overnight, and the new Principal, H. Parkinson, decided with the support of Council to suspend the entire student body for the rest of the term. Describing the incident, Simpson says that the students' nightly visits to the town of Ilosho were "sullying the College's reputation," and quotes the students: "The students said they refused to be confined like animals in cages and they wrote to the press on these lines." The students were readmitted for the second term of the year after individually signing a pledge to obey university rules. To this date, the wire netting still exists in some halls, and so does the porter's lodge, but ingenious students have evolved new ways of slipping in and out of hall unobtrusively, and the University authorities have the good sense not to try rigidly to enforce the regulations.

U.C.I.'s third and last British Principal was H. Parkinson, who came in 1956 from the Chair of History at the University College of the West Indies and remained in Ilosho until 1960. According to two Ilosho professors: "His regime was marked by the statesmanlike quality of his public utterances, by a remarkable but always controlled rate of expansion, and by his success in attracting to the College considerable benefactions from overseas." Under Parkinson, the teaching staff increased at an annual rate of over 10 per cent compared to 7 per cent under Simpson, while the student body grew by almost 25 per cent a year compared to a rate of 11 per cent under Simpson. (See Table I) Aside from achieving a rapid rate of growth, the Parkinson era reversed Simpson's heavy-handed attempts to change the balance of power in favor of administrators. Under Parkinson, the pattern of university governance by an oligarchy of professors operating through the Senate and its committee structure was consolidated, and the administration was again relegated to its original subordinate and rather inefficient role.

Nigerianization

The major historical significance of the Parkinson era, however, was that it constituted the transition from a British-dominated to a Nigerian-dominated institution. U.C.I. was being deliberately "Nigerianized" in preparation for Independence in October 1960. The early policy of Nigerianization meant accelerating the hiring of Nigerians on the teaching staff as much as possible without compromising high standards; promoting a few more Nigerian Senior Lecturers to professorships so as to darken the complexion of the hitherto nearly all-white Senate; appointing Nigerians to most senior administrative positions; and, most symbolically, choosing a Nigerian Principal to succeed Parkinson.

It might be expected that this process would have activated conflicts of interests between Nigerians and expatriates. In fact, for a variety of reasons,

TABLE 1 / NUMBER OF STUDENTS AND SENIOR STAFF,
UNIVERSITY OF ILOSHO

Academic Year	Senior Staff	Students	Student-Senior Staff Ratio
1948 (Jan.)	12	104	8.7
1948–49	50	190	3.8
49–50	62	288	4.6
50–51	75	327	4.4
51–52	84	338	4.0
52–53	117	368	3.1
53–54	121	407	3.4
54–55	144	476	3.3
55–56	146	586	4.0
56–57	163	563	3.5
57–58	181	747	4.1
58–59	217	1005	4.6
59–60	233	1113	4.8
60–61	278	1256	4.5
61–62	297	1644	5.5
62–63	329	1689	5.1
63–64	431	2018	4.7
64–65	499	2284	4.6
65–66	485	2687	5.5
66–67	488	2729	5.6
67–68	548	2559	4.7
68–69	619	2900 (est.)	4.7

this did not happen to any significant extent. Most foreign staff at the University accepted the principle of "africanization" (as it was known in the early days) in preparation for Independence, both in the country at large and at university. Africanization was easy to accept as most were transients without any permanent stake in Nigeria. Nigerianization in the University took almost entirely the form of filling vacancies left voluntarily by their prior, foreign incumbents. Even the few expatriates who stayed on for longer periods did not suffer from africanization, as the pressure for accelerated promotions for Nigerians soon generalized to accelerated promotions for everybody. This "promotion boom" did not get started on a big scale until after 1960, but it was a clear consequence of the policy of africanization, and, for a number of years, it was easy to sustain without much cost to the university because of the rapid rate of overall expansion. The more senior expatriates who were professors and heads of departments had security of tenure for as long as they cared to stay, and when moral pressure against their monopolization of power began to build up in the 1960's, the problem was solved by introducing the "American" principle of multiple professorships in various departments, instead of the old British pyramidal system of one chair per department.

Instead of creating cleavages along lines of "race" or citizenship, the transition to independence opened the Pandora's box of ethnic competition between the Nigerians. The University became a microcosm of what was happening in the country at large. The rapidity of the British departure created an acute scramble for scarce resources between educated Nigerians. Class conflicts did not play a significant role, first because the stratification system in the "modern sector" of Nigeria was still extremely fluid and ill-defined, and second because the competition was fiercest at the very top, i.e. for the few hundred elite positions in the bureaucracy, the political machine, the professions, and the academic world. Independence made very little difference in the lot of the overwhelming majority; the elite were the principal, not to say the sole, beneficiaries, and, hence, competition was almost limited to the top of the social hierarchy.

In addition to the relative insignificance of class conflicts in the pre-independence years, Nigeria was characterized by an enormous degree of ethnic heterogeneity, and by *greatly disparate rates of economic and educational development between ethnic groups,* especially between the "advanced" Southern groups on the one hand, and the "backward" Middle Belt and North on the other. Thus, in this highly artificial and loosely integrated multi-national state of Nigeria, it was almost inevitable that ethnicity would become the principal line of cleavage in political alignments. Many foreign observers optimistically and naively expected that the process of education and "Westernization" would reduce the significance of ethnicity among the educated elite. In terms of their *values,* the elite is indeed often urbane and universalistic, but their behavior is determined more by their interests than by their values. The ethnic constituency is the easiest to activate politically, and ethnicity is the most clear-cut and useful criterion to gain preferential access to scarce resources, to maintain one's position, and to eliminate most qualified competitors.

A more detailed examination of ethnic conflicts at Ilosho is presented below: here is a sketch of the nature of ethnic alignments which came to the fore-front of University life in the last 1950's, and remained ever since. The Nigerian intelligentsia is overwhelmingly Southern, composed of two of the three numerically largest groups in Nigeria, the Yoruba and the Ibo, plus a number of Southern "minority" ethnic groups, such as the Bini, Ishan, Ibibio, Efik, Ijaw, Itsekiri, Urhobo and so on.[7] These "minorities," being much smaller groups than the Yoruba and Ibo, only have a sprinkling of members in the intelligentsia, but their total representation is roughly pro-portional to that of the Yorubas and Ibos. On the other hand, the Northern groups, including both the "Middle Belt" of small "pagan" groups, and the solidly Muslim far North, composed largely of Hausa, Fulani and Kanuri, are almost totally excluded from the Western educated elite. Until quite recently, a Northerner had roughly only 1/200th the chance of a Southerner of entering university.

At the University, the Yoruba had from the start a dual advantage. The Yoruba were the first ethnic group to acquire Western education in sizeable numbers in the second half of the 19th century; thus there is a small Yoruba elite of third and fourth generation university graduates with a long-standing intellectual tradition, and whose children are best equipped to compete in secondary schools and universities. Secondly, and more importantly, U.C.I. was located in the heart of Yorubaland, close to the capital city of the Federation, which is itself enclosed in Yoruba territory and on the site of the provincial capital of the Western Region. The advantage of being close to the center of political power and among one's "own people" gave Yoruba academics both a political advantage and a much greater sense of security. This advantage was partly cancelled during the First Republic by the fact that the major party in the Western Region, the Action Group, was in opposition in the Federal Parliament, but a segment of the Yoruba intelligentsia aligned itself with the Nigerian National Democratic Party (NNDP), part of the coalition Federal government before the military coups of 1966. Given the strongly territorial nature of ethnicity, all non-Yoruba in Ilosho are "strangers," and not significantly less so if they are, say, Ibo or Efik as compared to Scottish or Canadian.

However, the conception of the University was always a "national" one,[8] and the campus has been regarded as a neutral, extra-territorial enclave, a kind of international settlement. The exotic nature of the University helped to make it an ivory tower rather than a Yoruba institution rooted in Yoruba soil. Nevertheless, the Yoruba staff inevitably found themselves much more "at home" than the relatively isolated members of other ethnic groups.

In the total University community, the Yoruba have always been the largest single group, but never a majority until the 1966 crisis when most Ibo went "home." Until 1966, the Ibo were consistently the second largest Nigerian group, and, in fact, close seconds to the Yoruba. The Yoruba, for example, have made up 42 per cent of all students who entered the University between 1948 and 1966, and the Ibo 31 per cent. Among the Nigerian Senior Staff, these proportions were nearly the same.

The main line of ethnic cleavage was thus clearly between Yoruba and Ibo, with the "minorities" and most of the expatriates tending to side with the Ibo and to "gang up" against the Yoruba. Until 1966, the Yoruba at U.C.I. were in political subordination, mainly because expatriates then constituted a vast majority of the ruling oligarchy of professors and wielded great power despite a by then predominantly Nigerian Council and University administration. Also, the Yoruba were largely excluded from power in a Federal Government which was, to all intents and purposes, an unlikely alliance of conservative Muslim feudalists from the North and Christian Ibo intellectuals, politicians and bureaucrats from the Southeast..

The foreigners, and notably the more senior British establishment, rode the storm of independence with great success, because instead of allowing the situation to degenerate into a white-black conflict, they squarely entered the game of Nigerian ethnic politics and overwhelmingly sided with the Ibo against the Yoruba. It would be tempting to give a machiavellian interpretation of this alliance in terms of an astute perception of group interests, but the situation was far more complex. Most expatriates identified more closely with Ibo colleagues than with other Nigerians in part because of cultural reasons. The Ibo intelligentsia in their relations to Europeans have generally presented themselves as admirers and emulators of Western culture, and consequently have helped establish the stereotype of the Ibo as "progressive," modern, dynamic, enterprising, Western-oriented, intelligent people, in contrast to their allegedly conservative, backward fellow countrymen. At the same time, many Ibo, coming from a traditionally stateless society lacking some of the more spectacular accomplishments of their Western and Northern neighbors, have felt culturally on the defensive *vis à vis* the Yoruba, the Bini, and Hausa and the Kanuri, and have not exhibited the pride of some of these other groups in their traditional cultures. Instead, the Ibo stressed the qualities that made them successful in the modern sector, e.g., in commerce, the professions, the civil service, and the academic world. Many Europeans were not insensitive to this subtle form of cultural flattery, and found it most comfortable to associate with those Nigerians whose values seemed to be most like their own. The Yoruba, on the other hand, especially the educated elite, often exhibit a tranquil and urbane self-confidence which makes them take the superiority of their way of life for granted, and show a deep sense of cultural pride and nationalism. The Yoruba gentleman often behaves with the same kind of self-assured supercilliousness as his British counterpart, and the latter has typically not responded kindly to this. Mutual aloofness, if not downright dislike often resulted.

The Principalship

The major bone of contention at U.C.I. was the Principalship. Suitable Nigerian candidates were still scarce in the late 1950's; most Nigerian academics were still in the junior ranks of the teaching staff, and only three were of professorial rank. The issue quickly resolved itself to a choice between a Yoruba and an Ibo contender. The latter, O. P. Nwanneh, the Professor of History at U.C.I., became Vice-Principal in 1959, and, supported by the British establishment, he assumed the Principalship the following year. This choice was not purely political: Nwanneh was indeed more distinguished academically than his Yoruba rival and was the most plausible choice at least within the ranks of the U.C.I. staff. Nevertheless, since this decision fell in line with the existing dominant alignment of British-Ibo against Yoruba, the ethnic cleavages within the University were aggravated.

When Nwanneh became Principal in 1960, he inherited a well-established institution of some 1250 students and nearly three hundred Senior Staff, and during his six tumultuous years in office, the University doubled again in size. Academically, U.C.I. was slowly gaining recognition as an institution of international caliber, and in December, 1962 the University of Ilosho Act was passed by the Nigerian Parliament, transforming U.C.I. into the autonomous University of Ilosho (U.I.). Henceforth U.I. conducted its own examinations and granted its own degrees. The link with the London-based Inter-University Council (I.U.C.) was maintained, however, and continued to the time of writing; this remaining colonial link perpetuated a powerful British influence in the selection of teaching staff, since the main function of I.U.C. is to solicit references on candidates and serve as an assessment panel. In practice, this meant that British and British-trained Nigerian candidates have had a much more "direct line" of entry into Ilosho than candidates from elsewhere. This link with I.U.C. also perpetuated a strong prejudice, shared by British and British-trained Nigerians alike, against degrees from non-British universities, especially American, Canadian, Indian and Eastern European ones.

The University of Ilosho Act also appointed Nwanneh as Vice-Chancellor (as the post of Principal was renamed) without specifying any time limit on his tenure. Thus, barring removal by Council on grounds of "misconduct or of inability to perform the functions of his office," Nwanneh became in effect Vice-Chancellor until his retirement or resignation. Nwanneh's British predecessors were also appointed without limitation of time, but the assumption was that they were all transient in Nigeria, as indeed they turned out to be. Now that the office was occupied by a Nigerian, it acquired a much greater potential permanency.

The New Universities

The year of Independence (1960) also marked the opening of a second and rival university in the Eastern Region, which, much to the annoyance of

Ilosho, preempted the title "University of Nigeria." Within the next two years, three more universities were opened. This proliferation of universities had a number of consequences for U.I., the most important being that there were now five institutions of higher learning, all with aspirations to academic excellence, competing with each other for an extremely scarce supply of qualified students and staff. The head-start of Ilosho enabled it to be in a much stronger bargaining position than the other four universities and to retain a substantial edge over them in terms of quality; but Ilosho lost many of its teachers and senior administrators to the other schools. In principle, a country of the size of Nigeria can well support five universities, and, eventually, the investment will undoubtedly pay. However, one can argue that the establishment of more universities was premature, since even Ilosho had not reached the critical size of 5,000 or more students when economies of scale begin to reduce the staggering cost of higher education. Consequently, all Nigerian universities suffered from being far below optimum size, and from having large numbers of vacancies on their teaching staff.

The establishment of the four new universities was dictated as much by political as by academic considerations. Each region, and each major ethnic group dominant in the three main regions wanted a university of its own. Geographical dispersal was not a major consideration; three of the five universities were located within 150 miles of each other in Yorubaland.

The Eastern University, which became defined as "Ibo," grew very rapidly to equal roughly Ilosho within a few years, but the Civil War closed it down from 1967 to 1970. In the North, political pressures resulted in the foundation of a University in an old Hausa city, close to Kaduna, the administrative capital of the Northern Region. As there are very few qualified students from the North, the University grew more slowly than either of the two older universities. Pressure developed to have a university at the site of the Federal capital, and so it too was founded some 100 miles away from Ilosho. Yoruba political pressures resulted in the establishment of a third university in Yorubaland, literally on the other side of the fence from the U.I. campus. All three of the newer universities had difficulty in attracting staff and in getting established as quality institutions, and they remained about half as big as their older sisters.

Although the newer universities slowed down the pace of development of Ilosho, they enhanced its prestige. U.I. became the apex of the Nigerian university structure, with by far the best established post-graduate programs. The Nigerian teaching staff at the other universities were drawn very heavily from Ilosho graduates, and the younger universities successfully raided U.I. with the offer of promotions and higher salaries. In the end, all the universities suffered under acute shortage of teachers. The superiority feelings of Ilosho students and staff members *vis à vis* "sister" universities also led to severe resentment, particularly between Ilosho and the Eastern university, the most successful of Ilosho's competitors. To the British or British-trained staff at Ilosho, the "Ibo University" represented the epitome of American academic mediocrity, as it was patterned after the American land-grant college and linked with Michigan State University.

Political Crises and the Civil War

During the Nwanneh regime, U.I. thrived from crisis to crisis. Ethnic conflicts gained steadily in intensity, and a long-standing feud between Nwanneh and the Registrar, B. M. Babalola, brought the University to the brink of collapse; but U.I. managed to survive the turmoil as well as the sudden departure of most of its Ibo staff in the months preceding the Civil War with only minimum damage to its quality. The civilian Federal Government in its five years of existence gradually sank into a morass of nepotism, corruption, ethnic particularism, and bureaucratic parasitism. Under a façade of parliamentary democracy (hailed in the West as a model of good government), an opportunistic alliance of Northern feudalists and Southern politicians organized themselves into what Stanislav Andreski aptly called a "kleptocracy," [11] pillaging the public purse for personal gain with considerable complicity from the Civil Service.

Had this ruling elite not been internally divided between fiercely competing ethnic segments, and had it not attempted to eliminate from a share of the spoils a substantial segment of the Yoruba elite, it might have stayed in power longer. By 1965, however, the Government had lost control of the Western Region and no amount of thuggery and election rigging could save the corrupt coalition. Yorubaland slipped into a state of chaos and anarchy in which rival political gangs of the Action Group and ruling NNDP engaged in daily rounds of arson and assassination. In January 1966, a military coup led by Ibo officers overthrew the civilian government, and after a bloody purge of most non-Ibo politicians who had been involved in the kleptocracy, reestablished a measure of order. The coup was soon interpreted by non-Ibos as an attempt by the Ibo to dominate the entire Federation, and, in July 1966, a counter-coup largely led by officers drawn from non-Muslim Northern minorities assumed power. The coup itself was less bloody than the first one, but, soon thereafter, in September, a wave of widespread anti-Ibo pogroms in the Hausa cities of the North killed several thousand Ibo and led to the exodus of more than one million Ibo from the North and West to the safety of their ethnic territory. Ibo army officers, with the complicity of Ibo intellectuals at the universities, including Ilosho, plotted for the secession of the Eastern Region, and having declared the independence of

"Biafra," plunged Nigeria into civil war from June, 1967 to January, 1970. After they lost the gamble that Chief Obafemi Awolowo and the Yoruba would side with the Ibo against the North, the Ibo had no chance of winning the war, but they fought with suicidal obstinacy at a cost of several hundred thousand lives, until their defeat and surrender in January, 1970.

The surprising thing is that the University emerged as unscathed at it did from this turmoil, remaining an island of safety and comparative sanity. Even at the height of fear and unrest in 1967, U.I. retained its "extra-territorial" status, and was often used as a place of refuge by Ibo townsmen during times of greatest uncertainty. The campus, under the special military protection of a 30-man infantry platoon, remained free of serious acts of violence during the war. Ironically, the most serious waves of violence on campus occurred both before and after the War. On October 14, 1965, students protested against the blatant rigging of election results by the ruling NNDP in the Western Region. The Western Regional Government retaliated by sending in riot police who went on a rampage, breaking windows and student property on campus, and indiscriminately assaulting and beating men and women students both inside and outside of buildings. This was the most blatant violation of the unwritten rule that the campus is off limits to the army and police unless university authorities request their presence. The next month, on November 16, the visit of Federal Prime Minister Balewa was marked by further disturbances. A few weeks later, Balewa, one of the few uncorrupt politicians of the First Republic, was assassinated by the officers who led the military coup. On February 1, 1971, a relatively trivial set of student complaints resulted for the first time in U.I. history in a riot fatality. When protesting students began throwing stones at the administration building, breaking windows and overturning the Vice-Chancellor's new Mercedes Benz, the riot police were called in by the university authorities. While the Vice-Chancellor and three of his staff hid in a toilet in fear of their lives, the police attempted to disperse the students, first with tear gas and rifle butts, and then with gunfire. The police claimed to have shot in the air, but one student was killed and four other persons seriously wounded. The University was closed for eleven days.

Academic Politics

As a Vice-Chancellor, Nwanneh played a complex role in a rapidly changing situation. He managed to be disliked by most of his colleagues, but even his detractors acknowledged his scholarship, his intellectual ability, and the success with which he attracted Ford and Rockefeller Foundation money to U.I., and thereby contributed to the institution's continued growth. Certainly Nwanneh had a powerful personality, but his autocracy was tempered by his numerous and prolonged absences from campus on various international conferences, speaking engagements, and fund-raising tours. Several senior expatriates who supported him accused him of finding it convenient to be away from campus whenever a storm gathered. In the end, at the time of the second military coup in July 1966, he was on leave in Britain; he stayed away for several months and finally resigned from the University in December without returning to it, but having taken to the Eastern Region his official car (which he returned several months and thousands of miles later).

Nwanneh's conception of his role was modeled after that of the President of an American university, i.e. of a true chief executive. During his years in office, he attempted to concentrate power in the Vice-Chancellorship through a variety of devices, but his success was relatively limited because, by 1960, the basic oligarchical structure of the University was well established. For the first two or three years of his term, Nwanneh was heavily reliant on a triumvirate of powerful senior expatriates, one of whom was his Deputy. These three men, referred to as the "bar establishment" because they were frequently seen settling University business at the bar of the Senior Staff Club, were, to all intents and purposes, running U.I. during Nwanneh's absences from campus; even when Nwanneh was in residence, he delegated most of the actual decision-making to the triumvirate.

After two or three years in office, Nwanneh's position of power had to some extent consolidated itself. Nwanneh was not interested in the details of administration, but rather in building his position and using it for personal and political ends. For the first time, the headship of the University was becoming clearly and ostensibly a *political* office, both "nationally" and within U.I. This was, of course, a direct result of the fact that the incumbent was now a Nigerian with extensive ties of kinship, locality, ethnicity, clientship, friendship, and so on, with thousands of local people, many of whom exerted more or less open pressure on the Vice-Chancellor to use his position to serve their ends. The extent to which these particularistic pressures exist is largely unrelated to the personality and predispositions of the incumbent. No Nigerian Vice-Chancellor can successfully resist them and stay in office.

Nwanneh's political strategy was to surround himself with a retinue of trustworthy clients, to place his *protégés* in key administrative positions such as deanships, department headships and senior administrative posts, and to undermine the authority of those whom he could neither trust nor remove from their jobs. One of the most common charges against Nwanneh was one of "tribalism," i.e., the accusation that he systematically favored fellow Ibo. There is unquestionable evidence that Nwanneh did maneuver to get a good many Ibo appointed, promoted, and placed in key positions, such as the Deanships of Agriculture and of Medicine (the two Deans were also related to each other and to Nwanneh by marriage), the Headship of the History Department, and the newly created Academic Office. Nwanneh's own rationalization for that policy was that he was trying to maintain an "ethnic balance" at U.I.; there had always been slightly more Yoruba than Ibo on the Senior Staff, and Nwanneh was ostensibly aiming at parity between these two groups.

The reality of academic politics was far too complex, however, to be accounted for purely in terms of ethnicity. In the first place, since the Ibo were destined for the foreseeable future to be a minority of some 15 to 25 per cent of the total Senior Staff, Nwanneh could not rely solely on fellow Ibo, and, as we have seen, support from the expatriates was absolutely essential. Over the years, by building up his constituency of Ibo clients, Nwanneh emancipated himself increasingly from reliance on expatriates, but, even then, lines were never drawn purely on the basis of ethnicity. Nwanneh also appointed a number of Yoruba to senior positions, and he had personal feuds with some of the Ibo. For example, the typical pattern in promotions to professorships for which there were both Yoruba and Ibo candidates was to promote both, but to give the key executive position such as the Department Headship to the Ibo, as was done, for example, in Nwanneh's own History Department. In all ranks, the proportion of Nigerians on the teaching staff increased substantially during the Nwanneh era. In 1962, about 28 per cent of the staff was Nigerian; by 1967, this had risen to a little over half. If the non-teaching Senior Staff was included, then the Nigerian proportion was about 60 per cent.

This process became increasingly easy with the acceptance of the principle of multiple professorships in various departments. Nwanneh was a strong advocate of multiple professorships which served a multiplicity of functions, all to the advantage not only of Nwanneh but of the entire teaching staff. Modeled after the American system, the multiple professorship allowed for a much less pyramidal and autocratic departmental structure by creating several academic peers in any given department, instead of one Professor and Head, with a number of Senior Lecturers and Lecturers under him. A corollary of the system was that departmental headships were to rotate between Professors, except that existing Heads could retain their positions. The implied accelerated promotions for a number of Senior Lecturers ensured its almost universal support. In the words of one Professor, "it was a case of the elite against the public purse."Another effect, and indeed intention, of the new policy was to speed up the Nigerianization of the Senate by allowing for the promotion of qualified Nigerians without having to wait for expatriate incumbents to vacate chairs. Expatriate Professors also favored the system because it relieved any pressure on them to make room for Nigerians. It simply meant a bigger cake for everybody. Even in the lower ranks, additional promotions to professorships led to chain reactions of accelerated promotions, and consequently to lower expectations of seniority and scholarly productivity at various levels of appointment. This process still continues, and the rank of Associate Professor is currently proliferating for candidates who are not yet quite worthy of full professorships, but who some years ago would have been considered only for Senior Lecturerships.

The policy of multiple professorships and rotating departmental headships also resulted in a number of important structural changes in the distribution of power. It weakened the department headships; it greatly enlarged the size of Senate, thereby reducing its efficiency as a decision-making body and putting greater stress on the smaller oligarchy of deans and "committee professors" within Senate; and, finally, it strengthened the Vice-Chancellor by giving him more discretion as to which of the professors should be appointed heads of departments.

The major stumbling block in Nwanneh's control of the University administration was the Registrar, B. M. Babalola, a Yoruba whom Nwanneh did not trust. In Babalola's words, "the attempt to kill the Registrarship began around November, 1962 and has been the source of continual friction between us. . . . I should politely remind you [Nwanneh] that I have status in this University. . . . I am either a Registrar or I am not." Nwanneh, on the other hand, accused Babalola of being "concerned more with the importance of his own office than with the smooth running of the University . . . he does not seem to accept that responsibility and power go together. . . . During the past two years the Registrar has not given me this support: in fact at times he has indulged in acts of sabotage and disloyalty." Nwanneh's technique to undermine Babalola consisted in removing academic affairs from the jurisdiction of the Registry by creating an Academic Office led by an Ibo under Nwanneh's immediate authority, and otherwise by-passing Babalola altogether, and dealing directly with Babalola's subordinates.

The point of no return in the conflict was reached with the events of October 14, 1965 already described. Numerous students and staff accused Babalola of knowing that the police would come, and of having deliberately left the campus in avoidance of his responsibilities. By mid-1966, the feud had become a ludicrous farce with exchanges of countermanding memos, "leaks" to the press, telephone threats, calls to the police, the locking of the Registrar out his office, "sit-ins" by the Registrar in subordinates' offices, and a legal cross-fire of injunctions and counter-injunctions which lasted until December 1967, one year after Nwanneh's resignation.

The crisis came to a head in June 1966 when a trivial disciplinary action against an Intermediate Staff clerk accused of fornicating in a university office escalated to a violent strike and demonstration by the non-Yoruba faction of the University Workers' Union against Babalola, demanding his resignation. The Council, under Nwanneh's recommendation, obliged by suspending Babalola from duty "in view of the grave and open defiance of the constituted authority of the University and its effect on the morale and discipline of the University as a whole," and each side started legal action against the other. In November, 1967, the dispute flared up again. Babalola attempted to resume duty on the strength of a court decision, but G. Hickerson, the Acting Vice-Chancellor since Nwanneh's resignation a year earlier, locked him out of his office on the ground that the Chairman of Council had instructed him that Babalola was still on leave. Finally, the conflict was so acute that the head of the Federal Military Government, General Yakubu Gowon summoned first Hickerson and Babalola and then the entire University Council to his Dodan Barracks headquarters in Lagos. Gowon sat in as mediator in a closed meeting of Council on November 30, until the issue was settled. By that time, the dispute was being regarded by most Yoruba, both inside and outside University, as a national cause, and not to have reinstated Babalola could have provoked grave disaffection for the Federal Government in the Western State, as Babalola had allied himself politically with Brigadier Adeyinka Adebayo, the Military Governor of the West. The Council resolved the crisis by dropping all court proceedings and reinstating Babalola in office. At the special meeting of Council on February 2, 1968, that body welcomed Babalola back "after his long leave of absence and commended him for putting his leave to good use by obtaining a University of London Bachelor's degree in law." This was the most serious internal crisis in the University's history, and one of the few occasions when the Government deemed it necessary to intervene directly in U.I. affairs.

Despite evidence of both nepotism and "tribalism" during the Nwanneh regime, Nwanneh was also a scholar concerned with the quality of the University. His candidates were, in most cases, persons of demonstrated academic competence. The Yoruba staff often interpreted the Nwanneh regime as a case of pure and simple Ibo domination. After all, Nwanneh and Azikiwe, the Ibo Governor General (and after the proclamation of the Republic, the President) were known to have been close associates, and Akpe, the Chairman of the Council appointed by Azikiwe was also an Ibo. In fact, the situation was much more complex. Nwanneh vehemently opposed Akpe's appointment as Chairman of Council, at least in part out of ethical considerations. Azikiwe's appointment of Akpe over Nwanneh's objections and over a nearly unanimous negative "advisory" vote by Council itself, caused a deep rift between Nwanneh and Azikiwe, and Nwanneh's protest weakened his general political position in the country, though it certainly gained him support within the University.[12]

Much as Nwanneh attempted to behave autocratically, he always encountered sufficient opposition to be only partially successful. He was forced by external pressures to play an ethnic game and to rely on the support of an Ibo constituency; but he also had to keep sufficient support among senior and conservative expatriates who sometimes led him into unpopular ventures. At the same time, he had enough intellectual and moral integrity to antagonize some Ibo, including some highly powerful ones. Within University, some of his closest Ibo associates seriously compromised Nwanneh both through their political plotting for secession which led to the Civil War, and through their dishonest financial dealings. By and large, U.I. remained relatively free of corruption compared to the venality of the civil service and politicians outside, but the latter years of the Nwanneh era were characterized by considerable dishonesty within the University. Most notorious were the contracting deals made by some Council members on various construction projects of dormitories and other buildings. But on a smaller scale, senior Ibo academics pilfered university supplies and used official vehicles for private purposes.[13] When secession was imminent, Ibo academics not only abandoned their posts without any notification or resignation, but, in several cases, absconded with university property such as laboratory and office equipment, records, keys, and official motorcars. Later, two of them had relatives submit affidavits in an attempt to change their birth dates so as to qualify for a university pension. In fairness to the Ibo, it should be added that dishonesty was by no means confined to them. The private use of university vehicles was common, and a group of expatriates who were running the Senior Staff Club, its adjacent store, and the University Bookstore were also charged with attempts at private profiteering.

The University increasingly became a microcosm of the ethnic conflicts and the venality of the country at large. In the second half of 1966, after the second military coup of July and the anti-Ibo pogroms of September, most Ibo felt unsafe in Ilosho, and either left the campus for the East or failed to return after the summer vacation. With three or four exceptions, all Ibo Senior Staff abandoned their posts in the fall of 1966, but a substantial number of junior Ibo staff and domestic servants remained, perhaps because they felt that their more humble status made them less conspicuous and vulnerable. Some 400 Ibo students also failed to return from vacation, but quite a few came back to continue their studies through the 1966–67 academic year, especially the final-year students. More Ibo left, however, after the outbreak of hostilities in mid-1967. A number of non-Ibo Easterners who went home during the long vacation of 1967 were prevented by the war from returning for the 1967–68 academic year, and some Ibibio,

Efik and Ijaw students who were suspected of not supporting secession were imprisoned or murdered by the Biafrans. Of a total of 766 new students admitted in 1967, only 43 came from the former Eastern Region and only 13 from the Ibo part thereof; 558 came from Yoruba country, and 140 from the Mid-Western State.

The University was facing a major crisis. Most expatriate and non-Ibo staff stayed at their posts, but nevertheless the departure of the Ibo staff seriously depleted many departments, already chronically understaffed before the crisis. The man, who, more than anybody else, can be credited for holding U.I. together was the Acting Vice-Chancellor, G. Hickerson, the long-time University Librarian, now past retirement age, and a New Zealander by nationality. That he should have succeeded is all the more surprising as he had been, along with other senior expatriates, closely associated with Nwanneh and identified with the anti-Yoruba and anti-Babalola faction. The Yoruba were, by default, far and away the largest group of Nigerians left at University, and many expatriates felt insecure. As an expatriate, and as an outspoken, short-tempered, energetic person who had often clashed with Babalola, with the Military Governor, and with other senior Nigerians within and outside the University, Hickerson was widely resented and attacked. There is little question, however, that his willingness to assume an onerous job in a critical situation, his demonstrated loyalty to the University, and his refusal to yield to the climate of panic and rumor-mongering went a long way in persuading a number of expatriates and even Junior Staff Ibo to stay, and in preventing the outbreak of disorders on campus. The University continued to operate under conditions amazingly close to normalcy. Student enrollment dropped by nearly 200 in the 1967–68 session, but by the following year, both students and staff exceeded pre-war levels.

In the initial weeks of the war when the Ibo troops advanced to within 150 miles of Ilosho and Lagos, rumors were rampant, and the campus experienced some confusion and considerable anxiety. There were numerous episodes of Ibo being intimidated, beaten up, and in a few cases killed by Hausa in town, and by soldiers at military road blocks off-campus, but the campus was under military protection and there was no violence at U.I. (A small military detachment of some 30 soldiers remained unobtrusively on campus for the whole of the war, and behaved very well, never intervening in University affairs.) The Military Governor of the Western State, Brigadier Adeyinka Adebayo, wanted to evacuate the some 1200 Ibo (mostly Junior Staff, servants and their families) who were still on campus in mid-1967, but Hickerson dissuaded him, and they stayed. A famous Yoruba playwright, and director of the U.I. School of Drama, was arrested on charges of plotting for Yoruba secession and detained for most of the war, but no other members of the University staff or students were interfered with by the government. Despite the war, a climate of nearly complete academic freedom reigned on campus, and both students and staff did criticize the government on several occasions, even to the point of accusing army officers of deliberately prolonging the war for private gain. Yet, short of clear sedition, as in the above case, the government did not intervene.

The Civil War radically altered the ethnic composition of both students and staff at the University. The Yoruba now accounted for some three-quarters of all students and of the Nigerian Senior Staff. By default as well as partly by design, the staff vacancies left by the departed Ibo were predominantly filled by Yoruba. The war, in effect, transformed U.I. from a Nigerian university dominated largely by an Ibo-British coalition but with strong Yoruba opposition, into a *de facto* Yoruba one, with the expatriates, especially the British, a disorganized and insecure minority. The departure of most Ibo did not reduce the amount of ethnic factionalism, however. Rather, the focus of strife changed from Ibo-Yoruba conflict, to the much more intricate game of factionalism within the Yoruba group.

As Nwanneh had hinted in his letter of resignation, it was very likely that his successor in the Vice-Chancellorship would be a Yoruba, and indeed this was the case.[14] A new set of ground rules was evolved to settle this highly crucial political issue of succession. The new Vice-Chancellor, to be chosen by a Joint Committee consisting of five members of the Senate and five members of the Council, was to be appointed for a period of three years, renewable once. This limit on the term of office obviously reduced the power of the Vice-Chancellorship as compared to the indefinite tenure which had obtained in the past. Also, the selection procedure by the joint committee institutionalized the principle of a strong academic voice in the choice.

After considerable discussion the Joint Committee adopted ten selection criteria for the new Vice-Chancellor: a candidate must have a good university education, a very high academic standing, and preferably have held a senior teaching or research post at a university; he must have had wide administrative experience and be capable of dynamic leadership; his stature must command national and international respect, particularly in the academic world; he must command respect and loyalty among his staff and students at U.I.; he must be a man "not likely to foster personal, racial, ethnic, political, religious or other national interests"; he must be morally sound and "free from financial embarrassment"; his health must be good and his personality "pleasant, strong but non-aggressive"; he must be a man of courage who takes decisions "on the merit of facts and principles, and not on the basis of pressures from individuals and groups"; he must preferably be under 55 years of age and married; and "above all, he must be a man of unassailable integrity." The Joint Committee considered the suitability of 16 candidates, including at least two expatriates from other African countries, narrowed the field to a short list of three, and finally offered the post to a fairly non-political Yoruba diplomat, who first accepted it, but then turned it down to accept an important international appointment. A second Joint Committee was formed and the procedure was repeated. On the second round, the process became much more political, with various Yoruba factions organizing around three or four major contenders. In the end, an internationally know psychiatrist from the town of Abeokuta, and a Professor in the Faculty of Medicine, C. T. Akinode, was chosen and assumed office in February, 1968.

Akinode took over a university of nearly 3000 students and some 600 Senior Staff, with a nearly completely Nigerianized administration and a teaching staff that was slightly over half Nigerian, the Yoruba constituting by far the largest ethnic group, and indeed a large majority of all Nigerians. As the field work was conducted during his regime, we shall reserve for a later chapter an account of it and close here our historical overview of the University's development.

NOTES

[1] Leo Africanus wrote: "Here in Timbuktu, there are great store of doctors, judges, priests and other learned men, bountifully maintained at the king's cost and charges. And hither are brought divers manuscripts or written books out of Barbary, which are sold for more money than any other merchandise." Quoted in Basil Davidson, ed., *The African Past*.

[2] The decision to use a fictitious name for the University prevents my referring to the two books written by former Principals about their institution. Similarly I had to delete all titles containing the real name of the University from the bibliography. This was obviously a cost to be paid for the sake of anonymity, but the specialist will experience no difficulty in identifying the University and thus finding the bibliographic sources. Names have been changed in the quotations in conformity with the rest of the text. Both books contain a more extensive historical account than I shall present here, but they are somewhat in the nature of semi-official accounts. This is especially true of I. S. Simpson's book. L. B. Macaulay's book is a much more candid, insightful, and personal document, but Simpson writes very much from a British and colonial perspective, and fails to capture the complexity of the society in which he was a host. Both books are revealing as accounts of the role and attitudes of two key British administrators of the University in its formative years, and of their relationship (or lack of it) to their host society. I have made an extensive use of these two books in this chapter, but not only as secondary sources, i.e. as pieces of historiography to be taken at face value. I have also used these two books as

primary sources, i.e. as sociological documents equally revealing of their authors as of the events they describe. A third book by two Ilosho dons also deals more briefly with the growth of U.C.I. and with problems of university education in Nigeria.

3 Simpson gives a corroborating account of the ritual in his book.

4 Thomas Hodgkin confirms that the African elite supported the importation of the European university pattern in Africa. He writes: "The leaders of African opinion in the 1940s unhesitatingly rejected substitutes. They were interested in the establishment of universities which would be equal in all respects —as regards status, academic standards, research facilities, value of degrees granted—with university institutions in the metropolitan countries." It should also be noted that some local academics, Nigerians and expatriates, were from the start critical of the values implicit in the foundation of U.C.I.

5 The term "tribalism" is used widely in Nigeria, by Nigerians and non-Nigerians alike, and has the derogatory connotation of unwarranted favoritism or discrimination based on ethnicity. It is of course invidious to call ethnic groups or nations "tribes" if they happen to be located in Africa, and therefore I shall refrain from using the word "tribe" and all its derivatives except in quotation marks where the context requires the use of the local term. At the analytical level, I shall speak of "ethnic group" to designate a collectivity sharing a common language and culture, of "ethnicity" to refer to the abstract principle of commonality of culture, and of "ethnic particularism" or "ethnic prejudice" to mean a preference or dislike based on ethnicity. Terminological confusion must also be avoided concerning the words "nation" and "nationalism." By "nation" I shall mean an ethnic group which is subjectively conscious of its separate identity; by "nationalism" I shall mean a political ideology based on the principle of ethnic self-determination (i.e. what in Africa has often been called "tribalism"). Consistent with this usage, Nigeria is *not* a nation but rather a *multi-national state.* When the context makes it awkward to avoid the terms "nation" and "national" to mean the multi-national state, I shall use those words in quotation marks. The Yoruba, Ibo, Hausa, Bini, Kanuri, etc. are ethnic groups and, to the extent that they are politically conscious of their separate identities, nations.

6 Elsewhere, Simpson justifies car allowances by stating that the Nigerian climate is such that "walking is only possible for short distances."

7 The term "minority" is confusing in Nigeria, because no single ethnic group comes close to constituting a majority of the total population. Of some 60 million Nigerians, the Yoruba, the Hausa and the Ibo constitute ten to twelve millions each, for a total of some 35 to 36 millions. In Nigerian usage, "minorities" refer to all other 200-odd ethnic groups ranging in size from three or four millions to only a few thousand people. Collectively, however, the "minorities" are far more numerous than any one of the three large groups. The three major ethnic groups are *regional* majorities (but then so are nearly all ethnic groups if the geographical unit is small enough). Each of the three main groups makes up only about one fifth of all Nigerians.

8 Here I am using the term "national" in its common but misleading sense to

apply to the multi-national state of Nigeria. In fact, I should say that the concept of the University was always *international*.

[9] The famous Ashby Commission Report (1960) gave the stamp of respectability on these political considerations. In the words of the Report: "We believe it would be a grave disservice to Nigeria to make modest, cautious proposals, likely to fall within her budget. . . . Our recommendations are massive, unconventional, and expensive . . ." Philip Foster (1970) writes: "Doubtless [the three regional] universities were created as a result of pressure from regional elites to have their own tertiary institutions, thus indirectly contributing to the 'ethnicization' of student populations. . . . The Ashby Report, although well meant, constituted one of the most wrong-headed pieces of advice given on educational policy to any African government over the last decade."

[10] Cf. Stanislav Andreski (1968:92–109) writes: "The essence of kleptocracy is that the functioning of the organs of authority is determined by the mechanisms of supply and demand rather than the laws and regulations; and a kleptocratic state constitutes a curiously generalised model of laissez-faire economics even if its economy is nominally socialist. . . . Nigeria presented a very close approximation to this ideal type. . . . Normally kleptocracy is not 'pure' but intertwined with coercion by armed force; so that strategy and tactics as well as price theory are needed to explain the functioning of a system consisting of a mixture of venality and gangsterism. . . . ."

[11] The Chairman of Council was supposed to be appointed by the Governor General on the advice of Council. On the day Council was to take an advisory vote in the election of its Chairman, Azikiwe had his chauffeur deliver a letter asking Council to recommend Akpe. Council turned down Akpe by a vote of 8 to 2, one of the two favorable votes being presumably Akpe's since he was already a member of Council. Azikiwe, incensed over Council's vote, disregarded it and appointed Akpe as Chairman, as indeed he had the legal authority to do.

[12] Nwanneh himself all but admitted that financial malpractices did take place. In an address to Congregation in June 1966, he said: "It was alleged that a number of people were converting to private use research grants made to them by foreign agencies and Foundations. . . . It is unimaginable that misuse of research grants on the scale portrayed by a section of the press can escape the vigilance of the Bursary, the Audit and the Registry. . . . There have also been allegations relating to the functioning of the University Bookshop. . . . It has always been my policy to investigate any irregularities. . . . Already two committees have been appointed, one to investigate the anomalies in the recruitment of junior staff and the other to investigate the management of our Agricultural Farm. Their reports are awaited. I shall certainly set up other committees if and when necessary to *investigate any allegations that are based on facts.*" (Italics are mine.)

[13] The text of the letter, dated December 15, 1966, reads as follows: ". . . I returned to Nigeria in October to find that the large majority of the academic and administrative staff of Eastern origin had, for reasons of personal security, returned to the Eastern Region. Hundreds of Eastern students also left the

campus. The continued and isolated killings of Easterners in Lagos and parts of the Federation served to confirm the fears of the great majority that they can best find security within their own borders. . . . But the fundamental issue is not that of personal security. One must face the fact that since the events of recent months Nigeria is bitterly and grievously split into regional groupings, each deeply suspicious of the other. In consequence a Nigerian holding an important position outside his own Region is bound to be an object of suspicion and attack. . . . Recent events have heightened tension to a degree unknown since the British unification of the Niger territories some seventy years ago. No doubt, in time, we shall transcend tribal barriers and it may be possible for Nigerians to work in any part of the country regardless of their Region of origin. It will be unrealistic, however, to pretend that this is the case today.

"Because of this my position as Vice-Chancellor has become very difficult and I feel my usefulness is curtailed. It is this consideration which has really influenced my decision to resign. I am convinced that the University will be better served at this difficult time by a Vice-Chancellor who has the fullest support of the people of the Region in which the University is situated."

CHAPTER TWO

University and Society

University and the City

U.I. is at once an extremely important part of Nigeria and an exotic implant. The physical setting of the University reflects this situation. Located some 4.5 miles north of the large Yoruba city of Ilosho on the most important road and railway in Nigeria connecting Lagos with Kano, the campus, or "compound"[1] as it is also referred to locally, occupies 4.5 square miles of tropical rain forest. Total University assets are estimated at £13.1 million, £8 million of which consist of the value of land and buildings at cost, and the rest of cash and investments. At today's replacement value, University assets certainly exceed £20 million. The campus is surrounded by a wire mesh fence, but from the main road few of the buildings are visible behind the lush green curtain of vegetation. Until the main gate is reached the campus looks very much like any of the surrounding forest, and indeed well over half of the University land is still undeveloped.

Beyond the main gate lies a different world, lacking the bustling cacophony of squatters' markets, the congested, odorous and colorful mud house compounds of the Yoruba metropolis with its hordes of children, its mangy stray dogs and poultry, its noisy record shops blaring the latest "soul" hits, its hustling hawkers and crippled beggars, and its groups of prostrate Muslims assembled for communal prayer. As the U.I. *Calendar* justly claims: "Some of the most striking things about the University have been its splendid physical layout and attractive buildings." A 50-yard-wide dual carriage way shaded by jacarandas stretches for a half-mile, leading to the gleaming white clock tower, the main assembly hall, the administrative buildings, the bookstore, and Queen Elizabeth Hall, the women's hall of residence.

The avenue is called Oduduwa Road after the Yoruba Creator-God, the first Oni (King) of Ile Ife, who through his 16 sons gave birth to all

Yoruba and indeed to all mankind. But that, and the fact that the clock on the "ivory tower" seldom comes within 15 minutes of the correct time, are the only indigenous touches to greet the visitor on first glance. More striking than the natural splendor of the forest backdrop, the cultivated beauty of the English gardening enhanced by tropical vegetation, and the harmonious proportions and lay-out of the long white four-story buildings, is the low density of human habitation in contrast with the town of Ilosho. This is a world in which people live indoors and move around by car if they can possibly afford it, be it in the dilapidated, overloaded Morris Minor or Datsun taxis that commute in a steady stream between campus and town. In contrast to the exuberant gaiety of the human kaleidoscope of Dugbe market downtown, the campus has an air of manicured serenity. The campus comes to life between seven and eight in the morning when townsmen come to work and when little caravans of uniformed school children walk by, carrying their books and lunches on their heads, and after 3 p.m. when the commuters leave until the next day. Every 50 minutes, there is a brief flurry of students hurrying from one class to another. But, most of the time, the campus seems to lay dormant in the soporific steambath of the 85–90°F, 80–90 per cent relative humidity weather.

For all its magnificence, the campus is not built for human convenience. More precisely, it is only built for the convenience of the affluent Senior Staff who can afford private motorcars. Its harmonious spaciousness was achieved at the cost of scattering low-rise buildings over a wide area, considering the relatively small number of students. By way of comparison, U.I. with some 3000 students and 2800 acres has a density of about one student per acre,[2] while the University of Washington, (which admittedly is largely a non-residential university) crams 33,000 students in some 500 acres, or some 66 per acre. Even though much of the U.I. campus is still undeveloped, the built-up area stretches for some 2 miles by 1.5 miles, not to mention the teaching hospital some $3\frac{1}{2}$ miles away from the main campus. On the main campus alone, students often have to walk five or six miles a day to complete their daily rounds of classes, library, and meals, sometimes rushing over half-a-mile between lectures.

Let us look successively at the place of the University in the city of Ilosho, in the Western State (formerly the Western Region), the Federation of Nigeria, and finally the world at large. Locally, U.I. can be said to be *in* Ilosho but not *of* Ilosho. The city of Ilosho comprises a total of anywhere from 750,000 to one million people. It was founded as a war camp in the early 19th century, during the period of turmoil caused by the Yoruba civil wars and the slave trade, and its strategic position led it gradually to supplant Oyo as the most powerful Yoruba city-state and to become the largest city in tropical Africa. In recent years, Lagos has probably outstripped Ilosho in population, but Ilosho remains a close second and is approached in size by no other Nigerian city.

Ilosho (along with other large Yoruba towns) has been termed a "city-village" insofar as it consists overwhelmingly of a huge conglomeration of traditional or semi-traditional mud-walled one-story houses interspersed with empty spaces for open-air markets, interconnected by a bewildering maze of winding alley ways with only a limited network of paved roads suitable for wheeled transport. The now ubiquitous corrugated-iron roof, electric lighting, and the public fountains with their communal water taps are the most visible non-traditional elements in this sprawling and seemingly unplanned and unstructured city. Closer inspection shows that the city is indeed complexly structured in terms of kinship, politics, and economic organization, and that what looks to the naive Western eye as spatial untidiness reflects in no way social disorder; clearly, Ilosho is a non-Western city in almost every respect. Unlike many other African cities such as Dakar, Accra, Nairobi, or Salisbury, which grew during the colonial period and which are fundamentally tropical versions of European cities, Ilosho and other traditional cities of Nigeria (such as Abeokuta, Ogbomosho, Oshogbo, and Oyo in Yoruba country, and Kano, Sokoto, Zaria and Katsina in Hausaland) are truly African cities with a few exotic accretions of which U.I. is the most sizeable. The standard of living is very low (less than £30 per capita per annum in Nigeria as a whole, and perhaps twice as much in the South) and high density presents serious sanitation problems, but Ilosho is nevertheless a viable and obviously thriving concern in both social and economic terms. Poverty and disease have been the lot of nearly all humanity for nearly all of its history, and only recently have they become defined as "problems." It takes a foreign eye to regard Ilosho as problematic.

Emerging from a vast sea of rusty corrugated iron are a few conspicuous islands of what has been rather misleadingly termed "modernism," concentrated in the Northern part of the city. These include a "modern" shopping district with its impressive but incongruous office skyscraper (Cocoa House), a Barclay's Bank, the Central Post Office, Railway Station, and Police Barracks, a large cinema, foreign consulates and the British Council, a street of Lebanese-owned textile and general stores, and two supermarkets which serve as the shopping Meccas for both the local and the expatriate elites. In particular, the luxurious, air-conditioned Kingsway Store with its rolling staircase is the closest approximation to American culture in Ilosho, and a major attraction for visitors from the "bush."[3]

A second major cluster of European-style buildings in Ilosho comprises the Western State Government buildings, the University Teaching Hospital (where the clinical departments of the U.I. Faculty of Medicine are located), several banks, and a few residential districts for the elite, that are still sometimes called "reservations" after the term used by the British to designate the colonial ghettoes. Most of these Western-style 3 or 4 bedroom houses are now occupied by the Nigerian elite, but practically all expatriates who reside off campus also live in them. On the main road connecting downtown Ilosho with U.I. are also found the exorbitant (£8 per day per person), air-conditioned Premier Hotel, and the airport (also used as a grazing ground by Fulani herdsmen who bring their stock to the adjacent cattle market).

ECONOMIC LIFE

The biggest exotic island in and around Ilosho is undoubtedly the University "compound." Despite its alien character, its importance to the city is enormous. With close to 5,000 employees on its payroll, U.I. is one of the few large employers in the city. Given the almost total absence of large-scale industry, the only sizeable competitors for wage employment in the area are the Western State government, the Federal Civil Service (including the Police and Railways), and, since the Civil War, the Army. Some 20,000 people reside on the campus, and can be said to rely almost entirely on the University for their subsistence; but to this number must be added many more people who work there, or provide services to U.I. but live off campus. Allowing a conservative average of ten dependents per wage worker, some 50,000 people, or some 5 to 6 per cent of the population of Ilosho live directly from the U.I. payroll. At least an equal number of people derive at least some income from the University by trading, domestic work, and other services or goods provided to the relatively affluent University community. Altogether, at least 10 to 12 per cent of the town live from U.I., and many more benefit indirectly from it.

The economic importance of the University as an employer is further enhanced by the fact that U.I. employs a relatively high number of highly paid personnel. In other words, the University with its 600 Senior Staff members earning for the most part between £1,000 and £3,500 per annum probably accounts for around one third of Ilosho's population in that income bracket. Thus the U.I. community constitutes the largest single concentration of wealth in the town. Indeed, in an economy where the vast majority of the adult population is not in any kind of regular wage employment and participates only marginally in the money economy through the sale of surplus agricultural products, petty retail trade or small-scale handicraft production, even the most menial University jobs at £12 a month put the wage earners in an economically privileged position. In addition to the wages of U.I. employees, the city also benefits to some extent from the purchasing power of the students, which, although not large, is substantially above that of the average townsman.

Large numbers of people provide a wide variety of services for the University community. Just outside the main gate, there is an open-air marketplace with approximately 60 to 70 stalls and a few permanent stores selling foodstuffs, medicines, and other items of current consumption. In addition, there are several canteens serving cooked foods, bookies for pool betting, a mechanic and petrol station, a bicycle repair shop, and two tobacco stands. Hundreds of landlords rent rooms to U.I. junior employees who, for the most part, have to live off campus. Nearly all Senior Staff families employ a minimum of two domestic servants and frequently three or four, many of whom live on campus since Senior Staff houses are typically equipped with two separate rooms still referred to as "boys' quarters."[4] On campus itself, there are at least a dozen small open-air markets, the principal one being in Obatala Village, the crowded housing settlement for Junior Staff, and others gravitating around the Senior Staff Club and the student halls. Hundreds of hawkers and peddlers make the rounds of student and staff residences selling a wide array of goods, such as fruits and vegetables, leather goods, textiles, and wood carvings. Many itinerant craftsmen also offer their services, notably barbers and tailors, and a wide array of pastors collect money for charities of varying degrees of legitimacy.

During the year 1968, a total of 410 trading permits were granted (at a fee of 7 s. 6 d a year) by the University; 170 of the licenses were granted to men and 240 to women, the men concentrating mostly in the curio trade and leather goods, shoe- watch- and bicycle-repairing, tailoring, barbering, and photography, and the women dominating most other trades especially foodstuffs, palm wine, tobacco, toilet articles and other items of current consumption. (See Table II) By ethnicity, 71 per cent of the traders were Yoruba, 14 per cent Bini, 10 per cent Hausa, and the remaining five per cent Ibo, Efik and Urhobo. The category "Hausa," as used in the South is a loose one; it broadly includes all Northern Muslims of which the Hausa are by far the largest group but which also includes Kanuri, Nupe, Fulani and many others. The "Hausa" traders on campus specialize almost exclusively in the curio trade (other than woodcarving, which is a Yoruba near-monopoly), and deal mostly with expatriates. Many of the traders are highly specialized, not only in the type of food or service provided, but also by sex and ethnicity of the trader, and even ethnicity of the clientele. There are some barbers, for example, who cater almost exclusively to the wealthier expatriate clientele.[5]

Most of these retailers who operate on campus are, of course, linked with downtown wholesalers and "petty wholesalers" in the larger Ilosho markets, so that University trading is complexly integrated in the general economy of the city. Many of the women who peddle textiles from door to door, for example, purchase their goods from wholesalers in the large Oje cloth

TABLE 2 / Occupation of Licenced Traders on
U. I. Campus, 1968

Occupation	Number of licences
"Petty Trader" *	179
Other foodstuffs	56
Curios, carvings, leather goods	42
Clothing and tailoring	37
Hair dressers and barbers	24
Palm wine sellers	22
Empty bottle collectors	15
Shoemakers	8
Watch, bicycle and radio repair	5
Book and newspaper sellers	4
Pool (gambling)	4
Photographers	4
Medicine sellers	2
Miscellaneous (car washer, firewood etc.)	8
Total	410

* The category "petty trader" consists almost exclusively of women, and refers to the typical one-table stallholder who sells a mixture of fruits, sweets, bread, biscuits, chewing gum, kola nuts, soap, toothpaste, cigarettes, ball point pens, matches and similar small items of current consumption.

market held every 16 days in the heart of the traditional section of Ilosho.

Finally, a class of people derive profit from illegal or at least shady activities and services involving the University. Prostitutes in the Mokola section of Ilosho are reputed to cater to the student clientele (the latter being referred to in student *argot* as "Mokolites"). Organized gangs of petty thieves break into campus houses with great regularity. In a six-month period in 1967–68, for example, there were 36 reported burglaries or attempted burglaries on campus. This situation in turn provides employment for a number of night watchmen. (Burglar and night watchman are not necessarily incompatible occupations.)

The University is dependent on the city for its water supply, although it has its own water storage tanks. The chronic shortage of water is a severe problem. During the dry season, water distribution is typically limited to one hour in the morning and one hour in the evening, but is occasionally disrupted altogether for two or three successive days. Even during the rainy season the supply is erratic. The supply of electricity, a Federal concern, is also plagued by almost daily power failures, to the great annoyance of students. In the evenings preceding examinations, power failures are greeted in the halls by loud howls of protest audible from several hundred yards' distance.

The University farm, with considerable livestock (cattle, hogs, poultry) and some vegetables, sells milk, eggs, meat and vegetables to members of its staff, but the main purpose of the farm is experimental and pedagogical, since it is attached to the Faculty of Agriculture, Forestry and Veterinary Science. Its output must achieve, by far, the highest production costs in Nigeria, and in any case is grossly inadequate to feed the campus population. Students take their meals in their respective halls of residence, and these in turn are supplied by the Catering Office which acts as a distribution agency for the goods brought in by various outside contractors.

Members of the staff buy their food and other supplies through private channels, either on or off campus. Most of them find it necessary to go shopping in town at least twice a week, both in the "modern" shops and in the open-air markets such as Dugbe and the one near the main gate. In fact, for most expatriates, these shopping expeditions downtown constitute their only significant contact with the outside world, and, even then, most confine their movements to the air-conditioned, sanitized environment of the Kingsway and Leventis stores.

Politically, there are relatively few ties between the University and the city. The Oba (traditional ruler) of Ilosho is the nominal landlord of the University; he is always invited to U.I. functions, and he occupies a prominent place in the protocolar hierarchy. By and large, the municipal level of government does not greatly affect the University.

University and the Western State

The links between the University and the Western State are mostly political and social rather than economic. U.I. is located in the heart of the Western State, by far the largest of the twelve states created by the second Federal Military Government. Ilosho is the administrative capital of the Western State, and, hence, has a substantial provincial bureaucracy and military garrison. Since U.I. is a federally supported institution, the University has few formal ties with the Western State government, except insofar as the latter has jurisdiction over a secondary and two primary schools on campus.

Informal social and political links between University and State government are, however, numerous and crucial. U.I. is the Mecca of the Yoruba intelligentsia, and the Western State incorporates the bulk of the Yoruba nation. The Yoruba members of the University staff naturally have many ties to other people in the region, most particularly with other sectors of the elite in the professions, the civil service, and more recently the army.

The Yoruba staff at U.I. is divided into a number of smaller groups which often compete against each other in a complex and shifting pattern of alliances. These interest groups and cliques almost invariably include many outsiders to University, as group membership is based mostly on locality, "old boy" school ties, and kinship. Thus, the most senior academic from, say, Ijebu or Ekiti Division will typically be a prominent member of his town's "progressive association," play an important role in the "old boys'" association of the secondary school from which he graduated, be close friends with highly placed bureaucrats, politicians, lawyers, and army officers from his town and old school, and be regarded by vast numbers of less fortunate kinsmen and fellow townsmen as a "big man" who is expected to use his influence to dispense patronage and promote the interests of his clients.

Non-Yoruba academics are also involved in solidarity networks, but, except for the Ibo before the Civil War, and perhaps the Bini since the establishment of the Mid-Western Region (now State), none of the other ethnic groups exerts much political influence at U.I. or at the Federal level. Among the "minorities," the link of ethnicity is paramount in that these groups are too small to afford the luxury of further fragmentation along the lines of locality, kinship, or school ties. Among the Ibo, there was considerable internal differentiation by area of origin and secondary school ties, but the crisis of 1966–1970 resulted in a great upsurge of national consciousness and solidarity *vis à vis* all non-Ibo. The Yoruba, on the other hand, are proverbially divided, a fact recognized by both themselves and their rivals. These internal subdivisions go back to the traditional fragmentation of the Yoruba nation into a multiplicity of city-states (with Oyo as the only truly large one) and to the bitter Yoruba wars of the 19th century. Consequently, Yoruba politics have always been of a bewildering byzantine complexity. At U.I., the very size of the Yoruba group and the fact that they are "at home" make for a division into half a dozen or more major factions, fluid in membership and shifting in patterns of coalitions.

Expatriates have frequently been caught in the political cross-fire between various Nigerian factions and have been identified, if only peripherally, with one group or another. Most foreigners were traditionally seen as pro-Ibo, and a minority as pro-Yoruba. An interesting case of involvement of U.I. in regional politics is that of the International School. The Western State Commissioner for Education was also a Lecturer in Mathematics on leave of absence from U.I. Arguing with considerable evidence that the International School was an elitist institution catering mostly for the needs of foreign children and unsuited to the needs of Nigeria, and accusing the school administration, especially the British Principal, of various practices which suggested racial discrimination, the Commissioner mounted a press campaign against the School, against its Board of Governors, whose Chairman was the Vice Chancellor of U.I., and against the U.I. Council, which claims ultimate responsibility for the School. The School was established originally during the Nwanneh era with the strong support of the British "bar establishment." American foundations gave most of the initial grant, but over the years the school ran at a deficit, and U.I. made up the difference, indirectly at the taxpayers' expense, since the University is supported principally by the Federal Government. Thus, the argument was that the Nigerian taxpayer was subsidizing the education of the elite, both Nigerian and expatriate.

University and Country

The links between the University and the country as a whole are more important than the more local ones. Before turning specifically to U.I., a few general remarks are necessary to contrast the position of universities in "developing" as distinguished from "developed" countries. Paradoxical as it may seem, the universities of the Third World, though often still feeble and exotic transplants, play a much more prominent role in their respective countries than in the industrial states. In financial terms, the costs of first-rate higher education are much the same everywhere, and indeed may even be higher in Africa because the relatively small size of universities does not permit economies of scale. This means that, relative to their scarce resources, poor countries often spend much more on their universities than rich countries.

All modern states, "developed" or not, rely in the last analysis on university research and teaching for the training of bureaucrats, technicians and professionals whose skills are indispensable to the machinery of government and business. Even though underdeveloped countries can only absorb a relatively small number of high-level manpower, they rely on the university-trained at least as much as developed countries. To a greater extent than in industrial countries, many of the "new nations," especially in Africa, are run by a bureaucratic mandarinate. The small number of university graduates and of universities enhances the status and the importance of both, so that the "national" university, fledgling though it may be, plays a relatively much bigger role than even the oldest, largest and best universities of industrial nations.

Along with the greater relative importance of the "developing" university goes, of course, the relative prestige, power and wealth of its teachers. In Nigeria, a university professor only earns about half of his American counterpart, but, relative to the standard of living in the two countries, the Nigerian is some ten times better off than his American colleague. With a basic salary of £3000 per annum plus fringe benefits amounting to at least another £1,000, the Nigerian professor earns roughly 120 times his country's per capita income. If we assume that his nuclear family consists of six members, he and his immediate family are roughly twenty times as well off as the average Nigerian. The American full professor at a major university may earn from $15,000 to 25,000, or some 7 to 10 times the U.S. per capita income. Allowing a family size of five, his family is roughly twice as well off as the average American family.

In terms of prestige and power, academics in the Third World and especially in tropical Africa also outrank their colleagues in industrial nations. In Nigeria, young lecturers in their thirties get appointed to top government positions to which only the most senior and well-established professors could aspire in Britain or America. A professor in Nigeria is regarded as the equal of the most senior civil servants and the peer of a cabinet minister. With a population of 60 millions, the teaching staff of all Nigerian universities numbers some 2,000 persons, some 300 of whom are professors. Student enrollment is still under 10,000. By comparison, the United States with a little over three times the total population (205 million) has over half a million university and college teachers and seven million students. As a concrete example, Nigeria has a score of professional sociologists and anthropologists compared to some 20,000 in the United States. In proportional terms, then, the American academic establishment is at least 100 to 200 times more developed than in Nigeria.

An American professor of economics at a small university or college is likely to be known among a few hundred colleagues and students and to lead a life of modest comfort and secure obscurity in a sedate, middle-class neighborhood. If he writes a successful textbook, he may, with luck, belong to the top ten per cent of the income distribution. His African counterpart is apt to be a national celebrity, a key government adviser, and the principal influence behind the latest development scheme or five-year plan, and so he belongs to the top 0.01 *per cent* of his country's income distribution. Furthermore, the American professor is unlikely to know *anybody* among the top power elite in Washington, whereas the Nigerian will typically have some personal acquaintance with a sizeable percentage of the top politicians and civil servants, and be linked with quite a few by ties of kinship, friendship, marriage, "old-boyhood," or some such close connection. In short, Nigerian academics are an essential segment of a very small "national" elite, which, although ridden by factionalism, is nevertheless integrated by a dense network of personal ties. In industrial countries, academics are nearly anonymous specialists in a vast scholarly establishment which is only peripherally linked (and then in an almost ancillary fashion) with either the power elite or the propertied classes.

A direct consequence of the involvement of Nigerian academics with other sectors of the elite, and especially with the political (and now military) elite is that universities are much more politicized than in industrial countries. Staff and students are not necessarily more politically conscious, but universities are very much in the forefront of the political game, both "nationally" and locally. Everything that happens at the university, down to the smallest student group protesting about the quality of food in their dining hall, hits the headlines of newspapers and is a matter of widespread concern and public debate. Senior appointments to the teaching or administrative staff of the university often activate ethnic or other forms of factionalism outside the academic world, and sometimes degenerate into a public controversy of the first magnitude. Academics can be, in effect, tenured politicians, relatively immune to the vagaries of popular elections and military coups, so long as they do not engage in open acts of subversion. This is not to say that most academics play politics, but rather that they have the opportunity to do so if they choose, and with less risk than almost anybody else.

Let us now turn more specifically to the University of Ilosho. The relationship between U.I. and Nigeria is, of course, one of mutual interdependence. The University is the kingpin in the training of Nigeria's high-level manpower in all the "modern" sectors of the society. Nearly all the top personnel who are not foreign-trained, are Ilosho graduates, of whom the University produced 3,636 from 1948 to 1968. The other Nigerian universities are gradually undermining that monopoly, but they themselves are heavily dependent on Ilosho for the recruitment of their teaching staff since Ilosho is still, to all intents and purposes, the only center for the training of post-graduate students, and, hence, of university-level teachers. In fact, Ilosho itself hires a good many of its own higher degree holders.

THE MANDARINATE

The training function of U.I. goes much beyond the imparting of technical skills. Indeed that function is not necessarily paramount, because, with the partial exception of Medicine and Agriculture, the intellectual baggage with which the student leaves the University often bears very little relationship with the tasks he will be called to perform as a civil servant or manager of a firm. *The University is in fact training a bureaucratic elite that resembles the mandarin class of imperial China.* It creates learned gentlemen versed in an esoteric and recondite intellectual tradition which is little more relevant to the realities of their society than the Confucian classics were to pre-revolutionary China. In a sense, the problem of relevance is further aggravated in Africa because that intellectual tradition is not only esoteric but entirely alien. Nevertheless, the very difficulty of acquiring these skills ensures a double selection of students in terms of intellectual quality and socioeconomic background. A university education (and, in Nigeria, even a secondary education) takes money, time, and brains. The average Nigerian graduate is undoubtedly of higher quality than his American counterpart, irrelevant though his skills might be.

The University, as the main source for the country's bureaucratic mandarinate, molds not only the minds of its students, but also their entire life style. The University sets the pace for the emergent class culture of the elite; it creates powerful bonds of friendship between its former students, and thus contributes significantly to what little solidarity and class consciousness the elite shows across ethnic, regional and religious lines. Fragile though the integration of Nigerian society is, what there is of it is largely in the top echelons of the occupational hierarchy, and the role of U.I. as a "national" university has been paramount in this respect.

Despite bitter conflict and sectionalism among the elite, the whole structure of the state rests in the hands of the few thousand bureaucrats, technicians, managers, professionals, academics, army officers and politicians who, between them, control the entire machinery of government and the monetary sector of the economy. This elite is not yet solidary or closed enough to constitute a class; ethnic conflicts within the elite are still often more salient than class conflict between elite and "masses." The important fact about this elite, however, is that they are not a land-owning aristocracy or a capital-owning bourgeoisie, but controllers of the bureaucratic machinery. They are what in the Soviet Union have been called the *apparatchiks* or what Milovan Djilas more blandly called the "New Class." There are, however, two major differences between the New Class in "people's democracies" and in many African countries. First, in the capitalistic framework inherited from the colonial powers and in the neo-colonial relationship which has persisted in many countries since "independence," the bureaucratic elite has acquired a peculiar character of "political entrepreneurship" which, as Andreski has noted, can easily degenerate into organized "kleptocracy." Second, bureaucrats in much of Africa owe their positions not to political party loyalty but to their possession of the proper diplomas and degrees. Like the Chinese mandarins, African bureaucrats in countries such as Nigeria, Kenya and Ivory Coast are both more venal and more intellectually selected than their colleagues in European socialist countries or in African countries like Algeria, Guinea and Tanzania which tend to approximate somewhat more closely the socialist model.

This intellectual selection and the salience of the diploma as passport to elite status place the universities in an especially crucial position. As the main trainer of the ruling elite, U.I. serves a dual and contradictory function. On one hand, it is a major avenue of upward social mobility, but on the other hand it powerfully contributes to the emergence and crystallization of a new class structure; the ruling elite of Nigeria is still much more open than in the "advanced" capitalist countries.

Not only is U.I. a major trainer of the elite, but academics themselves are an important sector of that elite, and, by virtue of their spatial segregation on campus, a highly visible and corporate one. Academics are in an ambivalent position *vis à vis* other segments of the elite and *vis à vis* the country at large. In a system where social status in the "modern" sector is so closely linked with formal education, university dons are accorded a very lofty position. The Ph.D. is the ultimate prestige symbol, and honorary degrees from U.I. are the ultimate mark of recognition. At the same time, the security, long vacations and numerous other benefits which academics enjoy are the target of much envy and hostility both from other sectors of the elite and from the general public. Most commonly this hostility takes the form of virulent press campaigns against elitism, tribalism, nepotism and other "irregularities" at U.I. and in other universities.[6]

The same type of links between members of the University and non-academics exists at the Federal level as at the regional one. Ethnic solidarity, for example, operates at both levels. Previously, we have stressed the role of Yoruba academics in the Western State, because U.I. is located there. But both Yoruba and non-Yoruba academics and university administrators have links at the Federal level as well.

U.I. was always jealous of its reputation as a federal institution because this helped vindicate its higher status *vis à vis* its merely "regional" sister university, and gave it a more cosmopolitan aura. In fact, the composition of the staff and students was never representative of the whole of Nigeria. U.I. has always been an overwhelmingly Southern and Christian university, the latter by virtue not of official clericalism, but of the very small representation of Muslims and traditionalists among the students and Senior Staff. Until the crisis of 1966, U.I. retained a fairly proportional mixture of Southern ethnic groups, and, although rent by ethnic conflicts, maintained its multi-national character, as did the ruling elite at large.

Within U.I., the Civil War broke the ethnic balance, making it *de facto* a predominantly Yoruba institution, and it is still too early to foresee the extent to which Ibos will be reintegrated. No doubt, *some* reintegration will take place, but it will probably take several years before the pre-war balance is re-established, if indeed it ever is.[7] In the 1966–69 period, the *de facto* "Yorubaization" of the University certainly weakened the claim of U.I. to be a federal body. At U.I., as in the entire federation, the Civil War undermined, at least temporarily, the already fragile web of cross-ethnic ties among the elite which was precariously holding multi-national Nigeria together. Only the force of arms prevented total disintegration, and it was an army officer in his early thirties and without academic experience who had to mediate a deadlock in the august University Council during the Babalola crisis and thereby avert the threatened collapse of the University. If the war "proved" nothing else, it certainly showed that the fate of the University is linked with that of country.

BUDGET

In one very direct and obvious respect, U.I. is dependent on the Federal Government, namely for its budget. Out of a total operating expenditure of £3,454,000 in 1967–68, exactly two-thirds (66.7 per cent) came from a Federal Government subvention, while 11.8 per cent were contributed by student fees, 20.0 per cent by outside grants, mostly foreign foundations, and the remaining 1.5 per cent from interests on endowments and miscellaneous fees. During the civilian regime, the budget of the universities was passed by Parliament, but under the military regime, the Federal Ministries of Education and Finance are responsible for the allocation of funds. The most crucial part of the budget exercise concerns the delicate negotiations between U.I., the National Universities Commission (N.U.C.) and the relevant ministries.

During the Civil War, cuts in the educational budget made the exercise even more competitive and traumatic than is normally the case, but the basic principles remained the same. At every step, you request more than you need in full expectation that your competitors will do likewise, and that the final allocation will be much lower than the request, any gains over the previous budget being at best marginal. The "disadvantaged" units which had a late start (e.g. the Faculty of Social Sciences versus the Faculty of Medicine or the newer universities versus U.I.) try to close the gap, while the ones that had the headstart try to present the best possible case for maintaining the existing disparities. Being the best established, U.I. gets a lion's share (some 31.5 per cent in 1967–68) of the total university budget of over £7 million, a fact which is resented by the other institutions, and justified by U.I. on the grounds that it has an expensive Faculty of Medicine and does much post-graduate and research work. In view of the fact that nearly everybody is in principle in favor of more education, every university can make a convincing case for getting more money. Thus, the final outcome is to a large extent determined not so much by the intrinsic merits of the case as by the state of personal relations between key members of the university, the N.U.C. and Government. The same competitive process takes place within each university, and the links between budget allocations and power relationships are obviously reflected in the internal structure of the University. Thus, within the Faculty of Science at U.I., the biggest department by far is Chemistry, a fact not unrelated to the position of its former head as Deputy Vice-Chancellor and a member of the expatriate "bar establishment" during the early Nwanneh era. Similarly, in the Faculty of Arts, the mammoth size of the History Department is obviously linked with the fact that two heads of the University were historians.

The University and the World

Finally, U.I. is also part of a world-wide community of scholars that transcends political boundaries. Many universities are so mediocre that these international links are tenuous, but U.I. has sufficient international standing to be indeed a meaningful participant in the world of international scholarship. These international links do not affect the entire university community but only the teaching staff. In the first place, U.I. is still heavily dependent on foreign universities for the recruitment of its staff. The other Nigerian universities are not yet in a position to train a significant number of students to the doctoral level, and, while Ilosho has begun in the last few years to hire many of its own successful doctoral candidates, nearly all of the expatriate staff and about half of the Nigerians received at least part of their university training abroad. The Senior Staff is indeed much more cosmopolitan than at most universities in the "developed" countries. Of the 483 Senior Staff members from a 1968 list, whose nationality could be ascertained, 69.7 per cent were Nigerians, 15.3 per cent British, and 3.3 per cent American. In the remaining 11.7 per cent, another twenty-seven nationalities were represented; 2.5 per cent came from eight other African countries; 2.3 per cent from five Asian states; 2.5 per cent from four other American states (mostly West Indians and Canadians); 2.9 per cent from seven Western European countries; and 1.5 per cent from three European Socialist countries.

Expatriate teachers are, of course, most internationally oriented, in the sense that few expect to stay in Nigeria more than a few years; for the most part, they expect to return to their country of origin, and they regard U.I. as a stepping-stone in a career that will, they hope, culminate in a professorship at a prestigious university back home. The U.I. policy of paid annual home leave for expatriate staff allows the latter to maintain close ties, both of kinship and scholarship with their home countries.

Except for a score or so of Nigerian scholars who have achieved a world-wide reputation, and who spend much of their time plane-hopping between conferences and symposia, Nigerians, on the whole, have fewer sustained

overseas contacts than expatriates. Nevertheless, their intellectual orientation is much more European or American than African. As academics, they
are much more internationally oriented than the average British, French or
American professor at home. No doubt, this is in good part a reflection of
the greater degree of academic development and self-sufficiency in Europe
and America. But, whatever the reasons, the Nigerian scholar sees himself
very much in the context of world scholarship. The University as a whole
is extremely conscious of its international standing, and this theme appears with
great regularity in official addresses of Vice-Chancellors. Similarly, to the
individual scholar, his discipline and his professional association are very
important reference groups. The achievement of international scholarly
status is perhaps the most important criterion of prestige within U.I.,
superceding even successful academic politics as an avenue of promotion.
The University's status depends so heavily on retaining "stars" that academic criteria remain quite important despite powerful particularistic
pressures.

This international orientation of Nigerian scholars is strikingly evident
in the fact that, in a number of academic issues such as reforms in the
curriculum or in the structure of departments, the place where a person
received his higher education is often a much better predictor of alignments
than nationality, ethnicity or any other factor. Of the foreign-trained staff,
the largest number have attended British universities, with the American-
trained as poor seconds, and no other country sufficiently represented to
constitute an alternative academic model. Thus, one frequently sees an
alignment between Britons and British-trained Nigerians versus Americans
and American-trained Nigerians. Since U.I. was modelled after British
universities, the first group tends to be conservative, while the latter tends
to be reformist. In theory, most Nigerians state that U.I. should develop
along its own lines rather than emulate either model, but in practice, the
concrete referents in people's minds tend to be those institutions where they
themselves were trained. The American-trained claim to have democracy on
their side while the British-trained view themselves as custodians of quality.
Both positions carry considerable power of legitimation. The British-trained
find it difficult to defend elitism and the American-trained are hard-put to
make a case for mediocrity of which other Nigerian universities, especially
the American influenced Eastern one, are generally put forward as good
examples.

Another source of links between U.I. scholars and the outside world is
the growth of a Nigerian intelligentsia in exile. Consequently, many Ilosho
academics and students have friends and relatives overseas, often as students
at British, American, or other foreign universities.[8] One of the vicious circles
which poor countries face is that without enough trained personnel they

cannot develop, but without development their capacity to absorb university graduates becomes quickly saturated. Nigeria and Ghana, which among tropical African countries, have a relatively developed educational structure without a corresponding level of economic and industrial diversification, are already experiencing the beginning of a "brain drain." Several thousands of their nationals are, for a mixture of political, intellectual, economic, and familial reasons, staying abroad semi-permanently, and indirectly helping the rich countries to widen the gap betwen them and the home countries of the African expatriates. Meanwhile, Nigeria continues to hire at great cost trained personnel from Europe and North America. The existence of an international market for trained brains thus puts Nigerian scholars in a world-wide academic circuit in which the "developed" universities' competitive advantages are reinforced by certain "push" factors in Nigeria such as the burden of extended family obligations or, notably in the case of Ibo scholars, political difficulties.

FOUNDATIONS

A last important set of ties between U.I. and the outside world has been established through the Foundations. Between 1948 and 1966, U.I. received some £3.85 million in external aid; 76 per cent of that aid came from private foundations. with the giant American ones, Ford and Rockefeller, accounting together for nearly £2.5 million.[9] In terms of both capital grants and recurrent expenditures, the foreign foundations thus played a vital role in U.I.'s development, especially since Independence. In 1967–68, for example, the foundations contributed almost exactly one-fifth of U.I.'s total operating expenditures. They subsidized a number of academic posts both for overseas visitors and for Nigerians; they provided funds for numerous pieces of research; and they helped create or expand several institutes, programs and departments. The Institute of African Studies, several visiting chairs in the Social Sciences, much research in agriculture and chemistry, and some of the research and clinical programs in the Faculty of Medicine (e.g. in Virology and Psychiatry), were financed by foundation grants, not to mention the International School and capital funds for buildings and library development.

The Nwanneh era, which coincided with the first years of independence, marked the beginning of large-scale involvement of the American foundations at U.I., and hence of American influence on Nigerian academic development. The overall effect of this on U.I. was mostly positive; besides the obvious effect of speeding up the growth of the University at a time when Britain was curtailing its responsibilities, the American influence meant a diversification of intellectual ties and horizons for U.I., and a departure from the hitherto almost exclusively British pattern. Nevertheless, initial reluctance on the part of the University to look into gift horses' mouths led to some problems. The major one was that the foundation grants were all either once-for-all capital grants, or operating grants for limited periods, typically of three or five years. The assumption was, of course, that after withdrawal of outside support, the University would absorb the burden in its ordinary budget. Thus, the University frequently found itself in a position of having to continue to develop in a direction which it did not choose, and without any considerate overall planning or systematic discussion of priorities. Individuals well connected to the foundations initiated requests for funds which were formally channeled through the Vice-Chancellor's office and the Senate Development Committee, but, in practice, negotiations were often virtually completed before the matter went through the Senate, and the latter found itself in a difficult position to refuse gifts. By 1966, when the long-range implications of these commitments for U.I. became increasingly evident, an Academic Planning Committee was set up to insure that the University would retain control over its own development and screen grant applications before they went to the prospective donors.

Nevertheless, a number of other problems remained, and numerous conflicts were activated by foundation projects. First, the aims of several of the projects were questioned. We have already mentioned the crisis provoked by the International School. The Institute of African Studies, devoted primarily to archeology and indigenous arts and culture, was also a target of attack when the University assumed financial responsibility. The arguments against the Institute were that it was an expensive luxury devoted to antiquarian subjects having a low order of priority for the present needs of Nigeria. It was also argued that by relieving its staff of teaching, the Institute gave its members an enormous competitive advantage over teaching colleagues in the regular departments, since promotions were based overwhelmingly on research and publications rather than teaching.

Foundation funds also gave rise to charges of "empire-building." Indeed, the semi-autonomous status of many of the projects often placed their directors in a privileged position not only in terms of research opportunities and financial independence, but also in establishing a semi-private political fief outside Senate control. With the strong tradition of Senate sovereignty, this was widely resented. The abortive Centre for Demographic Studies was a case in point. It was viewed as an attempt to create an empire for a particular person who was heavily imbroiled in a complex case of political factionalism which also involved the Nigerian Institute of Social and Economic Research (a Federal Government concern, autonomous of U.I. but located on campus) and the Chair of Economics. The Rockefeller Foundation, as sponsor of the Centre, was thus viewed as taking side in what was in part a Yoruba-Ibo conflict. In addition to the exacerbation of ethnic and other forms of factionalism, foundation-sponsored projects have sometimes given rise to such allegations as misappropriation of funds or misuse of vehicles. Accounting for grant monies has been at best dilatory and inaccurate.

At a more ideological level, some of the more radical Nigerian staff also view with suspicion the alleged political motivations of the foundations. Are not the foundations infiltrating African universities to serve the needs of American imperialism in the Cold War? Why, for example, is Rockefeller Foundation supporting so many visiting chairs in the sensitive social sciences like Sociology, Political Science and Economics? The fact that Rockefeller supports not only American visiting scholars but also professors from socialist countries like Poland does little to alleviate these charges of neo-colonialism.[10] Many Nigerian academics are, of course, equally if not more suspicious of the motives of visiting scholars from people's democracies despite the fact that they come mostly from the smaller countries like Poland, Czechoslovakia and Hungary rather than the Soviet Union or China. (In fact, Nigerians strongly discriminate against fellow Nigerians who have degrees from eastern European universities, the hierarchy of degrees being roughly as follows: 1) Oxford-Cambridge-London, 2) British "redbrick," Ilosho, better-known American like Harvard, Yale, Berkeley, Chicago, or Columbia, and continental Western European, 3) other American, Canadian or Australian, and 4) Eastern European, Asian, Latin American or other African.)

Some local foundation representatives played a significant personal role in the affairs of the University, especially during the Nwanneh era. A Ford Foundation official was alleged at one time to have exerted a powerful influence on the Vice-Chancellor, and later a Rockefeller Foundation representative became Dean of Social Sciences and, as such, was a key person in the early development of that Faculty to which his Foundation gave much support.

Finally, the American foundations create resentment, among Nigerians and non-American expatriates alike, in that Americans enjoy a higher standard of living and "overpay" their servants. Since visiting American scholars typically receive normal United States salaries, they earn roughly twice as much as their Nigerian and British colleagues. Furthermore, they live in foundation-built houses, which, next to the Vice-Chancellor's lodge, are the most luxurious on campus, although they are only marginally superior to the houses normally allocated to staff of professorial rank. Housing allocation is an important source of conflicts at U.I.

Having sketched the historical development of the University and its place in the broader context of Nigeria and the world, we may now turn to a more detailed analysis of its internal structure and processes.

NOTES

[1] The term "compound" is widely used in Nigeria to designate a set of traditional dwellings usually enclosed within a mud wall, and housing an extended, virilocal, polygynous family. By extension, the term also refers to any set of buildings having some organic unity and usually but not necessarily fenced or walled in, e.g. "the hospital compound," "the police compound," etc. The campus is thus frequently called the "U. I. compound" and the near-by University Teaching Hospital is referred to as the "U. T. H. compound." More in keeping with the traditional meaning, each of the Senior Staff houses on campus with its servants quarters, and its large hedged-in garden is also called a compound. The status of the male Senior Staff member (who is addressed by his social inferiors as "master") is assimilated in the minds of many unwesternized Nigerians to that of head of a localized segment of patrilineage in the traditional pattern of residence.

[2] This figure is misleading in that the students make up only one sixth or seventh of the campus population. An estimated 20,000 people live in the University "compound." This includes the Senior Staff with their families and servants, and some of the Junior Staff with their families. The resident Junior Staff is heavily concentrated in the small overcrowded area of Obatala Village where they live in University quarters and where a large (1000 pupils) primary school is located. We shall deal in greater detail with the physical lay-out of the campus when we describe the status system.

[3] Here again, I am using the word "bush" in the local meaning. As used by English-speaking Nigerians, "bush" could be be translated as "rustic," "backward," or "peasant-like." "Bush" is the antonym of "sophisticated" and "urban." The Yoruba are a very urban-oriented culture and look down on the rural population. By extension, the term "bush" is used to designate anything not "in" among elite circles. Thus, incorrect English grammar is "bush," and so are certain rustic styles of hairdress or clothing for women. For example, the cassava-resist indigo wrappers worn by most Yoruba women as everyday dress, and much in vogue among expatriate women, are considered by Nigerian students and urban sophisticates as "bush." Invidious sub-ethnic distinctions are also made by the use of the word "bush" as an epithet. E.g. snobbish Lagosians regard all other Yoruba as "bush"; the Ijebu and Egba sub-groups of the Yoruba regard the more northernly sub-groups as "bush"; and the most remote northeastern Ekiti Yoruba are regarded as most "bush" by all others. The traditional near-nudity of some of the "Middle Belt" ethnic groups is often considered by urban Yoruba with the same kind of horrified incredulity that anyone could be so "primitive" as one might have expected from a Victorian petty bourgeois in 19th century England. We shall deal later with ethnic stereotypes.

[4] This colonial terminology consisting of addressing adult servants as "boy" and "girl" is still widespread, about equally so by Nigerians and expatriates, but

is widely resented by servants. More sensitive and politically conscious Nigerians and foreigners are beginning to avoid this usage, however.

⁵ When I asked my own barber, a Yoruba, why he specialized in expatriates, he replied that cutting Nigerians' hair was "a waste of time," and that there was "no money in it." Nigerian hair was more difficult to cut, you had to pull more on the comb, and he could "finish 3 or 4 whitemen" in the time it took him to cut a Nigerian's hair. When I then asked him why he was charging me 4 shillings instead of the regular 1s 6d or 2s, charged by itinerant barbers to students, he laughed and said "You are a rich man." Price in Nigeria is a function not only of supply and demand, but also of the status of the buyer. The affluent, whether Nigerian or foreign, are expected to pay more because they can afford it and not to do so would be a mark of stinginess. This pattern of generosity is common in many traditional African societies where the maintenance of high status involves considerable redistribution of wealth in the form of hospitality and gifts, and, hence, militates against the formation of social classes along economic lines. Many African societies, though highly stratified, are very "un-Marxian" in this respect. Among the Yoruba, for example, it has become customary to extend not only food, drink, kola nuts, entertainment and lodging to guests, but also gifts in cash. I witnessed a foreign anthropologist visiting Yoruba friends and being given a £1 note as gift from his host, even though in this case the host was much less well off than the guest.

⁶ One of the more restrained front page editorials entitled "Policy of Privilege or Prestige" and dated April 13, 1969 is a good example of the major themes of press attacks against the University:

We are well aware that it is not Professor X alone who is a victim of the latest reckless policy on the question of appointments and promotions of both senior academic and non-academic staff. There are others, both expatriates and Nigerians.

We do not desire to indulge in personal villification or assail the integrity, professional or otherwise, of the men who run Ilosho. However, we are ethnically [sic] bound to expose all these irregularities first in the interest of the public who pay for its running and secondly, because of the likely adverse consequences on the reputation of this institution.

It is our strong belief that the university
1. Has not acted judiciously, fairly and honestly over certain appointments and promotions made recently in that these exercises do not take into account certain basic principles like competence, ability and seniority;
2. Has indulged in too many wastes especially over purchase of equipments and instruments for research projects;
3. Acted in a questionable manner by allowing a Ford Foundation Fellow to draw a year's salary in advance from the Special Development Fund whereas the fellowship covers the salary and other allowances of this staff while in the United States;
4. Is operating the Fund in other ways to suggest that it is an instrument of privilege and even of punishment;
5. The renewal of the contract of an expatriate woman and her subsequent appointment to a higher post completely flouts the principle of academic excellence;

6. Should not have yielded to outside pressure in appointing a Nigerian academic staff who had unsuccessfully gone through two Department interviews;

7. Has filled new postings in a manner of haste and rush and without advertising these positions.

It is also hoped the university would continue to bear its international outlook at all levels without in the words of Vice-Chancellor Akinode himself, sacrificing its new acquired African personality and distinctive features.

[7] Shortly after cessation of hostilities, U. I. authorities declared that all former students and staff who left because of the war would be readmitted. Students began coming back within weeks of the end of the war, but the reintegration of Ibo staff is going to take much longer as most of their old posts have been filled, and as many Ibo in exile are not eager to return to Nigeria as yet.

[8] A 1966 Nigerian government register of students listed 4532 "potential graduates" for that year. Of these, 46.6 per cent were enrolled at Nigerian universities, 26.4 per cent of British institutions, 10.9 per cent at North American universities, and the remainder in the rest of the world. Only 8.0 per cent of them came from Northern Nigeria which comprises over half of the Republic's population. Of the half of the Nigerian students who reside abroad, many do not return to their home country, and concern about this incipient "brain-drain" led the Federal government to appoint a commission of inquiry into the matter.

[9] For the data on foundations, I am heavily indebted to C. Le Moignan's excellent thesis on the subject, to which the policy of anonymity adopted here prevents me from referring formally since the thesis was presented at Ilosho.

[10] From personal experience, I should say that most of the American staff of the foundations tended to be "non-political liberals" who took a purely technical view of their role in Nigeria, and who considered that they were there to do a job and to support the local establishment rather than to "rock the boat." On the whole, they have pushed africanization more strongly than the British staff, if only because their status has been much more transient, the typical stay being two years. Compared to the British and British-trained Nigerians, they have tended to push for the democratization of the university structure, reflecting their bias toward an American type of higher education. Scholars from the "people's democracies" have impressed me as being among the most conservative or at least apolitical, taking the most technocratic view of their roles, and having a very autocratic and pyramidal conception of the university, such as was characteristic of pre-war continental Europe. Personally, I was never aware of the Rockefeller Foundation exerting any kind of political pressure on me, even though my position was clearly to the left of that of most of my fellow Americans. I did find out, however, that a Rockefeller staff member reported to U. I. officials prior to my assignment at Ilosho that I had been involved in a political crisis in my previous assignment in Nairobi, and inquired of U. I. whether they still wanted me. Notwithstanding this, however, the Rockefeller Foundation not only reappointed me but gave me a research grant to conduct the present study.

CHAPTER THREE

Status: The Three Estates

U.I. is a highly stratified community, combining some of the features of a colonial caste society with those of traditional status systems in indigenous societies. The interplay of numerous criteria of invidious differentiation makes for a status system of much greater complexity than is found in the universities of industrial countries, and also for much wider socio-economic gaps between strata. First, relative to the larger society, virtually every member of the University community, including the Junior or Subordinate Staff, is in a privileged position. Even University employees in menial positions are in regular and fairly stable wage employment, and enjoy some fringe benefits such as health care and pension and death benefits. Domestic servants are in a somewhat more precarious and unprotected position, but many servants are still better off than their average fellow Nigerians in the subsistence economy. U.I. thus exemplifies the common condition in tropical Africa where the low productivity of subsistence agriculture makes almost any kind of wage employment, however lowly, preferable to living in the overpopulated, overstocked "bush," and puts the small urban proletariat on the lowest rung of the privileged strata rather than among the downtrodden masses. In a pre-industrial society, almost every employed townsman enjoys a higher standard of living than the average peasant. The relative decline in the material conditions of the proletariat seems to appear with the early phases of industrialization, as in 19th Century Europe.

Keeping in mind the relatively privileged position of the entire University community, the enormous disparities in life style and socio-economic conditions within it become all the more startling. The University comprises three sharply differentiated status groups, which, for lack of a better term, we shall call *estates*. These are 1) the Senior Staff, 2) the students, and 3) the Intermediate and Subordinate Staff, often referred to more succinctly as Junior Staff. These three groups are certainly not castes, because they lack all three basic characteristics of castes: there is mobility between them, the first estate being recruited in part from the second; the groups are not in any sense endogamous; and membership is not ascribed by birth. Nor are these three groups social classes in the usual sense. Kinship ties cut across all three groups, and a very wide spectrum of social origins is represented in the first two groups, all the way from third or fourth generation university educated families to small-scale subsistence farming.

Yet, the groups are distinct and unambiguous in their membership; they are self-conscious and act corporately through a variety of institutions and voluntary organizations; they are in an unequivocal hierarchy of prestige and power; and they are separated by wide gulfs in income, education, values, life style, family organization, leisure-time activities, and indeed almost all aspects of social behavior. The three groups live in distinct worlds which meet for a number of special purposes, and are segmentally linked through important criss-crossing ties of kinship, clientage, locality and ethnicity, but which nevertheless remain sharply distinguished. The parallel with the estates of pre-industrial Europe is far from a close one, yet the term "estate" seems less misleading than either "class" or "caste."

Senior Staff

Reserving for later chapters a more detailed account of the institutional structure of, and internal distinctions within, each estate, we shall now turn to a brief description of the three groups and the links between them. The Senior Staff is composed of some 600 U.I. employees and numbers, with their dependents and relatives, some 3000. By now, between 60 and 70 per cent of the Senior Staff are Nigerians, including a little over half of the teaching staff, and some 90 per cent of the administrative staff. Senior Staff annual salaries range from £950 for Assistant Lecturers and Administrative Officers to £4250 for the Vice-Chancellor, nearly one half earning between £1000 and £1500. (The per capita income of Nigeria is somewhere between £25 and £30 per annum.)

The basic salary, however, accounts for only some 2/3 to 3/4 of the real income of the Senior Staff, who also receive numerous fringe benefits and perquisites. They are all entitled to a furnished house or flat which they rent at a highly subsidized rate, seldom exceeding 6 or 7 per cent of their salary. They receive loans for the purchase of private cars and, in addition, a generous monthly allowance of £13 to £16 10 s. to operate them; in 1969, for example, the University had £230,000 tied up in motor vehicle advances to the Senior Staff; the interest rate of 3 per cent per annum was raised to 6 per cent in 1966. Medical care is free, U.I. having its own clinic and hospital. Senior Staff children receive bursaries to attend the University primary and secondary school at much lower fees than outsiders. The University provides at nominal cost recreational facilities such as the Senior Staff Club with its restaurant, bar, T.V. room, table tennis, reading room, swimming pool and tennis courts. The expatriate Senior Staff receive a free annual first-class return boat passage to Britain for themselves and their families, and Nigerian Senior Staff get a special vacation allowance. All Senior Staff are covered by a retirement plan. The Vice-Chancellor, department heads, deans and Masters and Wardens of Halls get additional benefits because of their administrative work.

At work, the Senior Staff enjoy spacious, well-furnished, air-conditioned offices. (Air-conditioners are more prestige symbols than utilitarian items. They are kept going at full blast even overnight sometimes, and offices are frequently uncomfortably chilly for someone who is lightly clothed for the outside temperature. The rational adaptation to climate is obviously not air-conditioning with tight-fitting European clothes, but rather the loose Nigerian-style *buba* and good cross-ventilation in buildings.) Another Senior Staff privilege in the office and classroom buildings are the segregated toilets. This is resented by students, especially when there is no nearby convenience for them. Thus, a prominently placed notice on a toilet door read:

ATTENTION TO STUDENTS!!!
PLEASE, THIS LAVATORY IS FOR MEMBERS OF SENIOR STAFF ONLY. STUDENTS ARE STRICTLY WARNED *NOT* TO USE IT AT ANY TIME. ANY STUDENT FOUND CONTRAVENING THIS ORDER WILL BE DEALT WITH.

DEAN'S ORDER
30TH MAY, 1969

An irritated student added a penciled comment to the notice: "Apartheid in Nigeria??"[1]

Members of the Senior Staff enjoy a standard of living roughly comparable to that of middle-class Americans, with, in addition, the luxury of cheap domestic servants. The furnished housing provided by the University ranges from the modern one or two bedroom flat for bachelors or childless married lecturers, to the large three or four bedroom house with a half- to two-thirds acre garden, garage and servants quarters for married professors. Domestic servants typically number at least two or three, at least among expatriate staff: a cook (sometimes called "head boy") who also acts as supervisor; a "small boy" (often in his late teens or early twenties) who does most of the cleaning and laundry; and a half-time gardener. In addition, there may be an adolescent girl to serve as nursemaid, and, less frequently, a chauffeur. In the larger Nigerian Senior Staff families the pattern is somewhat different; often there is only one person specifically hired as a servant to do most of the heavy work, while adolescent daughters, nieces or poor relatives share the rest of the work with no well defined boundary between the status of servant and poor or junior relative.

One of the most important and visible symbols of Senior Staff status is the private motorcar. In fact, more than anything else, it is the mark of elite status in Nigeria. Extremely high import duties and the high cost of petrol make cars at least twice as expensive to purchase, maintain and operate than in the United States or Europe, and hence put them beyond the reach of all but a tiny fraction of the population. A few of the better paid members of the Intermediate and Subordinate Staff also own cars, but most of them cannot afford them; lacking the money to operate their cars, some owners keep their vehicles on piles all year long and use them only once or twice a year to impress their friends and relatives when they are on leave in their home town.

Among the Senior Staff, a private motorcar is regarded not only as a prestige symbol but as a basic necessity; and, indeed, while a car is not a necessity in any strict sense, life without private means of transport is difficult. Public transportation is relatively cheap but irregular, unreliable, overcrowded, uncomfortable and dangerous (because of a combination of poorly maintained vehicles, overloading, treacherous roads, and inexperienced or reckless drivers). As already noted, the campus was planned for the convenience of a motorized Senior Staff; spaciousness and airiness were purchased at the cost of long distances between buildings. Even shopping for basic necessities involves long walks and a great waste of time without a car. There is no single centrally located market for "one-stop shopping" on campus, but rather a multiplicity of small clusters of stalls each offering a very restricted range of goods and services; e.g. the shoemaker and the bicycle repairman may be a mile or more apart. The "Senior Staff Shop" deals almost exclusively in expensive imported goods beyond the reach of most people. Trips to town are frequently unavoidable. The bicycle mitigates the problem, but the city is a hot, hilly five miles away, and there is a high risk of theft.

A number of Senior Staff families have two cars, especially if the wife is also employed. The prestige of the car ranks from the small, low-priced Volkswagen, Morris Minor or Renault 4, to the middle-class Peugeot 404, to that supreme mark of affluence and conspicuous consumption throughout Africa, the Mercedes-Benz.

Students

Students are an economically much more heterogeneous group than the Senior Staff. Some 97% of the 3000 students are Nigerians, 2% come from other African countries, and one per cent from the rest of the world, mostly Western Europe and North America. Of the Nigerians, just over one-tenth come from elite homes with well-to-do, professional and university educated parents, but the vast majority come from families which are better off than average, but nevertheless far from wealthy, even by Nigerian standards. Nearly one third are sons of farmers. For most students, going to University involves severe financial difficulties both for themselves and their families, and the payment of fees means acute duress for at least half to two-thirds of them. Opportunities for outside employment during vacations are extremely limited, and a student is often forced to drop out of school for a year or two, and take up a job as a clerk or teacher to save enough to continue his studies. At the same time, the student knows that the university degree is his passport to elite status, even though the returns on the educational investment tend to decline over the years as the number of university graduates increases steeply. Thus, the student, while often from a background of poverty or near-poverty and frequently in severe financial straits during his stay at the University, is also an heir presumptive to elite status. He knows that only three years and his final examinations stand between him and life-long security and comfort. This ambiguous situation of temporary indigence combined with a high likelihood of future affluence accounts for much of the collective behavior and attitudes of students.

U.I. is an almost completely residential university, i.e. nearly all of its students live in halls on campus. Although this increases the cost of education, there is little practical alternative, as few students could find housing in town under conditions of privacy and quietness necessary to university studies. In terms of physical accommodation, students are not nearly as well off as the Senior Staff, but much better off than most of the Junior Staff. The student halls, as originally conceived, were quite roomy and comfortable, with a single room provided for each student. In short order, however, enrollment pressures forced the uncomfortable doubling up of students in small rooms.

The student enjoys a standard of living which is very considerably above that of the mass of his fellow countrymen, a fact which provokes envy and criticism. The press, for example, often attacks students, especially when they demonstrate against housing conditions or food at the University, on the grounds that they are pampered, spoiled, elitist children behaving as "hooligans" (a favorite press epithet against student demonstrators). Students are fed a well-balanced diet which is partly indigenous, partly Westernized in content, but is undoubtedly of greater protein and vitamin content than the average student's home diet. The halls of residence, although over-crowded by a factor of nearly 100 per cent in terms of their original design and offering far from ideal study conditions, are still much more luxurious and less cramped than the quarters in which the vast majority of the popu-lation of Ilosho, including the U.I. Junior Staff, have to live. While two students share a small room, much of the Junior Staff in Obatala Village live with an entire family of ten or more persons in a room barely larger than a student room, and with inferior sanitary and water facilities.

The most significant structural divisions between students are by type and stage of studies. The two largest faculties by far are Arts and Science, followed by Medicine, Social Sciences, Agriculture, Education, and Libra-rianship. Post-graduate students make up about 5 per cent of the enrollment. The nearly 3000 undergraduates are divided into four class groups, namely the ones taking a preliminary year before starting on their degree program proper, and the three years of the regular degree course leading to the B.A. or B.S. In addition, some students in Education and Librarianship are enrolled in diploma rather than degree courses.

Junior Staff

The third estate consists of people linked with U.I. who are neither Senior Staff nor students. It includes mostly domestic servants of the Senior Staff, and the University employees known formally as the Intermediate and Subordinate Staff, but more commonly referred to as "Junior Staff." With some seasonal fluctuation, this includes a work force of some 3800 to 4200 University employees ranging in status from hundreds of casual workers (such as grass cutters and other unskilled staff) at £100 or so per annum to some twenty high level secretarial and clerical personnel in the £1000 to 1200 category, whose salaries overlap with the lowest category of Senior Staff. The arbitrary dividing line between Subordinate and Intermediate Staff is an annual salary of £458 a year. Only some ten per cent of the non-Senior Staff are in the Intermediate category, and some 80 per cent earn less than £300 a year. The Intermediate Staff consists almost exclu-sively of the secretarial, clerical, nursing and kindred semi-professional staff who typically have at least some secondary education, many of them having matriculated. Thus, except that the lower clerical personnel (such as typists) are in the "Subordinate" category, the distinction between Intermediate and Subordinate Staff amounts largely to one between non-manual and manual workers.

A few of the Intermediate Staff members earn as much or slightly more than the lowest category of Senior Staff, but they account for only one per cent of the non-Senior Staff, and if fringe benefits are taken into account, that little overlap disappears. Indeed, aside from a pension scheme and free medical care, the Junior Staff receive few of the privileges enjoyed by the Senior Staff. Most notably, they get no car allowance and are not entitled to subsidized furnished housing. There is some University housing for Junior Staff, but, besides being unfurnished and of far lower quality than that of Senior Staff, the housing is grossly inadequate in quantity. At most 15 per cent of the Junior Staff are housed on campus, mostly employees with the most seniority and those whose duties make their continuous presence on campus convenient to the University. They also pay relatively low rents, but housing is not part of the Junior Staff's contractual rights, and the waiting list is long. When a Junior Staff person gets any University housing at all, he receives a single room if he belongs to the Subordinate Staff and a small 2 or 3 room flat if he has Intermediate Staff status.

The contrast between Obatala Village, as the University housing estate for Junior Staff is called, and the rest of the campus is both striking and symbolic of the gulf that separates Junior and Senior Staff. Living conditions in Obatala Village are certainly superior to those prevailing in much of the town of Iosho; the houses have brick walls, cement floors, corrugated asbestos roofs, electricity, doors, windows and small verandas. Although they lack indoor plumbing, access to water taps is much closer than in most parts of towns. Dwellings are of two basic types: rows of single rooms with communal kitchens and latrines for the Subordinate Staff, and small duplex cottages for the Intermediate Staff. Even the latter do not approach in either size or quality the standard of the Senior Staff housing. Obatala Village has a Medical Clinic, a public primary school with an open playground and football field, and a Community Center. (The latter has until recently been used to accommodate the overflow of pupils from the school rather than for its intended recreational use, however.) In addition, many occupants use their verandas as stores and engage in small-scale retail trade to supplement their earnings. (In Southern Nigeria, as indeed in the rest of Coastal West Africa, many if not most women engage in retail trade; the vast number of traders relative to customers reduces profits to £5 a month or less in most cases.)

Compared to the rest of the campus, and especially the Senior Staff residential areas, Obatala Village is an overcrowded, malodorous, insalubrious and unsightly ghetto. It has been described as an "eyesore" by the Estate Officer, a health hazard by the Director of the Health Service and the Professor of Preventive and Social Medicine, and a "sordid situation" by the Vice-Chancellor, who in 1968, said he was "appalled at the sanitation and the general health and social conditions of the place." Indeed, the University authorities feel guilty and self-conscious about Obatala Village. Occupying some 50 acres, or two per cent, of the campus' 2800 acres, Obatala Village houses a population of 4000 to 4500 people in some 515 dwellings, 350 of which are single-room ones.[2] A 1969 housing survey gave a mean population of 7.0 persons per 120 square foot room in 145 one-room units, or an average of 17 square feet per person. One room had a phenomenal 19 occupants, and 12.4 per cent of the units surveyed had over 10 inhabitants. The overcrowded Obatala Clinic treats an average of 275 patients a day.

Physically segregated from Senior Staff and students, Obatala Village is fairly effectively tucked out of the sight of the casual visitor to University. It is located eccentrically beyond all the classroom and administrative buildings, the Library, the student halls, the several sections of Senior Staff houses, the sports grounds, and the mosque and Catholic and Protestant chapels. Its closest neighbors are the Farm with its malodorous piggery, poultry and cattle pen, and the Motor Transport and Maintenance yards. Yet, despite congestion, noise, drab architecture, and poor sanitation, Obatala Village pulsates with life unlike the "sleeping beauty" atmosphere of the Senior Staff sections, and seems much less out of place in Nigeria than the rest of the campus.

At least 85 per cent of the U.I. Junior Staff cannot be accommodated on campus at all. They mostly have to rent rooms in town or in some of the satellite villages closer to University. Typically, they have to pay a greater portion of their earnings for housing of a quality well below that in Obatala Village. Local Ilosho people who have relatives or own property in town are of course better off in that they often pay no rent.

Domestic Servants

In addition to the Junior Staff, the third estate also includes the some 2000 domestic servants of the Senior Staff who, with their dependents, live on campus in the "boys' quarters" attached to the Senior Staff houses. With their dependents, domestic servants make up a resident campus population of at least 7000 to 8000 people, i.e. approximately twice as many as in Obatala Village. But, unlike the inhabitants of Obatala Village, they live dispersed among the Senior Staff houses. Although the status of domestic servants is distinctly lower than that of all but the most menial of University employees, many domestics fare better than Junior Staff workers in terms of housing (though not in wages). They live under much less crowded conditions, if only because their masters attempt to restrict the population of their servants' quarters, but of course they lose much freedom of movement and action by living with their employers. (Many expatriates are especially sensitive to noise, and servants have to restrain their children, for example.) Lack of freedom, low wages, the relative frequency of inconsiderate treatment, and lack of security of tenure make servant jobs the least attractive form of wage employment, though often still a preferable alternative to rural poverty. Thus, servants constitute the bottom of the status hierarchy at U.I., with, however, further distinctions among servants according to the nationality and status of their masters.

The basic three-fold division of the U.I. status structure is not an analytical artifact which I imposed on reality. It is, in fact, explicitly recognized in the institutions of the University. Each of the three estates, as we shall see in greater detail later, has its own representative organizations and voluntary associations. The Senior Staff is collectively represented by Congregation, and the students by a Student Representative Council and after graduation, by Convocation. The Intermediate and Subordinate Staff have a University of Ilosho Workers' Union (U.I.W.U.), and the residents of Obatala Village elect a Council.

The social and institutional life of the University is thus clearly compartmentalized, both in its informal ties and in its formal structure. The vastly unequal distribution of power and wealth between the three estates makes for a clearly stratified social order, and also, of course, for a strong barrier to free and easy interaction and for a considerable amount of conflict between estates. Yet, the three groups are also tied together by a multiplicity of ties of cooperation and interdependence which binds them into a single community. As in all social systems, cooperation and conflict, order and rebellion, control and freedom are but the opposite sides of the same coin. In the remainder of this chapter we shall turn first to the major lines of conflict and cleavage between the three estates, and then to the different types of ties which cut across these estate lines.

Cleavages

The Senior Staff has a complete monopoly of all positions of power at U.I. Actually, only about one tenth of the Senior Staff detain an appreciable amount of power, namely half a dozen key administrators, the Deans, the Department Heads and a dozen or so additional Professors and Senior Lecturers who enjoy academic politics and committee work. But all those in power are Senior Staff. The majority of the Senior Staff are content to enjoy the social and economic privileges of their position and to leave to the more senior among them the task of running the University on their behalf and for their benefit. Although the Senior Staff is regularly under attack from below, it knows that its position is secure. As the apex of the country's educational pyramid, its skills are indispensable, or at least thought to be so. The scholars among them are also conscious of possessing skills that are marketable on a world-wide basis, and, hence, that, even though they may not be assured of as pleasant and luxurious an existence as at Ilosho, they are at least assured of a job elsewhere.

As privileged classes go, the Senior Staff is at best half-hearted in defending its position. In fact, it is ideologically on the defensive. The expatriates, and especially the British, have to live down a colonial past in which they had for the most part no direct association, but with which their "race" and ethnicity nevertheless identifies them. A number of them try to assuage their guilty consciences by advocating the reduction of class distinctions and the democratization of the University and of Nigerian society. Nigerian Senior Staff members are collectively, perhaps slightly more conservative than the expatriates, because most of them intend to spend the rest of their lives in Nigeria while the expatriates are mostly transients. Nevertheless, the Nigerian elite are conscious of being the inheritors of highly privileged positions previously reserved to British colonials, and thus find it difficult to defend their neo-colonial position *vis à vis* their less fortunate countrymen. Many Nigerian academics use the rhetoric of African socialism but are quite content to enjoy their perquisites and privileges.

Students are, if anything, even more conservative than the Senior Staff. Before independence, students saw themselves as the intellectual vanguard of the struggle for self-determination, and seemed radical, at last to the British staff. Now that independence has been achieved, students are behaving as a presumptive elite, and show few signs of radicalism other than quasi-ritualistic denunciations of foreign intervention and neo-colonialism. On domestic issues, Nigerian and indeed other African students are less radical than their counterparts in industrial countries. In fact, African universities lack an intellectual culture of radicalism, so that most students do not even acquire the rhetoric of revolution, much less the theory and practice of it.[3]

Consequently, there is no fundamental conflict of interest between Senior Staff and students. The students know that the vast majority of them will not achieve as exhalted a position as their teachers. But a university degree will insure them financial security and elite status, and given a bit of luck in examinations and another three or four years of post-graduate studies, a few students will be called to become Senior Staff. In last analysis, the Senior Staff is recruited, at least in part, from students, and there is thus no fundamental class conflict between the two groups.

Student Protest

If Nigerian students are rather conservative, they certainly are not passive or quiescent; on the contrary, they are often quite vocal, turbulent, and indignant, traits that are sometimes mistaken for radicalism. There have traditionally been two types of issues that have aroused Ilosho students to the extent of prompting public demonstrations. The first type has consisted of political issues, often complicated by ethnic conflicts and personal rivalries. Before 1960, the main issue was, of course, independence; during the First Republic, political corruption and the rigging of elections incensed students enough to bring about a violent clash with the police and a demonstration against the Prime Minister in 1965; the Civil War of 1967–70 brought forth demonstrations of patriotism and solidarity with the Federal Government and hostility to foreign powers, such as France and the United States, seen as supporting the Biafran secession. In April 1969, allegations of corruption against the Student Union officials led to a Student Congress, i.e. a general meeting where a motion of no confidence was introduced and defeated.

The second type of student protest at Ilosho and in other Nigerian universities has been even less radical, though sometimes more violent than the first. These have been the "bread and butter" demonstrations in protest against living conditions, notably overcrowding in the halls, the quality of food, the condition of facilities and services available to students, bursary and loan programs, and University rules regulating student behavior. In 1968, the residents of one of the halls rose in protest against conditions in their hall, including the state of disrepair of their television set. In February 1970, Ilosho students staged the largest and best organized demonstrations in U.I. history, in sympathy with students who had protested against conditions at another university in the North, been attacked and beaten by the policy, and suspended by the University authorities. Ilosho students boycotted classes, barricaded the gates to the campus thereby preventing University employees from coming to work, and locked several of the administrative and classroom buildings, absconding with the keys. Threatened with dismissal, the students gave in, returned the keys and went back to classes after two days of demonstrations. The absence of the police and army averted any significant violence to persons.[4] A year later, on February 1, 1971, a much more violent riot in which the riot police intervened resulted in one fatality and several serious injuries. The students of one of the halls accused their cafeteria manageress of "maladministration" and of hoarding beer cans at a party. After attempting to have their grievances redressed by calling on the Vice-Chancellor and by going on a hunger strike, the students became impatient and the protest generalized to the other halls.

Collectively, the students began to attack the administration building, the riot police were called in, and the violence quickly escalated.

Student politics, involving the election of a Student Representative Council and of hall and University student officers, are animated and hotly contested, but take the form of conflicts between halls or between ethnic factions much more than of political alignments of right or left, or platforms for the defense of student interests against other groups. In short, student elections are largely apolitical in the larger sense, and tend to be divisive in terms of collective student action. Class position is clearly not an important source of conflict among students, partly, as already stated, because students are relatively privileged to start with, but also because, as in the other segments of the Nigerian population, ethnicity and locality are still more important bases of social solidarity than class.

LABOR UNION POLITICS

Among the third estate, the situation is somewhat different. Junior Staff workers, especially the Subordinate (as distinguished from the white-collar Intermediate) Staff, exhibit a much greater degree of class consciousness than the students, and do openly challenge the privileged status of the Senior Staff. The University of Ilosho Workers' Union (U.I.W.U.) has struck several times against U.I., and has on a number of occasions displayed a considerable degree of militancy along the lines of working class politics. In 1964, when a General Strike was called to force the government to publish and implement the findings of the Morgan Commission on wages, the U.I.W.U. joined the movement and indeed played an important role in it; this strike was not, however, directed against U.I. At the time of the Nwanneh-Babalola crisis in 1966, the U.I.W.U. struck and demonstrated, demanding the resignation of the Registrar.

Two main internal factors have reduced the effectiveness of Junior Staff action. The first has been, as with the students, ethnicity, a topic to which we shall return. Another less obvious fact has been the wide range of status, income and education represented among Junior Workers, all the way from the illiterate gardener or cleaner to the highly skilled, secondary school educated stenographer, private secretary or executive officer. With some exceptions, the Intermediate or clerical-level staff have taken little interest in Union affairs, partly because they felt more secure and partly because their higher status militated against solidarity with manual workers. The lower and the more insecure the workers' status has been, the more active they have proved to be in the Union, as shown by the great militancy of the catering staff in the student halls.

This inverse relationship has had an adverse effect on the U.I.W.U.

In a multi-ethnic situation, English is the common medium of communication, and, more importantly, of negotiation with the Senior Staff. Thus, in order to transact business with the Senior Staff, to draft petitions, and the like, the Union needs Western-educated men who can meet their superiors without too great a linguistic and technical handicap. Yet these are the people who are least likely to be involved and interested in Union affairs.

Obatala Village

Among the residents of Obatala Village, there is widespread bitterness at living conditions. The people compare themselves with the Senior Staff with whom they are in close daily contact, and blame the University authorities for their failure to improve conditions and relieve the overcrowding. Many Obatala Village residents have friends or relatives in town who live under far inferior material conditions, but it is not so much the absolute level of amenities, grossly deficient though it is, which embitters the Junior Staff as their relative deprivation *vis à vis* the Senior Staff, and the segregated and inferior nature of their facilities.

Thus, for example, the Obatala School, though one of the best primary schools in the Western State, compares very unfavorably with the neighboring Senior Staff School. The Obatala School, a Western State public institution catering to approximately 1000 pupils, is often described by residents as a "bush school." In an attempt to accommodate the overflow of pupils, some classes were held in buildings little better than shacks, and the Community Center was until recently taken over by the School, thereby depriving the adults of the use of a recreational facility. None of the school buildings have indoor plumbing, and a single communal tap is the sole source of water. In some of the buildings, there are no inside walls and different classes are separated only by flimsy movable wood partitions. By contrast, the Senior Staff School, a fee-paying school sponsored by the University Council is located on spacious landscaped grounds, and consists of modern, well-ventilated and lit buildings including an assembly hall, a library, administrative offices, and a common room for teachers. Some three-fourths of the pupils and half of the teachers are Nigerians. Many of the teachers are university graduates and possess a level of qualifications normally expected of secondary school masters.

In the British tradition, both schools have the children wear uniforms, though the Senior Staff School is much laxer in what it accepts as "uniform." The uniforms of the two schools being different, the class membership of the children is made even more strikingly visible than if no uniforms were worn. Perhaps the most notable vestiary difference between the schools, apart from the uniforms, and one which is laden with symbolic significance in Nigeria, concerns the wearing of shoes. The vast majority of the Obatala School children go barefoot—no particular hardship in the Nigerian climate—while, at the Senior Staff School, children who appear without footgear are sent home to dress "properly." Interestingly, the few children at the Senior Staff School who do come barefoot tend to be Americans rather than Nigerians. Another highly visible status difference between the two schools has to do with parental car ownership. Nearly all Obatala children walk to and from school, some of them coming from several miles off campus. At the Senior Staff School, between 50 and 100 cars, some of them chauffeur driven, clutter up the access road mornings and afternoons to pick up children who in most cases would not have more than one mile to walk.

In 1969, when the University was under attack for its educational elitism, new classrooms were built for the Obatala School to relieve the congestion, and the word "Senior" was dropped from the official name of the other school, but otherwise things remained unchanged.

Recreational facilities, except for the (until recently unavailable) 3-room Community Center, the little-used tennis courts (most residents cannot afford the luxury of the needed equipment), and a soccer field, are nonexistent in Obatala, and stand in sharp contrast with the nearby lavish Senior Staff Club. The vast difference in medical facilities is also an object of considerable bitterness. The far-superior Jaja Clinic with a comfortable waiting room and adequate laboratory, pharmacy and consulting rooms caters to the Senior Staff and students, while the grossly inadequate Obatala Clinic is reserved for the Junior Staff. The same four physicians take turns at the two clinics, so, presumably, the quality of medical services is substantially equal, but at Obatala the overcrowding makes for much longer waiting, and the facilities are grossly overtaxed. Patients have to wait on benches, tightly packed under a corrugated iron roof.

The major complaint of Obatala residents, however, is overcrowding of living quarters. Obatala housing is in great demand because of its nearness to the place of work and low rentals, considering the quality of the buildings. The problem is intrinsically insoluble. To provide housing for all of its Junior Staff at the *present level of space allocation* the University would have to increase the size of Obatala at least seven times. Aside from the vast capital outlay this would entail, the problem would only be magnified sevenfold instead of solved. The overcrowding would be just as great. Obatala would become a big slum instead of a little slum. If every Subordinate Staff worker were to be provided with a small 3-room cottage instead of a single room, then the amount of housing would have to be increased at least twenty times. This would mean the creation of a city of some 800 to 1000 acres which would engulf a third of the campus, and a good deal of overcrowding would still remain, unless drastic restrictions were imposed on who could live on campus. Such restrictions would be not only unpopular, but highly unlikely to succeed in their aims. With the combination of high fertility, polygyny, an extended virilocal system of traditional residence, and the close proximity of a city of around one million badly housed people, the population would always expand to fill the available space by a factor of twice or three times its intended use.

The Obatala resident does not see his predicament abstractly as one of population explosion and underdevelopment, but much more concretely as one of invidious class distinctions. His frustrations are enhanced by the fact that he has no effective power, nor even effective channels of communication with the authorities. Obatala Village is administered by the Estate officer on behalf of the University Council, and the Obatala Council is an ineffective body, largely because it is totally powerless. The Council is elected by the residents from among themselves, and its main function is to serve as an ambulatory complaint box between the residents and the U.I. administration. Elected officials derive no benefit from service on the Council; consequently, the motivation to serve is minimal and apathy characterizes both the elections and the sparsely attended meetings of the Council.

STUDENT-JUNIOR STAFF RELATIONS

Conflict and resentment are not limited to relations between Junior and Senior Staff. There is also a considerable amount of tension between students and Junior Staff, especially the ancillary staff in the halls of residence. Much of that conflict remains latent, but incidents and disputes erupt at frequent intervals. Students and the catering staff accuse each other of disrespect or even insulting behavior. The basis of the conflict is that most students regard themselves as superior to the Junior Staff from whom they expect a certain amount of deferential behavior. Servants in the halls, on the other hand, are extremely sensitive to their low status, and generally refuse to behave submissively toward students, since they regard themselves as University employees and not servants of the students. One index of their sensitivity, for example, concerns the style of uniforms provided by the University. Especially resented are short pants, a symbol of child status. For example, in a 1967 protest petition by the Catering and Hall Staff Association, an active sub-group of the U.I.W.U., their secretary wrote: "One cannot understand why people who are feeding animals in the Zoo are using trousers while those of us who are serving human beings are issued shorts and shirts for the purpose." This letter also expresses the principle that the status of servants is linked to the status of those served.

Age differences are a frequent source of friction between students and hall servants. The latter, being often much older than the students, expect deference based on the traditional criterion of seniority, while the students expect deference on the basis of their higher degree of education. Another cause of tension is the fact that some Junior Staff members, especially porters, exert a certain amount of authority over students. Students, for example, are supposed to enter and leave halls via the porter's lodge, and their visitors must register there. Porters are held responsible for the enforcement of visiting rules, while a number of students try to "smuggle" in their girl friends overnight, especially over the week-end. Sometimes "joking" relationships develop between porters and students, and some porters are known to look the other way when students violate residence rules. Room cleaners are sometimes bribed to "remove their eyes." But incidents of friction are not uncommon.

Sometimes, during workers' strikes in the halls, students resent the inconvenience and express their hostility against the Junior Staff. Thus, during the 1964 general strike over wages, the President of the U.I.W.U. and other members of a workers' delegation were assaulted by a group of students in one of the halls. Seldom if ever did students demonstrate any solidarity with the striking workers, especially as the latter have on occasions timed their labor stoppages for maximum impact toward the end of the academic year when the all-important examinations are imminent. This was the case with the June, 1964 strike.

Many unpleasant episodes between students and hall staff assume an ethnic flavor because they frequently take place between persons of different ethnic groups. Indeed, friction is likely to be maximized if, in addition to social distance and conflicts of interests, the barrier of ethnic and linguistic differences interposes itself and interferes with communication. Students of different ethnic groups can easily communicate through the medium of English, but most of the Subordinate Staff are not fluent enough in English to convey complex thoughts. Thus much of the student-Junior Staff interaction, insofar as they do not share a common mother tongue, takes place through the impoverished linguistic medium of Pidgin English. Misunderstandings are thus much more likely to arise across ethnic lines, even though ethnicity is not directly at stake. Also, in a society where ethnic distinctions are still more sharply drawn than class differences, there is a common tendency to interpret as ethnic conflict what may in fact be class conflict. Many foreign observers of Nigerian social reality tend to overstress the importance of ethnicity because Nigerians themselves tend to view most conflicts as expressions of "tribalism."

Two cases from student letters illustrate the propensity for trivial disputes to become interpreted in terms of ethnicity. A first student reports a clash with the Chief Cleaner in his hall:

The Chief Cleaner . . . started raving on me—that it is this Ibo attitude in me that is causing trouble in the country today. I told him I was no Ibo. I replied him with 'You are a fool,' and he said, 'your father is a fool.' I am very bitter here because . . . my father is not of the calibre that a mere steward should abuse. This particular steward . . . is naturally aggressive. Many have tolerated him in sympathy with the possibilities of that fault arising from the simple truths of genetics.

It is interesting to note here that the servant in question was Ibo, had asserted that the student was Ibo which he disclaimed, and that they both accused each other of "typical" Ibo behavior.

The other instance is that of an Eastern student who complains to his Warden of ethnic discrimination in room allocation. He alone of the elected members of the Student Union Executive does not have a room to himself, he claims, and, as he is also the only Easterner among the student officials, he can only conclude that ethnic discrimination is the cause of it:

I am not so inconsequential in this society as not to be listened to . . . I am the only one out of the eight Student Union Officials who is paired [i.e. who shares a room]. Your staff have said that they did so because I am from the East and not the Mid-West—I regard it as a tribal prejudice. . . . The staff concerned have always talked of me as an Ibo, and so, they have always been partial to me. If they have been suffering from Ibophobia, I am not. I am no Ibo, but I have always restrained myself from that mania; personally I have nothing against any man, Ibo or otherwise.

Here again is an interesting case of an attribution of Ibo ethnicity which is denied. These tensions were of course not unrelated to the Civil War. In both instances, a dispute based mostly on status claims, and which involved a student with a member of the Junior Staff and Senior Staff respectively, became reinterpreted in terms of ethnicity.

Inter-Estate Solidarity

So far we have stressed the cleavages separating the three estates at U.I. Now we must stress the other side of the picture which is of at least equal if not greater importance. The three estates are linked by a great multiplicity of ties which cut completely across social status distinctions. Sharp though status differences are, they are but one of several important bases of cleavage, and often not the most salient one. We shall turn first to the formal aspects of inter-estate cooperation, and then to the even more complex and no less crucial network of informal ties.

The tri-partite nature of the University community is officially recognized and is reflected in a number of formal structures which integrate the three estates. The first estate, or, more precisely, a small oligarchy within it, detains a near monopoly of power, but a small measure of representation and consultation is granted to the other two estates which are recognized as corporate entities, and formally incorporated as subordinate elements in the larger structure of the University community. The only segment of the community which can be said to be totally excluded from the formal structure are the domestic servants, who, as we have already seen, constitute a well-differentiated, lower-status subgroup within the third estate.

Symbolic recognition of the corporate-estate structure of the University, and of the unequal status of the three estates can be found in the great annual rituals of Foundation Day and Graduation, since 1969 combined into one, but previously held respectively in November and June. These highly elaborate gatherings are, at the same time, rituals of collective consciousness and solidarity in the Durkheimian sense, and dazzling displays of status distinctions. The pomp of British academic tradition blends with indigenous splendor to create an orgy of protocol and a colorful display of conspicuous consumption reminiscent of a tropical aviary. Academics in their crimson and indigo robes, traditional rulers in their embroidered *agbadas,* army officers in their parade uniforms, opulent dignitaries and their gold-bedecked spouses flutter around as so many birds of paradise to create a theatrical pageantry of status.

Not only do these events punctuate the life of the University; they are also among the most important social events in the whole of Nigeria, drawing together all the sections of the elite, including frequently the Head of State. They are a hybrid between a British coronation ceremony and the Great Sallah which marks the end of Ramadan in the traditional Muslim monarchies of the North. The Estate Officer is responsible for the elaborate protocolar and practical arrangements, a task which keeps him and his staff occupied for several months of the year. The vast majority of guests are either University Senior Staff or members of the top political, military, bureaucratic or professional elite, but a small contingent of students and Junior Staff are also invited as representatives of their estates, as well, of course, as the graduates and their immediate families at Graduation exercises. The seating is rigorously arranged according to status precedence, a task leading to endless arguments and occasional disputes as it is impossible to reduce to a single unequivocal and mutually agreeable order of precedence persons who belong to different hierarchies..

Even the parking lots are in a status hierarchy depending on their proximity to Congregation Hall. A steady flow of chauffeur driven Mercedeses and other prestige cars disgorges opulent passengers in front of the courtyard to the Hall during the hour which precedes the opening of the ceremony, and the Congregation Hall becomes, for the next two hours, the *rendez-vous* of the Nigerian elite. Admission is by gold-lettered invitation cards, carefully checked by the police at the entrance gate. During the Civil War, the police and the military were maintaining strict security, as a well-placed bomb could have thinned very considerably the ranks of the ruling class. The military governor, for example, came with a military convoy of half-a-dozen army vehicles mounted with machine guns, and the stage inside the Hall had almost as many policemen as dignitaries.

Another set of formal events at which status lines are clearly marked are the parties hosted by the student halls. Each student hall holds a formal and lavish party once a year, for which the University, the Master of the hall, and the students in residence all contribute funds. Every hall tries to outshine the others in the quality of the food, the elaborateness of the decorations, and the reputation of the "highlife," "juju" and "soul" bands hired for the occasion. The dining room and common rooms are converted into dance floors and tables and chairs are set in the illuminated courtyards between the dormitory wings. Dress is expected to be semi-formal, i.e. either Western suits and ties for men and cocktail dresses for women, or the full indigenous dress which is preferred by the majority of the Yoruba Senior Staff.

Each hall invites (with formal printed cards) some 60 to 100 members of the Senior Staff with their wives, and give them honored-guest treatment throughout the evening. Upon arrival, they are escorted by a student host to a special segregated section of the courtyard furnished with comfortable armchairs collected from the common rooms. They are then offered hard alcoholic beverages while the students have only a choice of soft drinks and beer. (Actually, little drinking takes place among either students or Senior Staff.) A special buffet table laden with a much greater variety and quality of Nigerian and English dishes than is available to the students is reserved for the Senior Staff to help themselves. Throughout the evening, very little mixing of students and Senior Staff takes place, as each group stays in its segregated area of the courtyard. The dance floors are mixed, but students dance with their dates, and the Senior Staff with their wives for the most part.

Some members of the Senior Staff attend the University-wide dances organized by the students half-a-dozen times a year in Congregation Hall, and so do many younger members of the elite from town such as civil servants and army officers, but students and Senior Staff tend to come in small groups of 4 to 10 friends who congregate around a table and dance only with each other throughout the evening. As the number of male students greatly exceeds that of female students, a number of non-elite girls from town also attend these dances.

The most democratic party which I have witnessed was that held by the Nigerian Institute for Social and Economic Research (NISER), a government-sponsored research organization located on the U.I. campus and closely linked with the Social Sciences Faculty. The entire staff of the Institute, from the secretarial staff to professors, was invited and there were no formal distinctions of rank in the seating, refreshments, or entertainment. Later in the evening, two or three members of the Junior Staff became inebriated, one of the rare displays of public drunkenness I have witnessed on campus, and this was a source of amusement to some of the Senior Staff who remarked with a note of tolerant condescension that those people were not used to this type of party.

Sport events are also integrated to some extent, but with preferential treatment granted to the Senior Staff. At soccer games or track events held on the main University sports grounds, for example, there is typically a crowd of several thousands spectators, mostly students and Obatala Village residents, who intermix freely, and stand around the grass field in the open sun. On one side, however, there is a small thatch-covered tribune with a row of easy chairs reserved for official Senior Staff guests (such as the wife of the Vice-Chancellor or the Master of a hall who is entrusted with presenting the cup to the victorious team) and other Senior Staff spectators.

With the exceptions just noted, the "social" life of the University, both the informal parties and the official or semi-official ones such as receptions at the Vice-Chancellor's, Senior Staff Club dances and the like, are strictly limited to the Senior Staff, and the amount of contact between the three estates outside the office, the classroom or the hall of residence is minimal.

Neither students nor Junior Staff are represented on any of the main statutory bodies of the University (Council, Senate, Congregation, Convocation), nor indeed, with one exception, on the standing committees thereof. Even on the Council and Senate Committees which deal specifically with matters of direct concern to the Junior Staff, such as the Intermediate and Subordinate Staff Sub-Committee of the Finance and General Purposes Committee, and the Students' Disciplinary Committee, the membership consists solely of Senior Staff. There is, however, a Consultative Committee for Community Development (C.C.C.D.) under the Chairmanship of a Senior Staff member. Several Senior Staff officials (such as the Registrar, the Estate Officer, the Chief Engineer and the Director of the Health Service) belong to it *ex officio,* but, in addition, each of the three estates chooses, by different procedures, three persons designated respectively as representatives of the Senior Staff, Junior Staff, and Student Residential Communities. The C.C.C.D. is a committee of the University Council, and, as its name indicates, it is powerless. Its main function is as a sounding board for complaints, and as a body making recommendations to Council.

Student attendance at meetings of the C.C.C.D. is minimal, largely because the Committee is primarily concerned with the kind of practical and material problems that is not of immediate concern to students, such as condition of the roads, water supply, repairs of buildings, allocation of staff housing, offensive odors and noise, the organization of the health clinic, and the like. Junior Staff representatives attend more regularly than the student members, but they are greatly outnumbered by the Senior Staff (which includes both *ex officio* and elected members), and lack of self-confidence in expressing themselves in English hinders Junior Staff participation.

Beyond this formal, statutory level of incorporation which, as we have just seen, is minimal, there are various mechanisms of semi-formal consultation. Since Akinode became Vice-Chancellor, he has on several occasions expressed concern about the need for greater student incorporation in the governance of the University, and has held regular weekly meetings with student representatives to discuss student problems, such as scholarships and loans. At a lower level, there is a Senior Assistant Registrar for Students' Affairs and Careers who, with his staff of subordinates, is in constant contact with students, mediates in disputes, acts on student grievances, guides students in seeking employment, moderates and supervises student elections, sanctions "official" demonstrations, and generally performs a liaison function between students and University administration. The students do not, however, directly participate in the administration of the University. The elected student officials in the Student Representative Council run scarcely anything besides a snack-bar and their own offices, and are a structure separate from, rather than incorporated into, the University administration.

At the Junior Staff level, the major liaison with University administration is through the Assistant Registrar for Establishments and Labor, who, symbolically, ranks lower than the Senior Assistant Registrar for students, even though he has a bigger, more difficult and more delicate job to perform. That Assistant Registrar is in almost daily contact with officers of the U.I.W.U., and is well aware of the need to maintain close consultation with the Union if labor disputes and strikes are to be avoided.

Concern about the ability and readiness of workers to strike has led the University to establish three non-statutory committees with both Union and administration respresentatives under the chairmanship of the Registrar: the Joint Consultative Committee, the Joint Negotiating Committee (which meets only in cases of labor disputes), and the Disciplinary Committee. There is little question, then, that the Union, despite its debilitating ethnic squabbles, exercises a substantial measure of power through actual strikes or the threat of strikes. Especially in a system which is as labor-intensive as U.I., strikes have an immediate paralyzing effect in essential services.

The Union has another important link with the Senior Staff through the person of a senior and prominent Yoruba professor who is perhaps one of the half-dozen most knowledgeable and powerful persons at U.I. A socialist by political disposition, he has been a leading opponent of the University administration and of Vice-Chancellors through the Nwanneh, Hickerson and Akinode eras. Besides being a permanent head of department, he is a voting member of two different faculties, has been intermittently the dean of one of them, sits in Senate *ex officio,* is a member of several key committees, is the elected Congregation representative in Council, and was chosen by the Union as its Patron. He is one of the very few persons at U.I. with an extensive understanding both of the formal and legal structure of the University, and of the complex informal structure in all three major segments of the community, especially the Senior and the Junior Staff; and he uses his sweeping knowledge and power with political skill. As representative of the first estate in Council, and patron of the U.I.W.U., he constitutes both a "friend in court" for the third estate and a formidable opponent to the administration within the first estate. Through his membership in both Senate and Council, and in several key committees of both, there is hardly any important decision to which he is not privy. To his power, he adds the prestige of an international scholarly reputation, and an unusual record of systematic opposition to whomever is in power. Mistrusted by nearly everybody on the Senior Staff, he is not aligned with any well defined clique and is both an important figure within the power structure and a formidable critic of it.

A final set of links of a semi-formal nature between the three estates is that of religion. The topic is important enough to deserve a chapter to itself. Suffice it to say here that the Protestant, Catholic and Muslim congregations on campus all transcend estate lines, and that these ties are much more significant at U.I. than one would find them at the typically more secularized universities of Europe or America.

PATRON-CLIENT TIES

Essential though the formal and semi-formal ties between estates are, by themselves they cannot give an even approximately accurate picture of the actual situation. Of at least equal importance, and of vastly greater complexity, is the multiplicity of informal ties between individual members of the three estates. These ties create a vast and extremely diffuse network of personal relationships across estate lines which often supercede "class" loyalties. Although one should not push the parallel too far, it is surely not accidental that this type of personalized political relationship of clientage is a prominent feature of most traditional Nigerian kingdoms.

The clientage system at U.I. is not purely and simply a transposition of the traditional order, because there are obvious differences between the two; but it is difficult to escape the conclusion that there has taken place, as in many other aspects of social change in Africa, a creative reinterpretation and adaptation of a traditional pattern to a "modern" situation.[5] These ties across estate lines are both more numerous and more important than in industrialized Western societies, though not necessarily than in the more agrarian Western societies of Latin America for example. The phenomenon to be described is thus not uniquely Africa, but rather more characteristic of complex agrarian societies. Weber termed this complex "patrimonialism," and found it prominently in Asian civilizations.

The patron-client relationship is an eminently personal tie, consisting of a private unwritten contract involving mutual obligations. This is not to deny that in the vast majority of cases some type of common group membership may have facilitated, if not largely determined, the establishment of the relationship. However, in the University context, these groups, most typically based on kinship, locality, or ethnicity are regarded as irrelevant if not downright illegitimate in the formal structure of the community; furthermore the links themselves are not corporate but personal. For example, an Ibibio student may be more likely to seek the protection of an Ibibio lecturer, or a junior brother will "naturally" seek the help of his senior brother in a higher position, but the ties themselves are strictly bilateral. One cannot even speak of a patron and his clients constituting collectively a corporate group. Thus, the structure of clientship is extremely diffuse and difficult to define with any precision, but nevertheless of great importance.

Three points must be stressed at the outset. First, the clientage system exists not only *between* the various estates but also *within* them. Thus, for example, a lecturer may become the client of a professor or a dean. Second, the degree of patronage to be dispensed being a function of power, it follows that only the more important members of the Senior Staff, especially the heads of departments, deans and senior administrators, have a clientele which goes much beyond the extended family obligations. Thirdly, while the demands made on senior Nigerians by their clients are often more numerous, more pressing and more difficult to resist because the ties are frequently closer, the system also includes senior expatriates. Many of them find themselves quickly enmeshed in a network of obligations before they have had time to develop defense mechanisms against demands by subordinates.

The first and often most potent basis of clientage which is largely limited to Nigerians involves the ties and obligations of kinship. The extended family is, of course, traditional in all indigenous societies, but in the modern context of the University, the network of obligations becomes even wider than it was. Traditionally, the senior relative would exercise authority and

expect deference from his juniors; in the modern context the economically
or politically successful person can expect any less fortunate kinsman irrespective of age to make demands on him. The relative recency of individual
success in the monetary sector, and the very scope of kinship obligations
insure that every member of the elite has scores of relatives who potentially
have claims on his hospitality, generosity or good will, many of whom will
actually attempt to validate these claims by becoming more or less dependent
on the "big man" in the family. Practically every member of the Nigerian
elite has close relatives—brothers, nephews, uncles—who are non-elite, and
who will expect him to share his resources with them in return for deference
and/or services. This still wide lack of coincidence between status in the
modern sector and the kinship system is a major factor creating powerful
links between estates, and differentiates the African situation from the more
stabilized class systems of Europe, Asia or America.

The many claims by relatives make for a considerable redistribution of
wealth, militate against elite closure, and constitute an important "social
security" system in a country that still lacks and can ill afford a more formal
state-run system. Many members of the elite increasingly resent and try to
minimize extended family obligations, but if they live within geographical
reach of their kinsmen, they can do little to avoid honoring the requests of
their impecunious relatives. In the nature of the case, dependency relations
tend to be self-reinforcing: the more one helps a person, the more one feels
obligated, and is expected by others to help him further.

In minimal form, kin obligations involve the extension of customary hospitality often for periods of weeks or even months. The Senior Staff person
living in a spacious home and in a gracious style would be regarded as
extraordinarily stingy and anti-social if he did not receive his relatives well.
Frequently a poorer relative will come and stay with a Senior Staff person
while looking for a job in town. Given the extreme scarcity of wage jobs,
he will naturally expect his elite kinsman not only to give him room and
board, but also to use his influence to find him a post, preferably at the
University. Meanwhile the poor relative will try to reciprocate the favors
by trying to make himself useful in the household and by a proper show of
deference. Sometimes the borderline between poor relative and domestic
servant becomes blurred. Thus nephews and nieces who have come to board
with their uncle to attend school in town will work in the household and
garden in exchange for room, board and school fees, although the exchange
seldom takes an explicitly economic form. Sometimes the relationship may
degenerate into a kind of domestic slavery, but more often the poor relative
constitutes a drain on the resources of the Senior Staff member.

Almost every Nigerian member of the Senior Staff (and indeed many
among the Junior Staff as well) has several relatives other than wife and

children living with him. He will typically pay the school fees and uniforms of any junior brothers remaining to be supported through secondary school, and will often contribute in addition to the expenses of one or two wife's siblings or father's brother's children. One or two of these junior relatives frequently live in the household as part-time quasi-servants. The more affluent Senior Staff person may have to carry the financial burden of a dozen to a score of more or less dependent non-elite relatives. The subsidization of schooling, which is in turn the passport to social mobility, is the most common, indeed a nearly universal, form of expressing family solidarity. In many cases, these obligations are in repayment of favors; thus, the person who may now finance his father's brother's son through boarding school may have had his own education paid for by that father's brother.

Where nepotism becomes more problematic is in the allocation of jobs, which, along with schooling, is one of the major demands of poor relatives on Senior Staff. Given a surfeit of secondary-school trained persons for middle echelon clerical occupations, and indeed a general surplus of labor at all levels in relation to the limited capacity of the money sector of the economy to absorb the products of the mushrooming schools, urban unemployment is extremely high, and competition to get any wage job at the University, even the most menial, is fierce.

In theory, University vacancies at all levels, from a professorship to a post of cook or cleaner, are filled according to an elaborate procedure involving advertisement in the local press for Junior Staff positions, and in the Nigerian and foreign press for academic appointments. Formal applications are sent to the Registrar, examined by a committee which also interviews the candidate and reports its recommendations to the appropriate appointments committee. Appointments are finally made by the Council, and in the case of academic posts on recommendation of the Senate. Elaborate procedures specify every step of the process in order to insure universalistic criteria of recruitment, so elaborate in fact that, if one were to follow them rigidly, hardly any appointment could be made at all. Even so, an attempt to apply the rules, or the pretense of applying them delays the most menial appointments by several weeks and the more senior ones by months. Thus, an ironical paradox develops: the universalistic rules endeavor to avoid nepotism, favoritism and tribalism, but in doing so they become so elaborate that they are self-defeating, and have to be evaded if vacancies are to be filled with some degree of dispatch and efficiency.

Far and away the most common evasive technique is that of the one-year temporary appointment, for which the regulations provide a faster and simpler procedure. These temporary appointments are supposed to cover either very exceptional or urgent cases where the regular procedure would not be appropriate, and, after one year of service, these "temporary" appointments may, and, in a vast majority of cases, are renewed and made permanent. Among the Junior Staff, no more than some 10 per cent of all non-daily paid casual workers are on temporary appointments at any given time, but some *two-thirds* of the new appointments made each year use the "exceptional" procedure, which is, of course, perfectly legal.

To return to the problem of nepotism, every person in authority is caught in the middle of a conflict between the universalistic normative system which he is supposed to abide by, and the insistent demands of his clients that he violate those rules for their benefit and in terms of totally different criteria which are often regarded as legitimate or indeed meritorious in the traditional context. Not to help one's relatives is selfish, and appeal to a formal and alien system of rules in order to avoid doing so is regarded merely as a poor excuse for not fulfilling one's duty or obligation to kinsmen. This is all the more the case as both patron and client know that, in practice, particularistic criteria are often the determining ones, and that, without the support of a well-placed patron, a person has next to no chance of getting a job for which there may be scores or even hundreds of at least minimally qualified applicants.

This is not to say that the universalistic rules are inoperative. At the very least, one has to go through the motions of following them even when one fully intends to pervert their spirit. Second, one has to know the rules in order to be able to challenge one's opponents on legalistic grounds. Third, the formal rules define at least the minimum level of competence, typically a minimum schooling requirement, required for the job, and thereby impose limits on the play of particularism. But within those limits, particularistic considerations are often paramount.

Among Senior Staff, there are vast differences in the ability to dispense patronage. The more junior lecturers and administrative officers, for example, do not sit on any important committees, except perhaps as non-voting secretaries, and exercise virtually no control over appoinments. Heads of departments, whether academic or administrative, on the other hand, can play a decisive role in the recruitment of all their subordinates. Masters of halls of residence dispose of the largest patronage empires, since each hall has up to one hundred positions for cooks, stewards, cleaners, launderers, gardeners and the like. The majority of Senior Staff in authority positions do not regularly use their power for patronage purposes, but a few, and by no means exclusively Nigerians, are notorious in this respect, as the ethnic composition of some departments or halls staff immediately reveals.

These patron-client ties between relatives ensure that throughout the University there is a wide network of kin ties between Senior Staff, students and Junior Staff. (There is much less nepotism in the admission of students than in the hiring of staff, because the criteria of admission are relatively clear-cut, and admission procedures are closely scrutinized by the various Faculty Boards, and by Senate where the multiplicity of particularistic interests results in their mutual cancellation.) The links between Senior and Junior Staff are especially significant since they span such a wide status gap. It is by no means exceptional, for example, that a dean's chauffeur will be his nephew, or that the department head's stenographer will be his wife's younger brother.

Patron-client ties are, of course, not limited to persons previously linked by kinship or marriage. After kinship, locality represents the next wider level of solidarity in the traditional order. The definition of the local groups varies greatly in scope depending on circumstances. It may range from a small town of a few thousand inhabitants to a major segment of an ethnic group numbering several hundred thousand people. Often, however, the most meaningful unit is a major town and its rural hinterland. Such local groupings frequently have a progressive association, which combines the functions of a chamber of commerce, a political pressure group and an employment agency; prominent members of the elite, including University Senior Staff, often play leading roles in such local associations which expect them to be their spokesman in whatever sector of the bureaucracy or business they hold a post. These town progressive associations often correspond in scope to traditional kingdoms, especially in Yoruba country, and they are linked with dialectical and sub-cultural differences. Locality is thus frequently a form of sub-ethnicity. Within Yorubaland, for example, or within an organization such as U.I. where Yoruba are numerous, both absolutely and relatively, this local level of solidarity is often more important than the wider but much looser concept of Yoruba ethnicity. One is not simply a Yoruba, but an "Ekiti man" or an Egba, or an Ijebu, or an Ondo, all localized sub-divisions of the larger group. These divisions are themselves fragmented into smaller units that are often traditional city states such as Ede, Iwo or Oshogbo, to mention again Yoruba examples.

Naturally, the politics of localism at the University are most developed among the most strongly represented ethnic groups, namely the Yoruba whose internal divisions are proverbial, and, until the Civil War, the Ibo. The smaller ethnic groups cannot afford the luxury of finer distinctions, but a person with a tie of locality has typically a much stronger claim on a patron's favor than someone who is merely a fellow ethnic. Next to kinship, locality is the most powerful basis of partonage and the most important predictor of clique formation within the main ethnic groups, especially the Yoruba.

Common ethnicity is a yet wider basis for a patron-client relationship than locality or kinship, and is perhaps most effective among the "minority" ethnic groups. The most senior representative of such a group on campus will often be regarded as the informal leader and spokesman for the group, and will frequently be put under greater pressure to promote the interests of his fellow ethnics than persons belonging to larger groups where these pressures are more diffuse. Often a senior member of a minority group will rationalize his ethnic favoritism as an attempt to redress the imbalance against the minorities imposed by the dominance of the larger groups. The final and widest basis of all for solidary patron-client ties is religion. The topics of ethnicity and religion are important enough to merit each a later chapter. Kinship, locality, ethnicity and religion are four major sets of ties which operate, in very important ways, both within and between each of the three estates. These relations which, across estate lines, take largely the form of patron-client ties, establish significant forms of solidarity, bridge the wide economic gap, and reduce the amount of conflict between the three main status groups.

The more senior professors in important positions of power may have a clientele running into the hundreds of persons who are indebted, dependent and loyal to them. Between teaching staff and students this model of relationship is of course completely accepted within the norms of academia, especially in a system which emulates the Oxbridge tutorial system with low student-staff ratios, small classes, and close ties between teachers and students. Both Nigerian and expatriate staff maintain such ties with students, and at that level, there is an accidental convergence of British academic norms and African traditional systems. Unless a lecturer expresses blatant ethnic favoritism *vis à vis* students, his preference for "his" students is fully legitimized in the official norms of the University. This is perhaps one of the reasons why accusations of nepotism and "tribalism" are fewest in such matters as admission of students and examinations.

The patron-client ties between the first and the third estate on the other hand do not have the stamp of legitimacy within the official norms of the University, and indeed they commonly seek to undermine or at least circumvent official rules. It may be thought that the bases for patron-client ties are such that the phenomenon is largerly restricted to the Nigerian Senior Staff. Expatriates do not have kinsmen, fellow townsmen or even fellow ethnics among Junior Staff. Only religion remains as a significant basis of corporate solidarity between foreigners and Nigerians. In practice, however, while it is true that the clientele of senior expatriates is probably less numerous and less insistent than that of their Nigerian counterparts, foreigners are also drawn, wittingly or unwittingly, into this vast patronage system.

Favoritism will then be based on personal liking and demonstrations of loyalty, more than on the basis of common membership in corporate groups. Furthermore, many senior expatriates are manipulated by their own subordinates or colleagues so as to make them behave in a way consistent with the interests of a Nigerian clique or faction. The pattern is clearest and most manifest to all parties involved in the case of domestic servants. The hiring of servants is done in good part through the recommendation of other servants, and the servants of expatriates maintain a vast informal employment agency, recommending each other for jobs, exchanging information about employers, and so on. This pattern may be so closely linked that parallel ethnic networks exist between groups of masters and servants. Thus, for example, a group of Americans who socialize with each other will tend to employ a group of Mid-Western Ibo servants who are closely related to each other by locality or kinship, and who keep placing each other with other Americans. The entire system is consolidated by the reciprocal "loan" of servants when large dinner parties are held.

Similarly, though in a manner of which the expatriate is frequently much less aware, foreign lecturers and professors are often used by Nigerian colleagues and Junior Staff to promote the aims of a particular group or faction. We shall examine later the effects of this on ethnic factionalism within the Senior Staff. At the Junior Staff level, Nigerians can often manipulate their foreign superiors all the more effectively as expatriates lack both sufficient knowledge of, and interest in, local Nigerian politics to enable them to see through their subordinates' game. Most expatriates are given a Nigerian ethnic label corresponding to that of their Nigerian friends and associates. Thus, they become known as pro-Yoruba or pro-Ibo. Many foreigners, when they discover that fact, are naive enough to be surprised, but their behavior often makes the labeling readily understandable.

Social Mobility

So far, we have reviewed the nature of the ties between the three estates. There remains to explore the question of social mobility between them. Despite numerous links of ethnicity, locality and kinship between the three status groups, social mobility of an individual between groups is extremely limited. Yet, paradoxically, the three estates are still widely open, more so, in fact, than Western-style social classes. How is this seeming paradox resolved? As the stratification system consists of a stepped pyramid wherein each ascending step is much narrower than one below, the probability of a person moving up to the next grade is very limited even though a sizeable proportion of those at the top have so climbed, if not in their own occupational history, at least as compared to the social status of their parents. Looked at from the top, the system seems relatively open and meritocratic; seen from the bottom the chances of mobility are infinitesimally small. Rates of mobility, and indeed their subjective perception by the people concerned, vary greatly according to one's position in the hierarchy and to the relative size of the strata from which one looks. African ruling classes recruit many of their members from lower strata, but as the ruling group comprises well under one per cent of the total population, it is much easier to take a sanguine view of the system's equity and democracy from the top than from the bottom.

Let us look at the details of how mobility operates at U.I. Between the second and the first estate the mobility is institutionalized, even though its actual amount is relatively small. U.I. Senior Staff is recruited from all over the world, but, holding qualifications constant, preference is given to Nigerians, and a fourth to a third of them have taken at least their undergraduate work at Ilosho. Looked at from the perspective of the Senior Staff, U.I. is a major, indeed the most important single avenue of entry into the first estate. From the viewpoint of the undergraduate, however, his chances of entering the University as a lecturer or senior administrator are approximately one in a hundred. Nevertheless, if he graduates, the student can look forward to elite status as a bureaucrat, manager, or secondary school teacher where he will typically get a starting salary of £750 to £900, or 25 to 30 times the per capita average for Nigeria. Even though the student has little prospect of becoming Senior Staff at U.I., he has a very high probability of entering at least the lower rungs of the same highly privileged social stratum. Insofar as the term "class" is applicable to Nigerian stratification, the basic distinction between students and Senior Staff is more one of age than one of class. Convocation, the body of U.I. graduates, along with the graduates of the other Nigerian universities, constitutes a roster of the people who run the modern sector of Nigeria.

The barrier between Senior and Junior Staff is much more fundamental, and mobility between them is exceptional both in a statistical and in a normative sense. According to a senior administrator, 37 Junior Staff members have been promoted to Senior Staff status in U.I. history, mostly in the Registry or in the laboratory technicians' categories. It is difficult to estimate precisely how many persons have served the University in the Subordinate and Intermediate ranks, but the total would certainly exceed 10,000 as the turnover is large at the bottom. Statistically, then, the chances of promotion from Junior to Senior Staff are roughly of the order of one to 300. This rough estimate does not tell us much about the actual situation, however, because there are vast inequalities of promotion opportunities within the Junior Staff itself.

At all levels, the amount of formal education is, by far, the most important determining factor of one's position in the hierarchy, and of one's chances of promotion. In theory, the University hires only literates, with preference to those who have completed six or seven years of primary education and who have a working command of English. In a country which is still 80 to 85 per cent illiterate, this means that the University is very selective, even in its most menial categories of employment. It also means that U.I. effectively screens out nearly all Northerners because the literacy rate in the South is many times higher than in the North (roughly 30–35 per cent and 3 to 5 per cent respectively), and because, in the North, Hausa rather than English is a *lingua franca*. This *de facto* discrimination is, of course, not intentional, but it is nevertheless very real.

In fact, not all U.I. employees are literate. Perhaps 10 to 20 per cent of the lowest job categories of the permanent staff, and 25 per cent of the casual daily paid workers are illiterate. In 1969, there was strong opposition by the Union, and especially by the caterers' group within it, to the University's attempt to dismiss some gardeners and caterers on grounds of illiteracy and insufficient knowledge of English. The University's argument was that English was the official language both of the country and of the University, and that, especially in the University Guest House which catered for V.I.P.'s from all over the world, even gardeners and cleaners had to be literate and speak English. The workers argued that gardening, cooking and cleaning were skills unrelated to either literacy or the ability to speak English. While the University is forced to retain its illiterate workers already on the permanent staff, basic literacy and basic English are now prerequisites for being hired. Increasingly this means that, even in purely ancillary occupations, complete primary education is the minimum standard. This even applies to the most desirable domestic servants jobs, namely those in expatriate households. Almost no expatriates in the South make the effort of learning any Nigerian language, although in the North many acquire a smattering of Hausa.

The Subordinate Staff employee with bare literacy and only a smattering of Standard English (as distinguished from the more widespread Pidgin English) has virtually no prospect of rising to a non-manual occupation, and of being promoted to the pay categories of the Intermediate Staff. The borderline between Subordinate and Intermediate Staff, though *economically* much less sharply drawn than that between Junior and Senior Staff, is perhaps socially and culturally *more* clear-cut. Intermediate Staff status means, in almost all cases, secondary as distinguished from primary education and an extensive knowledge of "proper" as distinguished from Pidgin English. The little mobility between Junior and Senior Staff which does take place occurs in the top echelons of the Intermediate Staff with highly skilled technicians or private secretaries who typically have matriculated at least at the "O" level and often at the "A" level,[6] and have had years of experience in running the routine part of a laboratory or an office that may involve coordinating the work of half a dozen or more clerks and messengers. The more gifted of these people (who, in local terminology, are called "executive officers") may be promoted to the rank of Administrative Officer, the lowest rank in the Senior Administrative Staff, and the normal point of entry of a University Graduate. In practice, then, opportunities for promotion from Junior to Senior Staff are extremely limited, and are to all intents and purposes non-existent for those who do not possess the rare combination of a good secondary education, an exceptional degree of native intelligence, and good political connections.

Language

The linguistic aspect of status in Nigeria, and indeed elsewhere in Africa, cannot be overestimated. English is the official language of Nigeria, the sole medium of instruction at the universities and secondary schools, and the common language of the educated "elite." It is, therefore, the prestige language *par excellence*. Mastery of English has replaced skin pigmentation as the most important symbol of "elite" status since Independence. It is no longer necessary to be white to gain access to the top, but it is more important than ever to speak the language of the former colonial masters if one aspires to escape any but the most menial and subordinate of positions. Interestingly, very few Nigerians, irrespective of their status, resent this linguistic neo-colonialism. The ruling stratum derives maximum advantage from this situation. Not only does it have a convenient means of elite communication across ethnic lines and a ready access to its international counterparts, but the oligopolistic and semiesoteric use of English is a powerful adjuvant to class domination. English is not only laden with prestige value; it is also the language of administration and of formal education beyond primary school, and therefore the language of power. Since fluency in English is the necessary (if not the sufficient) condition for upward mobility, English also has a negotiable monetary value on the labor market. To a considerable extent, the hierarchy of prestige, power and wealth in the modern sector of Nigeria (i.e. the sector which allows one to escape life-long poverty) is a hierarchy of ability to speak the King's English.

The continuum ranges from Pidgin, which is regarded by the "elite" as "bad" or "bastardized" English, and stigmatized as "bush," to the most assiduous endeavor to emulate an Oxonian accent. The degree of grammatical approximation to "proper" English is one of the most self-consciously used criteria of status placement used by Nigerians. Some members of the elite go as far as sending their children away to British boarding schools so they should learn not only "good grammar" as they would in a Nigerian secondary school, but also the "proper" accent. One of the main dimensions on which job applicants are rated in interviews is their ability to express themselves in English. The great majority of men and of younger women in the urban centers of the South speak at least Pidgin English, a widespread *lingua franca,* and Pidgin (which is an identifiable dialect of English, and not simply "broken" English) is also used extensively on campus as a medium of communication between lowly-educated persons of different ethnic groups, or between students and Junior Staff, or among students in a jocular context, such as to relate funny stories. Pidgin at U.I. is clearly associated with subordinate status, and more educated people will typically speak either their mother tongue or English in marked preference to Pidgin.

Among Senior Staff and students, ability to speak fluent standard English is taken for granted, and Nigerian intellectuals have sufficient status security to speak their mother tongue together if they share the same one. For example, Yoruba lecturers and students are as likely to speak Yoruba as English together, the main determining criterion being the presence or absence of non-Yorubas in the group, and to some extent the topic of conversation. It is considered bad manners to keep talking a language which excludes some members of the group, although a brief remark such as a proverb, a greeting or a joke may be interjected in an English conversation. The esoteric use of one's mother tongue is one of the main factors making for ethnic antagonisms, each group accusing the other of doing so deliberately and malevolently.

Between superiors and subordinates of the same ethnic group, preference is usually given to the mother tongue, unless outsiders are present, or unless the person of higher rank, who is often expected to initiate the conversation, wants to use English in order to stress his superiority. English, for example, may be the favorite language of reprimands. Differential ability to use English is an important mark of invidious status distinctions between Senior and Junior Staff; it reinforces social distance, and gives the superior a cultural as well as a power advantage over his subordinates. If the superior wants to make his subordinate feel at ease, he will use, if he can, a language in which both feel equally competent. In the case of ethnic differences, this is not possible, and the linguistic barrier is one of the more subtle factors making for ethnic mistrust. One cannot easily trust a person with whom one cannot communicate fluently and easily.

The use of English as a mechanism of ridicule and social distance can be quite devastating, and is relatively common. Thus, students often make fun of each other when one of them makes a grammatical mistake. The highest level of linguistic arrogance is probably found among clerical, white-collar workers. For example, I witnessed a young female clerk at the U.I. Post Office mercilessly ridicule and abuse a middle-aged man who was flustered in his attempt to order stamps in English. She told him not to waste her time and to go back to his wife in the bush if he could not speak proper English. (She was, incidentally, a Federal Government employee, not a U.I. employee, but this kind of behavior is not unusual at the Intermediate level of University staff.) A favorite way of humiliating a status inferior in Nigeria is referred to as "blowing grammar," i.e. using a complex vocabulary and sentence structure in English, and correcting other people's English. This behavior can only be engaged in with impunity by a person of a status superior or equal to that of the person whose English is being corrected.

Although many Nigerian farmers and urban working class persons who speak no English at all or only Pidgin deeply resent the linguistic snobbery of the upper stratum, they have not generally become aware of the political implications of the situation. The urban clerical lower-middle class, and, at University, the Junior Staff, far from challenging the *status quo,* try to emulate the linguistic behavior of the "elite," and the system becomes self-perpetuating. As knowledge of English continues to spread, its oligopolistic value declines correspondingly, but the result is not a more egalitarian society. Instead, the mandarinate restricts access by raising the formal educational qualifications expected at various levels of employment. Where a primary school certification was sufficient ten years ago, matriculation is now required; it now takes a university degree where previously an "A level" secondary certificate was regarded as adequate, and so on.

U.I. is the very pinnacle of this pyramid of linguistic snobbery, and the Senior Staff view themselves as the guardians of the intellectual and linguistic standards on which the entire structure of Nigerian privilege stands.

English is the sole official language of the University. It is used as a medium of instruction, in all deliberations of official bodies such as the Council, the Senate and their committees, and as a written medium for all official documents and correspondence. Nevertheless, a good deal of Yoruba, Edo, Ibo, Ibibio, Ijaw and other indigenous languages is used in offices, and, of course, in casual conversation in student halls, at home, and so on. A few Nigerian Senior Staff families have become predominantly English-speaking at home, and in the case of Nigerians married to expatriate wives, the children may not even know their father's native tongue. By far the more usual pattern, however, is bilingualism at home in Senior Staff or even Intermediate Staff families, with the parents consciously working on their children's fluency in English as a passport to elite status, but at the same time trying to retain some competence in the native tongue in order to maintain communication with less educated relatives. Among Subordinate Staff where competence in English is largely limited to Pidgin, the mother tongue prevails, even though many of those people are multilingual in Nigerian languages. Thus the average non-Yoruba Junior Staff worker will speak in addition to his mother tongue, Pidgin, a smattering of Yoruba if he has lived long in the West, and Hausa if he comes from the North.

English is both a prerogative of elite status and a mechanism reinforcing social distance. It erects a cultural barrier of overwhelming magnitude between elite and masses. In effect, it gives the elite the enormous advantage of freedom of communication with their equals across ethnic boundaries, and conversely it militates against communication between elite and masses except within the confines of the same ethnic group. English is thus an important element of elite domination, similar to the role of French as an aristocratic language in Czarist Russia.

Sex Status

So far, we have dealt with social status at U.I. only in respect to the occupational, economic and political structure of the University, and have disregarded two other aspects of status which are independent of the others, but quite important all the same. I am referring to the universal status distinctions of sex and age. Nigeria, like all of the world's societies is male-dominated, but in the South, women in the "traditional" sector probably have a wider degree of sexual and economic independence *vis à vis* men than in most Western industrial societies. In the traditional economy of the coastal cultures of West Africa, women control the vast bulk of the petty trade. This is not true in the "modern" sector. Western education, far from "emancipating" Nigerian women as it is commonly supposed to have done, has in fact reduced their status relative to that of men. Men outnumber women in elite occupations by a factor of at least nine to one. Among students, the proportion of women has increased from some 5 per cent in the early years to about 12 per cent today, but the discrepancy remains very wide. In the "modern" sector, women play a relatively less important role *vis à vis* men than they do in traditional Southern Nigerian cultures. This is reflected not only in the role of women in the system of production, but also in standards of sexual morality. Traditionally, there was little if any "double standard" of sexual conduct, such as was introduced to the detriment of women by the Victorian Protestant mission schools which trained "elite" women.

In addition, there has been widespread discrimination against girls in access to education, especially post-primary education. Among Muslims, there is a fear that Western education will "spoil" girls, the term "spoil" referring both to mental attitudes and loss of virginity. Among Christians, the prejudice against female education is not as strong, but given limited resources where only one or two children may be sent to secondary school, preference is systematically given to boys. It follows that, typically, only families affluent enough to send all their children to secondary schools will give girls anything like an equal chance. This is clearly reflected in the much higher class background of female compared to male students at University. In a sample of 3,167 students who entered U.I. between 1948 and 1966, it was found that 58.5 per cent of the fathers of women students were professionals or semi-professionals compared to only 31.5 per cent of the fathers of male students. Nearly three times as many men (32.4 per cent) as women (11.3 per cent) came from farming backgrounds.

Limited though female representation is among students, Junior Staff, and Senior Staff, it is interesting to note that, on the whole, there is much *less* sex segregation of occupations than one would find in industrial societies. Women are represented in a wide spectrum of occupations, and they do not come close to monopolizing any of them, except nursing. For example, typing and kindred clerical occupations at U.I. (and in the rest of Nigeria) are not the preserve of women at all; men outnumber women in the Intermediate staff by a substantial margin, though, of course, not as overwhelmingly as in such male preserves as driver, gardener, night-watchman, or messenger. Similarly, servants' jobs are held predominantly by men, although among Nigerian Senior Staff there is probably a fairly equal number of female and male servants. A good many of the male-only jobs are relatively low paying ones, and once a woman gains education and enters the money economy she is more likely to get an equal chance with men than she would in Western Europe or North America; but she has much less of a chance than a Nigerian man of acquiring the necessary education to compete with men in the modern sector, and even when she received Western education, her status compared to that of an educated man is probably lower than that of an uneducated woman relative to an uneducated man.

The occupational independence of Southern Nigerian women represents a carry-over from the traditional system, further facilitated by the fact that an educated Nigerian woman will have an abundance of cheap (and often male) domestic help. Thus, the educated Nigerian woman will find it much easier to contribute very substantially to the standard of living of her family. Many elite families earn double incomes, which in turn allow them to keep two cars and three or four servants who together will only cost one half or so of her salary after taxes.

The University structure reflects both the scarcity of women in wage employment, and the relatively high position of those women who "make the grade." There are no women on the University Council, but several women sit in the Senate and have been promoted to professorships and headships of departments, and there is a sprinkling of women among the administrative Senior Staff. Of the women at U.I., it may be said that they are clearly under-represented in the Subordinate level jobs, best represented in the Intermediate Staff categories (teachers, nurses, clerical workers), and somewhat represented at the Senior Staff level without any clear evidence of sex discrimination in advancement within that top category.[7]

Age Status

In conclusion, we must turn to the important question of age status. What African societies have lacked in economic class differentiation, they have amply made up in the extreme salience of both *relative* and *absolute* age as criteria of status. Nigeria is no exception. In almost every traditional African society, a person's absolute age, as sanctioned by rites of passage and membership in age groups, and his relative seniority *vis à vis* kinsmen and fellow villagers are matters of paramount significance to his role and status. In most Nigerian societies, an elaborate etiquette of age status symbolizes age as a principle of inequality. In the Yoruba language, for example, there is a "polite" form to be used by a junior in addressing his senior and a "familiar" form for seniors addressing juniors. The traditional greeting of a junior to a senior is kneeling with bowed head for women, and complete prostration with head turned sideways for men. This age etiquette prevails not only between generations, where the difference is great, but even between younger and older brothers.

Naturally, in the University context, traditional age etiquette is no longer fully operative and becomes attenuated, but nevertheless age deference structures remain quite obvious, and are still insisted upon by many educated Nigerians. Various evasive techniques are resorted to in order to escape age etiquette where it is no longer felt appropriate, such as speaking English where no distinction is made between a polite and familiar form. However, free and easy informal relationships, as symbolized in English by the reciprocal use of first names, are still exceptional between Nigerians, even when their academic rank is equal or nearly so. Greater informality and use of first names often prevails between Nigerian and expatriate colleagues, where the age deference structure does not interfere with the egalitarianism of the academic relationship; but Nigerians, especially of the same ethnic group and locality, who are therefore all the more conscious of their relative age, find it very difficult to treat each other informally as peers. Paradoxically, informality is easier across ethnic groups because then the consistent use of English allows one to escape the semantics of age etiquette, and because persons then find it easier to conceive of themselves as belonging to different and unrelated age structures. Within ethnic groups, consciousness of seniority is often extreme and frequently intrudes in the "modern" context of University life. Ethnic clique leadership for example will tend to go to the most senior person, or at least to the most chronologically senior among those of top rank in the academic hierarchy. Claims to political office, such as the Vice-Chancellorship are sometimes advanced on the basis of seniority. Aggressive behavior and over-talkativeness are resented from a person who is too junior, and sometimes academics in their fifties will contemptuously refer to rival colleagues in the forties as "small boys." [8]

Age deference is probably closest to its full traditional form among the Junior Staff, who being less westernized are also the most conservative. Prostration and kneeling between relatives is still a common sight in Obatala Village, but not among Senior Staff. Among students, age status plays an even smaller role than among Senior Staff, in part because age differences are smaller. Among male undergraduates, age is not important, but there is an important status difference between undergraduates and post-graduate students. Female students tend to be more sensitive than men to even minimal age differences between themselves, and to expect more deferential behavior. Relations between students and teachers are extremely deferential on a person-to-person basis, which sometimes does not preclude frankness or even rudeness in a situation of collective anonymity such as a large classroom.

Sometimes the age hierarchy corresponds to the status order in the occupational sphere, but, not uncommonly, the two dimensions are widely at variance with one another. Any great discrepancy between these two types of status is generally felt to create an uncomfortable situation. Thus most Nigerians will avoid hiring a domestic servant who is their senior, as this would make for an awkward strain in the relationship. Servants in Nigerian households are typically in their teens of early twenties, and thereafter have to find employment with expatriates or enter a different line of work altogether. Where the age difference runs counter the occupational hierarchy, as frequently happens between Senior and Intermediate Staff in an office, the result is often that the age difference will exert a tempering effect on the otherwise frequently authoritarian behavior of the hierarchical superior. The older subordinate on the other hand, will tend to treat his superior as if he were older than he is. In general, then, occupational status tends to dominate the relationship in work situations, but, even then, the effect of age status can seldom be discounted, and the interplay between the two factors is both subtle and complex.

Let us now, in the next three chapters, take a closer look at the internal composition of the three main estates at University.

NOTES

[1] It is interesting to note how high privacy in excretory activities ranks in the scale of segregatory efforts in rigidly stratified societies. Racially segregated toilets, and phobias surrounding their use, feature prominently in South Africa, and, until fairly recently, in the American South. The private toilet has high prestige value in the modern business corporation. And, of course, status segregation in bathroom facilities is also characteristic of many prisons, schools, hospitals and other such "total institutions." To push the point further, it is not only the excretion of food but also its *intake* which is status segregated in many societies. Status-linked commensality and avoidance rules on eating together are even more generalized than segregation in excretory functions. The latter seem to become status-regulated only in the most rigidly stratified systems.

[2] A sample survey done in 1962 put the Obatala Village population at 2,813, but that number has increased considerably since. Occupancy for the one-room units then averaged 4.5 persons, compared to 7 in 1969.

[3] A recent collection of studies on student politics in developing countries has shown that African students were among the least activist and concluded that lack of student "unrest" was associated, among other factors, with religiosity and an elitist university system with a relatively low rate of failure and a relatively low rate of unemployment among graduates. All these conditions still prevail in Nigeria, but the time is drawing near when the production of graduates will have exceeded the country's capacity to utilize their skills at a level commensurate with their education and, even more, their expectations. Already, there is a substantial "brain drain" of Nigerian students who postpone their return to Nigeria from overseas; and the steady decline in opportunities for graduates compared to a few years ago is beginning to produce considerable student dissatisfaction. In time, this may give rise to more political activity, especially if attempts are made to counteract this glut of graduates by restricting the output of the universities through more stringent examination standards. (Emmerson, 1968)

[4] This demonstration was at least in part political insofar as students had protested not only at their material conditions but also against their Vice-Chancellor and what they regarded as expatriate control of the University. Many other factors of regional politics, personal attacks on the Vice-Chancellor, and Student Union politics were also involved, but there was no fundamental questioning of the social order of the University, much less of the larger society, at any of the universities where sympathy demonstrations took place.

[5] For a classic description of clientage in a traditional Nigerian society, see Nadel's book on the Nupe, *A Black Byzantium.*

[6] In American terms, these are respectively the rough equivalent of graduation from the academic stream of a high school, and one year of university.

[7] It may be argued that anti-feminism at the top level is hidden by the fact that women who reach that level are much more selected than men, and therefore tend to be of superior ability. Thus, they should be doing better than, not

simply as well as, men. My own experience as a teacher confirms that women students tended to be both brighter and more motivated than the men, probably in good part because they come in far greater numbers from elite families where they had enjoyed great cultural advantages in preparation to university education. Educated Nigerian men tend to be insecure rather than domineering *vis à vis* women, and relations between the sexes are laden with an enormous amount of ambivalence.

[8] The term "small boy" is also used in reference to a young servant who is under the authority of a cook in a household. In any other context, it connotes very low status and contempt.

CHAPTER FOUR

The First Estate: Senior Staff

Collectively, the Senior Staff are the top stratum of the University. Together with their families, they make up less than 10 per cent of the University community; but they get the lion's share of the three main commodities which form the basis of invidious distinctions in stratified human societies: wealth, power and prestige. Their salaries range from three to ten times those of all but a tiny minority of the Junior Staff, and since their families tend to be considerably smaller, the per capita income differential is even greater. They enjoy numerous perquisites which amount to another third to one half of their salaries, and constitute, in effect, a state subsidy to the affluent. They monopolize all positions of power within the University, and exert considerable influence in the larger society. Finally, together with their counterparts in the civil service, the army, what is left of the political class, and the managers and directors of state corporations and private enterprise, they constitute the "high society" of Nigeria.

These characteristics, and the highly visible signs of affluence symbolized by "modern" housing, the private motorcar and imported foods, make the Senior Staff highly conspicuous in a poor country like Nigeria, and unambiguously identifiable as a group. Their privileged position has led some scholars to refer to them and their counterparts in other "modern" sectors of Nigerian society as an "elite." The word has many different connotations, and for that reason, I prefer to avoid it. To some, an "elite" connotes a closed group, which the Senior Staff certainly is not. To others, an "elite" implies a claim to superiority and an "elitist" outlook. This is perhaps the main reason why educated Africans resent the use of the term by Western scholars in reference to them.

Yet, though much more clearly identifiable than, say, the "upper class" in a European or even a Latin American country, "elites" in African countries are so heterogeneous in terms of social origins, ethnicity, religion, culture, and life style that they do not exhibit many of the characteristics generally associated with a "social class." Paradoxically, they are a sharply defined, highly privileged, but extremely heterogeneous and fluid group, which, for lack of a more adequate term, I shall call an estate.[1]

Aside from the commonality of institutionalized privilege, what do the Senior Staff (and by extension their counterparts in the larger society) share? The ruling stratum of most African countries, of which the academics are one key segment, are fundamentally a *mandarinate*. They are clearly not a bourgeoisie; in neo-colonialist economies that are still controlled by foreign interests, there is no appreciable indigenous class of owners of means of production. The new ruling groups of the "new" African states are first and foremost "owners" of the state apparatus, i.e., in the first instance, of the civil service and the means of organized violence (army and police). Historically, they are the successor class to the colonial administrators whose privileges they inherited, and like their predecessors their claim to office is based overwhelmingly on having passed certain examinations in a highly formalized system of education.

As in the classical case of the Chinese mandarin trained in the Confucian tradition, the Western system of formal education to which Africans have been exposed bears little relationship to the tasks of governance. At the same time, the sheer difficulty of the examinations, the physical and mental endurance necessary to undergo nearly two decades of "education," and the fiercely competitive and selective nature of the process insure a relatively high caliber of intellectual achievement.

The Senior Staff of the leading university of Nigeria is, in the nature of the case, the kingpin of the country's entire mandarinate. They are not only an important sector of the privileged mandarinate, but they possess the supreme power of granting the degrees which give access to the mandarinate. They are, in fact, both mandarins and mandarin-makers. The one major characteristic they share in common beyond the inheritance of colonial privileges is their extended exposure to a Western system of education, including, of course, university education. To them, the University is thus not simply a place of work, as it primarily is to the Junior Staff. It is the basis of their "class" position, the source of their institutionalized power, and, in the most fundamental sense, their *raison d'être*. They largely regard the University as theirs in a quasi-proprietary sense.

Beyond speaking English with one another,[2] holding (with a few exceptions) university degrees, monopolizing all the top positions at University, and enjoying the economic, political and social rewards attached to their jobs, the Senior Staff have few characteristics in common. The vast majority of the Senior Staff are at least nominally Christian by religion but, for many of them, especially expatriates, that fact is of little subjective significance.

Indeed, it would be difficult to conceive of a more heterogeneous group. The degree of national and ethnic diversity is much greater among Senior Staff than among either students or Junior Staff, as almost all of the latter two categories are Nigerians, or at least West Africans. Among Senior Staff, there were in 1968 twenty-nine nationalities, and about twice as many language groups. The Senior Staff communicate among themselves through the medium of English, but only a fifth to a fourth of them speak English as their mother tongue. English and Yoruba, and to a lesser extent Ibo, Edo and Ibibio are used fairly frequently, but most of the other 50 or 60 mother tongues are represented by fewer than five families each. In fact, in perhaps 5 to 10 per cent of the Senior Staff families, husbands and wives do not share the same mother tongue, and except for some of the British and American staff who can afford the luxury of monolingualism, nearly all Senior Staff are fluent in at least two and often three or four languages.

Cultural Differences

Ethnic and linguistic diversity are, of course, reflected in a wide variety of diet, life style, family structure, and other cultural differences among the Senior Staff. Some of the more visible differences distinguish Nigerians from expatriates, internally heterogeneous though both of these larger groups themselves are. Almost invariably, expatriates come to Nigeria as nuclear families, and thus their households tend to be far smaller than those of their Nigerian counterparts. This is true even of Asian expatriates who come from societies where the extended family is the norm. This difference is further accentuated by the fact that most Europeans and North Americans come from cultures where the fertility norm is two or three children per couple, instead of the much higher Nigerian ideal. While many Nigerian Senior Staff also control their fertility, their conception of ideal family size tends to fall somewhere in-between the traditional Nigerian norm of maximizing one's offspring, and the Western low-fertility norm. A number of Nigerians express surprise and even moral disapproval when expatriates tell them that they are deliberately restricting their offspring to two or three children. Many of the British staff further reduce their local family size by sending off their children of secondary school age to boarding schools at home.

By contrast, Nigerian Senior Staff families not only have more children, but are nearly all of the "extended" variety, i.e., include relatives other than husband, wife and their common children. However, few of the Nigerian Senior Staff families are of the virilocal,[3] polygynous type traditional of most Nigerian cultures. Among Western-educated Christians and indeed even Muslims, polygyny is frowned upon and regarded as incompatible with "elite" status, although extra-marital affairs are common among men and stigmatized only for women. The Western-style houses on campus are unsuitable to the establishment of virilocal, extended families including three or more generations of agnatically related males, their spouses and their unmarried daughters. The typical Nigerian Senior Staff household is thus neither "traditional" nor of the Western "neolocal" variety in that it often includes *some* relatives other than the adult couple and their children, but far fewer than in a traditional compound. Furthermore, the relatives present in the household are not necessarily married female in-laws of the male head of household as they would be traditionally. They may be male in-laws, for example. Often, the household will include a widowed parent, a couple of nephews and nieces of school age, or a younger brother, cousin, or sister-in-law, who help the mistress of the house with the housekeeping tasks and the child care.

These differences in family structure entail great dissimilarities in life style as well. For example, the larger Nigerian families make for more overcrowding of houses, and the "boys' quarters" (i.e., the two servants' rooms allocated to each Senior Staff house) are often in fact occupied by relatives rather than servants. Some Nigerian Senior Staff wives engage in a little retail trade for pocket money or children's expenses, a traditional woman's occupation in West Africa, and keep a stall on or near their compound. Nigerian families are more likely than expatriate ones to have a functional rather than a decorative conception of gardening, and to plant yams, maize and paw-paw trees rather than grass, roses, and shrubs. Dietary preferences vary widely, and, although expatriates have to pay a high price for not adapting to the excellent local staples, they prefer for the most part to eat exorbitant and low-quality imported foods, or the puny approximations to "European" tomatoes, carrots, beans, potatoes and cauliflowers that are cultivated in Northern Nigeria. Nigerians, on the other hand, typically eat a mixed diet that includes both local staples and imported prestige foods.

Master-servant relationships tend to differ, not only from person to person, but also by nationality. Europeans are sometimes shocked at the curt way some of their Nigerian colleagues treat their servants, and at the low wages they pay them. Nigerians do pay their servants roughly one half to two thirds (£4 to £6) as much as the average expatriate, but they also feed them which expatriates as a rule do not. It is also true that Nigerians tend to abuse their servants verbally and even occasionally physically with greater frequency than expatriates, but at the same time they treat them more as part of the family. Some expatriates, while never openly insulting or beating their servants, treat them coolly and impersonally, as non-persons paid to do a job and whose very presence can be ignored. For the Nigerian, the boundary between a servant and a poor relative, or simply a junior relative, is not sharply drawn, and the two roles are often combined. What an expatriate may interpret as discourtesy toward a servant may simply be an expression of the rigid age deference structure, and an assertion of authority over junior kinsmen.[4]

Leisure time activities also differ among various nationality groups. The expatriates make greater use than Nigerians of the recreational and sport facilities of the Senior Staff Club, especially the bar and the swimming pool. When expatriates entertain at home, they usually hold formal or semi-formal dinner parties to which invitations are extended several days in advance. Nigerians, on the whole, tend to prefer a freer pattern of informal visits, especially on week-ends when the houses of the more senior Nigerians become the venue for numerous visitors, often of the same ethnic group, from on or off campus. Certain traditional ritual events, such as the "naming ceremony" of newly-born infants or the granting of a chieftancy title, call for great social gatherings of kinsmen and friends, for lavish displays of expensive clothes and jewelry, and for bountiful hospitality. Other ritual events, such as weddings and funerals, happen with much greater frequency among them than in the expatriate group who typically come married and leave Nigeria long before old age. However, when a British Professor of Medicine died in 1969 he was buried with great pomp and academic procession in the University cemetery, an event which attracted hundreds of participants and was eclipsed in splendor only by Foundation Day ceremonies. Official University funerals are another Senior Staff prerogative, and student weddings are frequently performed at one of the U.I. chapels.

As Senior Staff houses are furnished by the University, individuality of taste is limited to decorations and accessories such as rugs, curtains and pictures. Although personal differences within each group are as great as differences between groups, there are nevertheless some national characteristics. A few Nigerians collect art from their own country, but the majority of amateurs of local arts and crafts are expatriates whose living rooms are often full of local wood carvings, mostly of the "airport art" variety, but occasionally outstanding pieces of work. The clientele of prominent Nigerian artists, whether they work in a "modern" or "traditional" style, consists primarily of expatriates, and U.I. Senior Staff constitute an appreciable proportion of the patrons. Many Nigerians, on the other hand, prefer to decorate their living rooms with framed photographs of themselves and their families, preferably in formal poses and in sumptuous "national dress" or in academic regalia, and their taste for tradition is largely confined to style of clothing.

Social Origins

The Senior Staff are as diverse in social origins as they are in cultures and life styles. Expatriates tend to come mostly from countries with a well-established class system, and are typically of middle- or upper-middle-class background, frequently coming from the urban bourgeoisie or the professions. Among Nigerians, however, the range of social origins is considerably wider as Nigeria has not yet developed a well-defined stratification system in the modern sector.[5] At one end of the social spectrum are a few academics who come from old Yoruba elite families from Lagos or Abeokuta, and whose grandfathers qualified as barristers, Anglican clergymen or physicians in England in the late 19th century. At the other extreme are academics whose parents are illiterate subsistence peasants, or more commonly, petty cocoa farmers with some cash income but little or no formal Western education. The bulk of the Nigerian senior staff fall somewhere in-between, coming from urbanized families and being the children of literate fathers who have gone at least to primary school and often to secondary school as well. Many academics are sons of clerks, petty or "executive" level civil servants, school teachers, clergymen, and similar urban white-collar or semi-professional occupations. The urban proletariat and the mercantile bourgeoisie, being both underdeveloped in Nigeria, are relatively unrepresented among the Senior Staff. Many people, however, owe their schooling in part to the supplemental earning of their mothers in petty trade, the most important remunerative occupation of women in Nigeria.

The following abbreviated life histories from three Nigerian members of the Senior Staff will give some idea of social heterogeneity. A was born in Southern Yorubaland, the son of a subsistence farmer who died when A was one year old. A's mother was the senior of two wives, and had three children of whom one died. A is the junior of two surviving brothers. His father's junior wife was childless. A's mother supported herself and her two sons by petty trading. When A was seven, the family moved to Lagos where A entered a Methodist primary school. A became informally adopted by a distant relative of his mother whom he regards as his foster father. That person was a prosperous trader and paid for nearly all of A's school through primary and secondary school. A entered a secondary school as a day student at age 15 and received his Cambridge School Certificate at age 20. For two years he worked as a clerk in the Civil Service. When A was 22, his senior brother, who was already at a university in the United States, sent him the money to come over, and, after a stay of several months in Britain trying to get an American visa, A joined his brother at the same university. A worked his way through school "washing dishes, scrubbing floors, driving taxis, running elevators, being a telephone operator." Two years later, his brother returned to Nigeria as an M.D., and established a practice in Lagos. When A was 27 he got his B.A., followed two years later by his M.A. At 33, he received his Ph.D. from another American university.

A married at 27 a Nigerian student at a neighboring university, and they have four children, all born in the United States, and hence with dual citizenship. A's wife is not a Yoruba; she was the daughter of a chief from the Mid-West, and her family objected to her marrying a "stranger." A would like his children to grow up as Nigerians, and is very critical of the European-oriented Senior Staff School on campus, and of Nigerians imitating Western ways. Nevertheless, as his wife speaks no Yoruba, English has become the home language. The children have, however, a Yoruba baby nurse who speaks Yoruba to them. In addition, A employs a "houseboy," and a younger sister of his wife also lives with them, and helps to take care of the children while his wife works at U.I. A supports financially several relatives: he pays the secondary school fees of his deceased sister's son, and he provides his mother and grandmother with subsistence allowances.

B is the son of a small Mid-Western cocoa farmer. Although B's father is a devout Roman Catholic, he is a bigamist. B's father had five years of primary education and is literate in English as well as his own language. B's mother is the senior of his father's two wives; she had four years of primary education and is also literate. She had three sons and one daughter while her junior co-wife had three daughters and one son. B is his father's first born. B's schooling was financed mostly by his father and his father's brother. He entered the local Catholic school at age 8, but five years later, went to a nearby town to join his father's brother, a bachelor and a carpenter and contractor by trade. B's uncle paid his fees for the remaining two years of his primary school. At age 16, B went to a Catholic teachers' training college in another town, his fees being paid by his father, with his uncle giving him pocket money.

Armed with his first teacher's certificate at age 20, B taught for two years in a Catholic school and became self-supporting. In his spare time, he studied for his Higher School Certificate, which he passed with flying colors, thereby earning a government scholarship and a place at U.I. where he entered at age 23. B received his B.A. three years later, his M.S.. in another two, and joined the U.I. staff at age 28. That same year he married a young woman eight years his junior. She is from the same ethnic group and is also a Roman Catholic. She has her Higher School Certificate and a Diploma in Education from U.I. Besides their baby boy, B and his wife live with one of B's younger brothers who is going to secondary school at B's expense. B also supports another junior brother through secondary school. The young couple employs two servants: a baby nurse and a "houseboy." B's wife teaches at a Catholic secondary school. B speaks three Nigerian languages besides his own and English. The home is tri-lingual: B's home language, English, and Ibo which he and his wife speak to their house servant. B intends to bring up his children bi-lingually.

C was born in Northern Yorubaland, the oldest son of a Baptist minister who received secondary education and religious training in Baptist schools. C's parents had eight children of whom three died. The five survivors are all male, and all of them went to American universities or colleges for their higher education. C has his Ph.D. and two of his younger brothers are close to getting their doctorates. At age 6, C entered school in the North where his father was posted as pastor. He then moved South and finished primary school as a day student in a Baptist school in Yorubaland, boarding with an older cousin, but his father paid his school fees. At age 12, C entered a Baptist secondary school as a boarder and, six years later, received his Cambridge Certificate. His father paid all his school expenses until then, but died the year C finished secondary school. Faced with the sudden need to support his younger brothers in school, C spent the next four years getting his teacher's credentials and teaching in Baptist schools. His mother supported herself through petty trade in cloth, books and bread.

At age 24, C received a scholarship to attend a Baptist College in the United States where, four years later, he graduated with his B.A. He then went to two large American state universities where he studied under scholarships and received his M.A. and Ph.D. after another four years of postgraduate work. While at the university, C was also supporting two junior brothers through Nigerian secondary schools. Now 32 years old, C joined the U.I. where, within three years, he rose to a Senior Lectureship. At 29, C married an old secondary school sweetheart from the same ethnic group and sub-group, who was also the daughter of a Baptist minister. C's wife also went to the United States, and got a B.A. at a Baptist college there; she is now completing a Ph.D. They have two sons, and intend to have no more children for the time being, a fact which distresses C's mother. Besides his wife and two boys, C's household includes his mother, who lives with him "on and off"; his wife's younger sister who is a school teacher; a "houseboy"; and a baby nurse. C also pays part of the secondary school fees of his father's brother's children.

Although both C and his wife are strongly americanized by their prolonged stay in the United States, they are proud of being Nigerians, dress in traditional clothes for formal occasions, eat a mixed traditional and Western diet, and use both English and Yoruba as home languages. The older boy was born in the United States; he has thus dual citizenship and learned English before Yoruba. C and his wife know some French but no other Nigerian languages besides their own.

Certainly, the absence of a commonality of family background among the

Nigerian Senior Staff and the relatively high (but probably declining) rate of mobility into that group preclude the use of the term "class" to refer to them. They are a meritocracy recruited through their stamina, perseverance, good luck and ability in "sticking through" with the formal educational system. Money is a facilitating factor in the acquisition of education, but the Nigerian "elite" are not, by and large, the sons of plutocrats. Most of them are "self-made men," although the next ruling generation will probably be less openly recruited than the present one. We shall return to the problem of educational recruitment in the next chapter when we shall deal with the students.

Representative Bodies

There is no corporate body which is fully representative of the entire Senior Staff, although some come close to it. The Senior Staff Club is open to all Senior Staff and the annual dues are quite nominal (£2. 10 s. for a couple; £1. 10 s. single), but many eligible people do not belong, or if they belong they only make minimal use of the facilities. Except for certain social events like Saturday dances held every few weeks, the Club, in terms of both its elected officers and the members who make regular daily use of the sports, catering, and recreational facilities, is largely an expatriate preserve. British and West Indian members are especially active in running Club affairs and patronizing the bar, while American families congregate around the swimming pool.

Convocation, the body of graduates and teachers of the University, includes the vast majority of the Senior Staff, but is much more inclusive since it also comprises thousands of former students. Furthermore, it excludes the administrators and technicians who do not hold a U.I. degree. In any case, except for the election of one member to Council and for an annual business meeting which often has to be cancelled for lack of a quorum, Convocation is devoid of power and of any clear functions. Thus, it has little meaning to either Senior Staff or graduates.

Congregation is a somewhat less shadowy body than Convocation and comes perhaps closest to being the corporate organ of the Senior Staff. It is convened thrice a year, and meetings also fail sometimes to achieve a quorum. When that happens, scouts are sent out throughout the campus to corral absentees to the meeting in order to be able to conduct business. Convocation includes all members of the Senior Staff who hold any university degree. Some members of the administrative and technical Senior Staff are thereby excluded, but some 90 per cent of the Senior Staff are members. However, since the teachers are in overwhelming majority in Congregation, that body has come to be defined as the organ of the teaching staff rather than the Senior Staff at large.

This is clear from both of the main political functions of the body, namely the election of one of its members to the Council, and the election of one third of the Senate seats from among its members who are not already *ex officio* members of the Senate (i.e., the professors and department heads). In practice, the elected Council member is a senior professor, so that Congregation representation on the Council has always been by an academic. As to the Senate seats, since the Senate is the academic ruling body of the University, there has been a convention to elect only teaching members of Congregation—Lecturers, Senior Lecturers or Associate Professors—to it. Thus, in practice, administrators and technicians have voting rights in Congregation, but are not eligible to the elective Senate seats.

Apart from elections, Congregation meetings are largely devoted to discussions of practical matters affecting the welfare of the Senior Staff such as pension funds, health services, and the like. In that capacity, Congregation acts as the collective organ of the entire Senior Staff. Also, as we have seen before, the Senior Staff has estate representation on the Consultative Committee for Community Development, with each of three main residential areas on campus electing one member.

The Four Segments

Functionally, the Senior Staff are subdivided into four major segments, namely the teachers (61 per cent of the total), the administrators (10 per cent), the research and technical personnel (24 per cent), and the library staff (5 per cent). Although each of these four branches has its own hierarchy of ranks, the teachers regard themselves as superior to the other three categories. Nearly four fifths (79.4 per cent) of the teachers have postgraduate degrees and nearly half (45.3 per cent) hold doctorates, while the other three categories are typically holders of only a bachelor's degree or specialized diploma. Furthermore, the teachers view themselves as functionally essential, and the others as ancillary to the central function of the University, namely to teach students. In keeping with the Oxbridge tradition of U.I., the teaching function of the University is stressed somewhat more than the research one, and the prestige of the teacher is quite high.

There is considerable resentment on the part of the teachers *vis à vis* the administrators, whom they regard as overpaid and overprivileged relative to them. The average salary of teachers is higher than that of administrators and technicians. Thus, for example, only the Registrar, Bursar, Chief Engineer, Librarian and Director of Health Service, as top administrators and technicians, draw salaries comparable to those of the sixty-odd professors. However, given their strictly academic qualifications, the administrators earn considerably more than similarly qualified teachers, a fact to which some teachers object. In October, 1968, for example, the Ilosho chapter of the Nigerian Association of University Teachers complained that administrators' salaries were too high compared to those of teachers. The administrators retort that since they are not hired to do an academic job, academic qualifications ought not to be the main consideration in their level of remuneration. Some teachers also resent some of the minor perquisites which administrators, they feel, unduly arrogated themselves. The offices of senior administrators are furnished with more expensive and modern furniture, for example, than those of many academics who make do with functional but antiquated equipment. Also, many of the administrators have reserved garages under their office buildings, while very few of the academics, including the professors, have such a convenience. This is not only a symbolically invidious difference, but a very real one in a climate where the sun converts a stationary motorcar into a fair approximation of a crematory oven in a matter of minutes.

Teachers jealously supervise the actions of the administrators whom they see as in a good position to usurp powers and prerogatives the teachers regard as theirs. The administrators, on the other hand, lacking the academic credentials of most teachers, find it difficult to challenge the prestige and power order of a system where the academics make the rules. The technicians and the librarians lack even the potential power base of the administrators, and their ancillary position *vis à vis* the teachers is taken for granted.

Of the four categories of Senior Staff, the teachers show the most collective consciousness. They frequently appeal to a normative system known as "academic tradition" to rationalize their behavior and defend their prerogatives. Internally, they jealously guard their powers *vis à vis* administrators and *vis à vis* Council, and externally they defend their autonomy and their academic freedom against the power of the state. In the past, especially in the early to mid-sixties, the local chapter of the Nigerian Association of University Teachers (N.A.U.T.)[6] was an active body, a frequent rallying center of younger lecturers in opposition to the Nwanneh administration, and a watchdog of academic freedom. In recent years, however, the N.A.U.T. has lost much of its vitality. This is due in good part to the more diffuse distribution of power within the University, and to the overriding nature of the Civil War and the ethnic and political crisis within the University from the mid- to late sixties.

By academic training, the most significant cleavage among the teaching staff is between the British-trained and the American-trained. Almost exactly

60 per cent of both the Nigerian and expatriate teachers hold their highest degree from a British university, but, for about half of the Nigerians, this means an external University of London degree taken at Ilosho under the "special relationship" arrangement of U.C.I. Nearly one fifth of Nigerians and expatriates were trained in the United States. The remaining fifth went to a large number of other East and Western European, Asian, African and South American universities, but none of the other countries is represented by a sufficient number of graduates to constitute a model to be emulated. (See Table 3) Thus, the concrete models of higher education which Ilosho academics, Nigerians and expatriates alike, have experienced and try to emulate mean in practice the British and the American, many

TABLE 3 / COUNTRY OF DEGREES HELD BY UNIVERSITY OF ILOSHO TEACHING STAFF IN PERCENTAGES (1968)

	Nigerians		Expatriates	
	First Degree	Highest Degree	First Degree	Highest Degree
United Kingdom *	74.6	61.1	52.7	58.9
United States	12.4	18.7	15.4	17.2
Other Western Countries	4.8	3.9	14.9	14.6
Asian Countries	—	—	7.4	2.1
Latin America	—	—	0.5	—
Communist Countries	—	—	5.3	4.2
Nigeria	8.1	16.3	—	0.5
Other African Countries	—	—	3.7	2.6
Total	99.9**	100.0	99.9**	100.1**

* Includes external University of London degrees taken at Ilosho under the U. C. I. system.

** Percentage does not add up to 100.0 because of rounding errors.

TABLE 4 / PROFESSIONAL QUALIFICATIONS OF UNIVERSITY OF ILOSHO TEACHING STAFF IN PERCENTAGES (1968)

Highest Degree Held	Nigerians	Expatriates	Total
B.A., B.S., *Licence*	25.6	14.1	20.0
M.A., M.S., B. Litt.	36.3	29.8	33.1
Ph.D., D.Sc., D. Phil.,			
M.D., M.B., Ch.B.	35.8	52.7	44.0
Unclassifiable	2.3	3.4	2.9
Total	100.0	100.0	100.0

individuals believing firmly in the exclusive virtues of the system of which they themselves are the product.

In terms of level of training, nearly four fifths of the teachers have post-graduate degrees, and almost half hold doctorates or their medical equivalent. (Table 4) There is an appreciable difference between Nigerians and expatriate, insofar as only slightly over one third of the Nigerians have doctorates compared to a little over half of the expatriates. Conversely, just over one fourth of the Nigerians have only bachelor's degrees compared to only one seventh of the expatriates. These differences are mostly accounted for by the fact that the Nigerians are markedly younger and more recently graduated than the expatriates, so that many of them, by the time that they acquire a level of seniority comparable to that of the expatriates, will have earned higher degrees. In 1968, only 13.8 per cent of Nigerian Senior Staff were over 40 years of age; 71.2 per cent had less than four years of service at University, and 61.9 per cent less than three years. Of the 62 Professors in 1969, only 24 were Nigerians, although the Nigerians made up some 60 per cent of the total teaching staff. (Table 5)

TABLE 5 / PERCENTAGE OF UNIVERSITY OF ILOSHO TEACHING STAFF IN VARIOUS RANKS (1969)

Academic Rank	Nigerians	Expatriates	Total
Professor	7.9	24.7	14.0
Associate Professor	2.0	2.9	2.3
Senior Lecturer	10.2	26.4	16.3
Lecturer	73.8	43.1	62.6
Assistant Lecturer	5.9	2.9	4.8
Total	99.8*	100.0	100.0

* Percentage does not add up to 100.0 because of rounding errors.

The Senior Staff are, of course, ranked by seniority and merit in a pyramidal hierarchy of some five major status categories and a score or so of salary steps ranging from £950 per annum for the most junior grade of Lecturer or Administrative Officer to £3000–3400 for Professors and £4250 for the Vice-Chancellor; in 1968, 84.5 per cent of the Senior Staff earned between £1000 and £2500 a year, but only 45.0 per cent earned more than £1500, and 12.1 per cent over £2500. (See Table 6) Differences in standard of living are determined not only by the salary of the head of the household, but also by the size of the family, the number of other dependents, and by whether the wife earns a second income, as many wives of Nigerian academics do, for example as secondary school teachers.

The academic ranks of Lecturer (below and above the "bar"),[7] Senior

TABLE 6 / PERCENTAGE OF UNIVERSITY OF ILOSHO SENIOR STAFF
IN VARIOUS SALARY CATEGORIES (1968) *

Pounds per Annum	Percentage
£ 3000 and over	10.8
£ 2750 to 2999	2.6
£ 2500 to 2749	3.7
£ 2250 to 2499	10.6
£ 2000 to 2249	7.8
£ 1750 to 1999	6.2
£ 1500 to 1749	8.4
£ 1250 to 1499	20.8
£ 1000 to 1249	25.8
£ 950 to 999	3.4
Total	100.1**

* This table includes *all* categories of Senior Staff.
** Percentage does not add up to 100.0 because of rounding errors.

Lecturer, Associate Professor,[8] and Professor, and their equivalents in the
parallel, non-academic hierarchies carry not only differences in salaries, but
vast differences in power, in prestige, and in various other perquisites of
which housing is the most visible. Originally the system was highly pyramidal, each department having typically three to ten Lecturers, two or three
Senior Lecturers and a single Professor. On the administrative side, the
numbers of positions was also steeply inversely proportional to rank. In
recent years, however, accelerated promotions, the creation of multiple
chairs in some departments, and the increasing use of the rank of Associate
Professor all mitigate somewhat the competitiveness between Senior Staff
and the power of department heads. These trends also make the University
establishment more top-heavy and hence more costly to the Nigerian taxpayers who, in last analysis, carry the burden of salary and rank escalation
among the Senior Staff.

Housing

Housing allocation is a source of intense competition among the Senior Staff
because the size, location and style of one's house are such highly visible
symbols of status. All Senior Staff are entitled to quarters provided for and
furnished by the University, and all Senior Staff housing can be described
as luxurious by Nigerian and even by European standards. They range in
size, however, from one bedroom flats to houses with three bedrooms and

study, not to mention the Vice-Chancellor's "lodge" with its vast private park which rivals the splendor of a colonial governor's mansion. Because of the high noise level, the least desirable quarters are the flats attached to student halls. Next in the scale of desirability are the four-floor blocks of Senior Staff flats and the small duplex-style "chalets." The fully detached three-bedroom-study-two-bathroom houses with their large private gardens, normally reserved for Professors and administrators of equivalent rank, are the most prestigious.

Even among "professorial" houses, a distinction is made between the "regular" ones and the more stylish ones built to accommodate the staff of the Rockefeller and Ford Foundations. Those houses are more modern in design and are equipped with air conditioners in every bedroom and in the study, with a private water storage tank (a precious asset during the dry season when the city water is cut off for many hours almost every day), with a spacious mosquito-screened verandah and with a greenhouse patio. These "American" houses have been the object of special envy not only because, next to the Vice-Chancellor's lodge, they are the best on campus, but also because the Foundation staff assigned to them are sometimes in the relatively junior status of Lecturer or Senior Lecturer. The Foundations follow a policy of scrupulous equality of housing and equipment among their own staff, irrespective of seniority, but while this may minimize rivalries among American housewives, it exacerbates the envy of the rest of the Senior Staff. The main factor which keeps those feelings from erupting more openly is that, since Americans, like the other "tribes," tend to socialize predominantly with each other, the in-door luxuries of the Foundation houses are shielded from most non-Americans. Even the domestic servants tend to stay with the houses, to be inherited by the successive waves of Americans, and to constitute a little occupational quasi-caste of their own.

In order to mitigate recriminations in housing allocation, the University has devised a "point" scheme which allocates credit on the basis of three main factors, namely rank, length of service, and family size (with a special allowance if the wife is herself on the Senior Staff). A special Housing Allocation Committee (H.A.C.), appointed by Council, consists of five academics and the Registrar. The Committee's task is to implement equitably the point scheme, which, in theory, is unambiguous since the Committee has published a detailed list of rank equivalents for every category of of Senior Staff. Nevertheless, the Committee is continuously bombarded with written complaints of insufficiency of space and requests for different quarters, and frequently accused in private of "irregularities" (a euphemism for favoritism).

Complaints about housing tend to fall into three basic patterns: they either challenge the adequacy of the existing rules, or they attack the

Committee's impartiality in applying the rules, or they list specific complaints or needs such as overcrowding, noise, and unpleasant odors. As the point system puts somewhat more weight on rank than it does on need (as defined by family size), the bulk of complaints come, of course, from the more junior grades with large families. For example, a married Professor with no resident children gets as many points (13 for his rank plus three for his wife) as a married lecturer with three children (seven points for his rank, three points for his wife, six points for his children). In addition, the Professor is more likely to have accumulated points for length of service at U.I. A recent modification of the rules to reduce the rank factor by abolishing a two-point credit for Department Heads was of course opposed by those adversely affected. One Department Head, for example, wrote: "There are several permanent Heads of Departments who do not wish their status further whittled down by being deprived of their two additional points."

Another defender of seniority privileges writes: "An assistant lecturer should normally be unmarried and without children. So, he should be entitled only to the smallest housing unit available. It is unwise to encourage that category of staff, young and poorly paid, to qualify for houses." A third more senior person states: "Giving credit for length of service is one of the most sensible and civilized features of the old points system." A person who transferred from the Civil Service to the University claims that his status requires bigger quarters: "This type of accommodation was commensurate with my status in the civil service as the acting Principal Research Officer."

Senior Staff of lower rank but with large families typically complain of lack of space. The problem is especially common with Nigerians. One person writes: "I would like to appeal to the Committee to give definite consideration to African members of staff who demand bigger accommodation for reason of harbouring relatives or children who are not theirs. The extended family problem is something which cannot easily be overlooked." Expatriates, on the other hand, whose families are, on the whole, much smaller object mostly to cultural conditions to which they are not accustomed, such as noise level, and stray poultry. In the words of one exasperated expatriate: "We live in an area which is reputed to be the noisiest on the campus. . . . We have neighbours who play their radios from morning to night, at times so loud that we cannot enjoy the music from our own record player. More people are keeping cocks in the garages opposite our bedroom. . . . Nurse girls and house boys [i.e. domestic servants] play noisy games outside our bedroom windows in the afternoon and do not move away when asked to do so. As we are in the minority in our desire for privacy and quiet, we should like you to move us to a small home in a quieter area."

The most serious complaints, alleging impropriety or partiality on the part of the Committee, are seldom expressed in individual letters, but are often voiced in private or taken up in the form of a collective complaint. Thus, in 1968, the local chapter of the N.A.U.T. expressed through their representative on the H.A.C. "their dismay at these unsavoury irregularities" in housing allocations. Another source of friction resulted in 1969 from the refusal by a Nigerian family to vacate a house which had been allocated to an incoming expatriate but which the Nigerian family had, as a special favor, been allowed to occupy temporarily. This was done in violation of regular procedure, and, in fact, without authority from H.A.C., so the attempt to relieve one family's problem resulted in a vast amount of ill will and in a jurisdictional dispute between H.A.C. and the Maintenance Department which had improperly released the house keys to the Nigerian family.

Housing, then, is a chronic source of friction and envy between individual members of the Senior Staff, and of organizational conflict between various departments of the University. Department Heads also compete with each other in their attempts to secure campus housing for some of their Intermediate and Subordinate staff, and, as the demand for non-Senior-Staff housing exceeds the supply by a margin of about eight to one, this sometimes leads to acrimonious debates between Department Heads as to which employee is more essential to University operations.

Differences in wealth and living standards among the Senior Staff, while appreciable, are relatively small compared to the gulf that separates them from students and Junior Staff. Similarly, in terms of prestige, there is a substantial difference between an established Professor with an international reputation, and a young Lecturer who has just received his Ph.D. But the young Lecturer of today can normally aspire within ten or fifteen years to a professorship if he does a minimum of research and publication. Such differences of rank as exist within the Senior Staff are thus not due to "class," but flow rather from the stage of professional life cycle in which the individual finds himself.

Distribution of Power

On the third, and probably the most fundamental, dimension of invidious status distinctions, namely *power,* the internal differences within the Senior Staff are much more substantial and consequential. In turning now to the central problem of power differentiation within the Senior Staff we are, in effect, dealing with the power structure of the University. As Robert Michels (1949), Gaetano Mosca (1939), Vilfredo Pareto (1935) and many other sociologists have noted long ago, the exercise of power in any but the most undifferentiated societies is always by nature oligarchical. U.I. is certainly no exception. Even though the Senior Staff constitutes less than the top tenth of the University community, the ruling oligarchy at U.I. is even more narrowly defined. At most, *one-tenth of that tenth,* can be said to have any effective power in the governance of the University. The "ruling class" of the University is drawn almost entirely from the Senior Staff. However, not all Senior Staff belong to the ruling stratum of the University. The vast majority are not called upon to make significant policy decisions, either individually or collectively.

The basic administrative unit of the University is the department which can be either academic or non-academic. Forty-nine academic departments or units are grouped under six faculties. By far the largest faculty is Medicine, subdivided into 22 departments and sub-departments; Science has seven departments; Arts, ten; Agriculture, six; and Social Sciences and Education, four each. In addition, academic facilities include the Library, the Institute of African Studies, the government-run Nigerian Institute of Social and Economic Research, the Institute of Child Health, and the Computing Centre.

Non-academic departments include the Registry, the Bursary, the Works, Maintenance and Transport Department, Catering, the University Press, the Health Service, the Bookshop, the International School (Secondary) and the Staff School (Primary). The Registry is by far the largest of the non-academic departments with a Senior Staff establishment of 27, and a number of sub-divisions such as Senior Staff Establishments, Senate Matters, Student Affairs and Careers, Examinations, Establishments and Labour, and the Estate Office. In addition to the administrative and academic departments, there are nine student Halls of Residence, one for undergraduate women, one for post-graduate students, and seven for undergraduate men. Each hall is under the authority of a Master or Mistress who is normally of professorial rank, a Warden who is often a Senior Lecturer or Lecturer of some years' experience, two or three Assistant Wardens who are more junior Lecturers, and a Domestic Warden, generally a woman, who supervises the catering staff. Each of the halls employs a small army of 50 to 100 servants (porters, cleaners, cooks, launderers, waiters, gardeners and the like) who cater for the students. Finally, there are some ancillary units like the Botanical Gardens, the Menagerie (Zoo), and the Farm, each with a large staff of junior workers.

Both academic and non-academic departments vary greatly in size, some having a score or more of Senior Staff members and hundreds of Intermediate and Subordinate Staff personnel, others with only two or three Senior Staff and half-a-dozen or fewer Junior Staff. Traditionally, every academic department had only one Professor; the teaching staff averaged one to three Senior Lecturers and three to six Lecturers. By 1968, eleven of the academic departments had more than one chair, not including the Visiting Professors and the Associate Professors. Most of the multiple-chair departments are in the Faculties of Medicine and of Science, with one each in Social Sciences and Arts.

DEPARTMENT HEADS

More than in any other position except the Vice-Chancellorship, the main locus of power resides in the Department Head. In the oligarchical but diffuse power structure of the University, the Department Head is indeed a strong feudal baron. To be sure, Faculty Deanships are also positions of great power, primarily through *ex officio* committee memberships; however, two factors stringently limit the power of Deans, namely the fact that they are elected by the teaching members of their faculties, and that their term of office is normally limited to one or two years. In larger faculties, such as Medicine, Science, and Arts, where there is a significant number of Professors (who alone are eligible for Deanships), there is a tradition of rapid rotation, and the elections are sometimes the occasion of important power struggles. A Deanship is first and foremost a political position, while a Department Headship, not being elective, is much less so.

Traditionally, a Department Head was appointed by Council both to the single chair of the Department and to the Headship, and he held both positions until his resignation or retirement. Persons so appointed are referred to as "Permanent Heads," and preserve their positions irrespective of any subsequent appointments of other Professors in their departments. The introduction of multiple professorships during the Nwanneh era did, however, erode to some extent the potentially despotic power of Heads. First, when a Headship now becomes vacant, no permanent new Head is appointed, the expectation being that all Professors in the department will take the headship for a year each, in order of seniority. The Vice-Chancellor has some power of discretion on whether to rotate Heads or not, but attempts by the present Vice-Chancellor to stop rotation have been strongly challenged as instances of "nepotism" or "tribalism."

Obviously, non-permanent Heads of those Departments which have multiple chairs are restrained by fear of retaliation in their use of arbitrary power against other senior colleagues. Even where the Head is permanent, the principle of multiple chairs, and, hence, of academic equality between Professors of a Department, often has the effect of making the departmental structure less autocratic. As departments become more "top-heavy" and less pyramidal in the rank distribution, their power structure becomes oligarchical rather than monarchical. Some cases of bitter enmities between Professors of the same department, degenerated to such petty actions as debarring colleagues from access to secretaries and even to departmental stationery. However, the genteel conventions of academic decorum usually prevail over such rivalries, and a *modus vivendi* based on mutual avoidance is often established.

Statutory powers of Heads are considerable. With the Intermediate and Subordinate Staff, Department Heads have considerable influence in hiring and disciplining, and the relationship is clearly one of command and subordination. With teaching colleagues, the norms of academia mitigate the Head's power to issue direct commands. By custom, he is supposed to treat fellow academics as colleagues and not as subordinates. Nevertheless, the Department Head has the power to assign courses to be taught and, perhaps most importantly, to recommend colleagues to the Appointments and Promotion Committee. A teacher has the option to present his own case for promotion over his Head's opposition, but unless he has powerful political support from the Vice-Chancellor, Deans or some important ethnic faction, he has almost no chance of success. The most notorious case of such a promotion in 1969 involved an expatriate Head who had weakened his position through his extreme reluctance to promote anybody, and who thereby created a powerful Nigerian, and predominantly Yoruba, coalition against him.

The extent to which Heads use their statutory powers *vis à vis* their teaching colleages varies widely. Some departments, especially the ones that have only a single chair, are still autocratically run. The Head has the discretion to call departmental meetings or not as he pleases, and in some departments he makes all decisions without even informal consultation with colleagues. More common is the oligarchical pattern where at least occasional meetings of the department are convened, but where most key decisions are taken by the Head in informal consultation with a few of his more senior colleagues such as Associate Professors and Senior Lecturers. In such departments, Lecturers play only a minimal role in the decision-making process. The most democratic departments are those where regular meetings of all teaching staff are held, and where most decisions are made consensually or by the majority vote of the entire teaching staff from Assistant Lecturers up. In no department is the decision-making process extended to either students or Junior Staff, even though it would be within the prerogative of the Head to extend representation at the departmental level to the second and third estates.

Academic departments compete with each other for shares of the budget, but otherwise disciplinary boundaries keep them apart and relatively noncompetitive. Most competition and conflict take place between faculties.

The non-academic departments present a very different picture. Their authority structure tends to be much more autocratic, in part because academic conventions do not operate, and clashes over power and jurisdiction both within and between administrative departments are much more endemic than in the academic departments. In theory, lines of authority and spheres of jurisdiction are well-defined, but, in practice, different interpretations give rise to complex power struggles between administrative departments, and to bitter wrangles over who has the power to do what.

THE REGISTRAR

The most fateful ambiguity in the history of the University has concerned the role of the Registrar. By British tradition, the Registrar is the chief administrative officer of a university; the University of Ilosho Act of 1962 vaguely defines the Registrar's responsibility as "the day to day administration of the affairs (other than academic and financial affairs) of the university," and this was later amended to delete the exception of academic affairs from his functions. He is a non-academic and has no direct authority over the teaching staff, who tend to regard him as a glorified clerk. Applications for jobs are normally channelled through his office, and Senior Staff records are kept there, but his role is that of clerical processing (and some would say of delaying and mislaying dossiers). The Registrar has some authority over students, but only such as is delegated to him by the Senate, and over the Intermediate and Subordinate Staff, but subject to the ultimate power of the Council. The Registrar is, in effect, the agent of both the Senate and Council, directly responsible to the Vice-Chancellor and, through him, to these two bodies. His function is simply to implement the decisions passed by them. His *de jure* powers are thus quite minimal outside his own administrative department, the Registry. Even within the Registry, the absence of a disciplinary code, such as exists in the Civil Service, restricts the sanctions he can use, as does of course the organized bargaining of the University Workers' Union. It was, for example, the suspension of an Intermediate Staff member by the Registrar in 1966 which in turn precipitated a strike and his own suspension by the Council.

Perhaps the most important aspect of the Registrar's job in terms of his power is the fact that he is *ex officio* Secretary to the Council, to the Senate, and to some of their key committees. As Secretary he has no voting rights, and his active role is largely limited to explanations, justifications or apologies about the functioning of the Registry in response to questions, or legal advice on procedural issues, as the Registrar also happens to be a lawyer. Nevertheless, the Registrar is one of the few members of the University who is privy to nearly all important decisions, and who thus is in a structural position to have a comprehensive overview of the system. Almost powerless *de jure*, he can use his wide range of information to good effect, and has in fact in the past made effective use of his political connections outside U.I. to suit his purposes within it. *De facto,* his influence, direct or indirect, is thus considerable, and, except for some Council members, he is the only non-academic who can be said to belong to the "inner circle" of the University power elite.

Vis à vis other department heads, the Registrar is also in an ambiguous position. His salary of £3250 is comparable to that of most heads of academic departments (except those in the Faculty of Medicine whose basic professorial salaries are somewhat higher). Yet, being a non-academic, the status he is accorded by most academic heads, and indeed even by the more junior teaching staff, is distinctly lower. As chief administrative officer of the University, the Registrar draws a somewhat higher salary and has higher status than other heads of non-academic departments, but he is more a *primus inter pares* in relation to the Bursar, the Chief Engineer and the Director of the Health Service than their hierarchical superior. The Librarian is in an even more ambiguous position, being both a quasi-academic and the head of a "service" department, but one that is the very repository of scholarship.

FACULTIES

Above the departments, the faculties are the next higher level of structural organization. Faculties are groups of academic departments that are intellectually related to one another. In theory, the faculties are equal, but like the animals in Orwell's fable, some faculties are more equal than others; their prestige ranking is a function of their age, size, expensiveness and "pure" versus "applied" character. In terms of budget, out of a total of £2,069,000 academic expenditures in 1967–68, Medicine accounted for 30.3 per cent; Science for 15.9 per cent; Agriculture for 12.1 per cent; Arts for 10.0 per cent; the Library for 6.2 per cent; Education for 4.4 per cent; and the Social Sciences, which have the dubious distinction of offering the cheapest education on campus, 3.1 per cent. The three "foundation faculties," Arts, Science and Medicine, claim priority by virtue of earlier establishment, and among them, the Faculty of Medicine is a law unto itself. Not only is it the largest by far in terms of teaching staff and number of departments (though not in student enrollment), but it also offers by far the most expensive training, and hence claims some 30% of the academic budget. Furthermore, the sheer physical separation of the Teaching Hospital compound from the main campus of the University, and the very special nature of clinical training of students and of the hospital environment make the Faculty of Medicine, especially the clinical section thereof, a state within a state.

A number of medical professors play important parts in the general affairs of the University, and both the present Vice-Chancellor and his deputy come from that Faculty; but many other medical teachers are first and foremost physicians whose lives revolve around the hospital rather than the main campus. Within the Faculty of Medicine, however, an invidious distinction is made between the Clinical Departments located at the Hospital, and the Pre-Clinical ones over on the main campus. This distinction is reflected in the fact that the Clinical staff draw salaries that, depending on rank, are from seven to twenty-five per cent higher than those of the Pre-Clinical teachers, and bitter animosity and resentment characterize the relationship between these two sections of the Faculty of Medicine. In particular, feuds between certain heads of departments in the two respective sections have assumed legendary proportions. Some of the teaching staff of other faculties are envious of the financial resources of Medicine and view that Faculty as an albatross around the University's neck. An important factor fueling the envy of other faculties *vis à vis* Medicine is the three-tiered salary structure of the U.I. teaching staff: for example, a non-medical professor earns £3000; a pre-clinical one £3200; and a clinical one £3400. While the medical staff find no difficulty in justifying their higher salaries, their arguments typically fail to convince their non-medical colleagues, and in such a highly status-conscious environment as U.I., even relatively minor salary differentials assume symbolic significance, and are widely resented.

The three younger faculties, Agriculture, Social Sciences and Education, are also the smallest. Agriculture has the longest history of the three, but the Social Sciences Faculty probably ranks first in prestige though last in terms of financial resources. Both Agriculture and Education suffer from the stigma of being applied fields, causing many academics in other disciplines to look down at them. The Social Sciences, while of distinctly lower status than the three foundation faculties, have gained in respectability in recent years, especially through the recognized importance of Economics, the best developed social science discipline on campus, and the international reputation of several of its professors.

Most departments belong to only one faculty, but a few have dual membership. Individual teachers may hold appointments in more than one unit of the University. This is especially true in the Social Sciences where a large number of the staff members of the Institute of African Studies and the Nigerian Institute for Social and Economic Research also teach in the Social Sciences Faculty. Each faculty is headed by a Dean, elected by the entire teaching staff of that faculty from among its full Professors. A Dean may, but need not, be a Department Head, and in departments with two Professors it sometimes happens that one is the Department Head while the other is the Dean of the faculty.

DEANS

Deanships are among the most politicized positions at U.I. The power inherent in them is, of course, mitigated by the short tenure in office (typically two years), and by being subjected to the vagaries of elections in which even the most junior of Lecturers has the same voting rights as the Professors. However, Deans are *ex officio* members of the most important committees of Senate, and, by themselves, they constitute a Committee of Deans under the Chairmanship of the Vice-Chancellor. That Committee of Deans is an important standing co-ordinating body, especially during the long vacation when Senate does not meet. Deans also sit on the two key Development Committee and Appointments and Promotions Committee of Senate where they collectively make up nearly half of the membership.

In the larger faculties, deanships are often hotly contested, and, although academic decorum prevents open campaigning, there is much discreet canvassing for support and caucusing on electoral tactics. The important role of Deans in the general affairs of the University make these elections matters of concern outside the faculties in question, most especially to the Vice-Chancellor, whose effectiveness is heavily contingent on his enjoying the support of at least a couple of the Deans of the larger faculties.

A Dean's first loyalty is expected to be to the teaching staff of his faculty who elected him, and if he incurs the displeasure of his colleagues he is likely to be voted out of office in short order. If the Professor elected as Dean of his faculty is known to be an opponent of the Vice-Chancellor, his election is often interpreted by members of the teaching staff as an indirect vote of no confidence against the Vice-Chancellor. A Dean's election in the complex game of University politics is seldom simply a personal victory; it is typically viewed as a collective victory for his faction and as a defeat for the other side. Most of the active politicking takes place within the confines of the faculty in question, but outside involvements and pressures occur as well, and allegations of such are even more common.

FACULTY BOARDS

The policy-making body of a faculty is its Faculty Board made up of all the members of its teaching staff under the chairmanship of the Dean, with the Administrative Officer serving as Secretary. During the regular academic session, each Faculty Board normally meets once a month before the monthly Senate meeting. Between Faculty Board meetings interim business is usually taken care of by the Dean with the assistance of a Board of Studies, an elective executive committee often composed of fairly junior teachers and devoid of any effective powers.

Most of the time of Faculty Board meetings is consumed with questions concerning students, such as course syllabus and curriculum, admission of new students into the faculty, examinations including the selection of external examiners and the composition of examining boards, and petitions from students for making exceptions to faculty rules. Meetings typically last one to two hours, and go into painstaking detail of often relatively trivial matters. The Faculty Board takes its collective responsibility seriously, and stringently limits the autonomy of its constituent departments.

Meetings take place in the air-conditioned comfort of the Senate Chamber, and though the style of dress is relatively informal, the style of debate is generally quite formal. The Chairman is addressed as "Mr. Chairman, Sir," and the Professors are often called by title rather than name (e.g. "The Professor of Political Science" or "the Head of Anatomy" rather than "Professor Jones"). Minutes are read and approved, and formal votes are taken where consensus has evidently not been reached. The Faculty Board is the main formal body of the University where the voice of the more junior teaching staff can be heard.

SENATE

All decisions of Faculty Boards are subject to approval by the Senate, the supreme decision-making body of the University in all academic matters. The 1962 University of Ilosho Act states that the functions of the Senate shall be "to organise and control the teaching at the university and the admission and discipline of students and to promote research at the university." It further specifies the Senate's power to establish faculties and departments, to appoint and promote teachers, to control syllabuses and examinations, to award degrees and set requirements for such, to organize halls of residence, to supervise the welfare of students and to regulate their conduct, and to regulate the use of academic dress.

In 1969, the Senate had 99 voting members, 32 of whom were Lecturers, Senior Lecturers and Associate Professors elected by Congregation, and the remaining two-thirds *ex-officio* members. The latter include all the Professors, the Librarian, and the few Heads or Acting Heads of Departments who were of lower than professorial rank. The Vice-Chancellor acts as Chairman, and the Registrar as Secretary. The Secretaries of the Faculties (i.e. the Administrative Officers) are in attendance but do not vote. Of the 32 elected members, only eight are Lecturers, while 19 are Senior Lecturers, and five Associate Professors. Thus, Congregation tends to elect the more senior of its non-professors to the Senate, which is composed overwhelmingly of seasoned academics of the rank of Senior Lecturer or higher. Of the 62 Professors (including the Visiting Professors) in 1969, 24 were Nigerians including the Vice-Chancellor and three of the six Deans. Twenty-four of the 32 elected members were Nigerians, making for a near-parity of Nigerians and foreigners on the overall membership: 51 of the voting members were expatriates and 48 Nigerians. Only one of the Professors and four other members were women. In short, the Senate is an oligarchy of some one-sixth of the Senior Staff and one-fourth of the teaching staff, consisting of all the Professors and some of the more senior non-Professors. It is a nearly all-male body, almost equally divided between Nigerians and foreigners.

Significantly, the one important issue which is hardly ever debated in the Senate, and then only in the broadest terms, is that of appointments and promotions. The Appointments and Promotions Committee (A.P.C.) report is presented to the Senate and routinely approved, so that in effect A.P.C. is the ultimate effective arbiter of the recruitment and status of the teaching staff. The extreme political sensitivity of this topic makes it too hot to handle in public discussion among such a large group. The Senate prefers by convention to abdicate the right to challenge A.P.C., rather than face the risk of acrimonious debate and the outburst of political passions.

Other conventions regulate the behavior of the Senate. A Dean is expected to show solidarity with his faculty and to defend its interests. Members of a faculty, however divided they may be internally, are expected not to express their internal disagreements or attack their Dean in front of the larger body, though this unwritten rule is occasionally violated when especially controversial issues arise. Reports of Deans are, however, regularly challenged by members of other faculties and the Senate retains close control over the Faculty Boards. Some Deans have developed the skill to present their faculty reports in a way which gets them smoothly through Senate, while others can scarcely open their mouths without raising storms of objections and queries, and getting their recommendations referred back to their Faculty Board for reconsideration. Referral back to committee or to Faculty Board, rather than voting things down, is the standard device used by Senate to dispose of a recommendation of which it does not approve.

In discussing both substantive and procedural issues, the tone of the debate is generally legalistic. Arguments are presented within a conceptual framework that might be described as "modified English Common Law." Within the constitutional framework of the University of Ilosho Act, precedent or lack of it is perhaps the most commonly invoked principle. This clearly gives the body a strongly conservative slant, as proposals for reform and change are regularly rejected simply on the ground that things have not been done like that before, and that doing so would raise all kinds of policy implications which need to be examined in detail before any action can be taken. The only significant change consciously voted upon by Senate during the one year of field work was the abolition of the June graduation ceremony which would henceforth be combined with the Foundation Day exercises on November 17. The Senate, through making a multiplicity of small decisions, often unwittingly creates precedents and thus brings about gradual changes in the system. But the entire decision-making process is heavily stacked against consciously planned change.

The main function of legalism in the Senate and indeed in the University at large is that it imposes some limits on the expression of particularistic political interests which, if left unchecked, could totally disrupt the institution. Allegations of favoritism, nepotism, and "tribalism," common in private, are clearly outside the bounds of propriety in the Senate and other official bodies of the University. Politically sophisticated members of Senate are often able to predict with considerable accuracy what stand their colleagues will take on given issues, and frequently attribute to them a variety of particularistic and "illegitimate" motivations for their position. Nevertheless, the entire debate takes place as if particularistic considerations were furthest remote from everybody's mind. The non-discrimination clause of the University Act is often cited.[9]

In actual practice, a wide variety of unstated considerations motivate the behavior of Senate members, the main ones being type of university training (British versus American system), faculty and departmental affiliation, ties of ethnicity, locality and kinship, personal links of friendship, obligations flowing from patron-client ties, political beliefs, and religious affiliation. The tendency is for members of Senate to interpret events disproportionately in terms of ethnic cleavages, but, while ethnicity is often an important factor, it is typically one of several and not necessarily the *most* important. In matters of curriculum reform, for example, the alignment is largely in terms of British- versus American-trained. The latter group are in minority and tend to favor academic reform away from the British model and toward a more American model. The British-trained majority (both expatriates and Nigerians) naturally lean toward the *status quo,* and being in majority often manage to prevent change, or at least to slow down drastically the rate of change. A good example of this inertia was the "course system" proposal which involved a relatively minor reorganization of undergraduate courses providing, among other things, for more flexibility for teachers and students. The implementation of the proposal was delayed several years despite the absence of strong arguments against it.

The Senate, then, is by no means a perfunctory body like Congregation or Convocation. Senate does spend much time on trivia that could more efficiently be dealt with by committees, by administrative action, or by giving greater autonomy to the Faculty Boards and departments. Yet, as the size of the Senate steadily increases through the proliferation of professorships and, hence, of the elective representation which is pegged at one-third of the total, its effectiveness as a decision-making body declines. Nevertheless, the Senate jealously guards its collegial prerogatives against possible encroachments by the Vice-Chancellor, the administrators, and the various faculties and departments. It is proud of its tradition of independence, and it views itself, with a considerable degree of justification, as a bulwark of academic freedom, of intellectual excellence, and of paramountcy of scholarship over politics.

However, the Senate has had to delegate more and more of its important functions to its committees. This was indeed the only structural alternative to either greater faculty and departmental autonomy or to greater powers to the administration. Faced with that dilemma, Senate, as an oligarchic body, opted for the choice that would retain the power collectively in the hands of its own members. In effect, by expanding its committee structure, it created an oligarchy within the oligarchy. In last analysis, the ultimate powers of the University are concentrated in the hands of the "committee Professors," including, of course, the Vice-Chancellor and the Deans.

The Senate has 18 standing committees and boards, one of which has three standing sub-committees. By far the three most important committees are the Appointments and Promotions Committee, the Development Committee and the Committee of Deans. All three have general, University-wide functions, while the other 15 committees and boards have much more circumscribed functions often linked with a special unit or institute of the University.

In addition to the committees of the Senate, Council has 9 standing committees and boards, and one sub-committee. An analysis of committee membership of both Senate and Council in 1968–69 reveals that 55 members of the teaching staff occupied a total 116 non-*ex-officio* positions on these 31 bodies. These figures exclude the non-academic members of Council, as well as the Vice-Chancellor, the Registrar and the Deans insofar as they hold most of their committee positions *ex-officio*. Of the 55 teachers on committees, 35 were Professors, and 31 were Nigerians. Since two-thirds of Senate and all of the Senate representatives on Council are Professors, it is not surprising that Professors make up nearly two-thirds of the committee posts. Nor is it surprising to find that, among Professors, Nigerians are over-represented since they have a more permanent stake in the University, and, hence, a greater incentive to become involved in committee work.

A closer examination of the data reveals an even more oligarchical situation than the above figures seem to indicate. Indeed, of the 55 academics involved, nearly half (24) were members of only one committee, often the one most closely related to their specialized area of competence. Another 14 persons belonged to two committees and 10 to three committees. This left only seven academics, four Nigerians and three expatriates, in addition to the *ex offico* members, holding between four and seven committee posts. The members of this overlapping directorate are referred to as "committee Professors," and along with the Vice-Chancellor, the Deans, the Chairman of Council and to a lesser extent the Registrar, they constitute the oligarchy of less than a score of persons who share the effective decision-making powers of the University.

The distribution of committee posts by rank is also somewhat misleading in that it understates the role of Professors. Not only do the twenty non-Professors on the committees hold on the average fewer positions than the Professors, but they belong almost entirely to specialized and peripheral committees. For example, there is not a single academic of lower than professorial rank on the Finance and General Purposes Committee of the Council, or on the Appointments and Promotions Committee and the Development Committee (and its sub-committees) of the Senate, which between them largely run the University.

About half of the Professors do not belong to any committees, largely because of lack of interest, and perhaps a good half of the remaining half are not active academic politicians. This leaves the oligarchy within the oligarchy, namely the Deans and the "committee Professors." This power group is by no means a unified one. Coalitions and alignments change with issues. It is thus impossible to speak of an "inner group" sharing power in a solidary fashion. Instead, the distribution of power, while extremely oligarchical, is highly diffuse and competitive within the oligarchy. There is no "power clique," no monolithic "establishment," conspiring to monopolize power and resources among themselves at the expense of the others.[10] Rather, the situation is one in which individualistic "stars" compete for power against one another with the support of powerful political patrons and power groups outside University and of junior clients inside it. Some of the spoils of the game of academic politics are distributed in the form of jobs, promotions and other favors to the respective clienteles of the oligarchs. The oligarchs enter into temporary alliances of convenience with other oligarchs, and there are some vaguely defined principles of solidarity based on kinship, locality, ethnicity, religion, and common educational experience which allow one to predict to some extent the broad lines along which alliances are formed. Ideology plays almost no role in the process at all. In last analysis, expediency in the pursuit of self-interest is the cardinal factor, and various ties of solidarity are activated to suit individualistic ends.

Let us take a closer look at the Development Committee (D.C.) and the

Appointments and Promotions Committee (A.P.C.). The D.C. is, in effect, the executive committee of the Senate; its membership includes the Vice-Chancellor as Chairman, and his Deputy, all the Deans, and six elected Professors, with the Bursar and the Librarian in attendance, and the Deputy Registrar as Secretary. Its terms of reference are, among other things, "to advise the Senate, and through the Senate, the Council, on the financial, academic and other aspects of the development of the University, . . . to formulate and review policies, and establish criteria, with a view to recommending to the Senate the order of priorities in the University's academic development, . . . to make recommendations to the Senate as to what changes in the academic organisation and administrative structure would make for greater flexibility and the most efficient and economical deployment of resources, . . . to scrutinise the annual estimates of expenditure submitted by Faculties, Departments, and others, . . . to consider all requests for authorisation of expenditure in excess of approved annual estimates, . . . to authorise applications for grants for research, . . . [and] to perform such other functions as Senate may from time to time determine." These functions are sub-divided between the D.C.'s three sub-committees on Academic Planning, Finance, and Research Grants. The last sub-committee, besides administering Senate's own little research fund, channels grant applications to external agencies, mostly overseas foundations, in which Ford and Rockefeller have pride of place. Although the sub-committee is not apt to turn down or discourage foreign donors of research funds, it does scrutinize the requests with an eye mostly to the possible financial implications and obligations that may grow out of the grants, and which the University may have to assume when the grants run out. The Academic Planning Sub-Committee recommends policies and priorities in the development of the University's academic curriculum, and drafts quinquennial plans establishing temporal guidelines for the establishment of new academic programs and departments.

The most unpopular of the sub-committees is the Finance Sub-Committee, the function of which is to mediate between the grossly conflicting budgetary demands of the various departments and faculties forever expanding shares of a fixed, or even, during the Civil War, a contracting cake. There are two main aspects to the "budget exercise," one external to the University, and the other internal. The first question is the size of the total University budget, and this is settled by high-level negotiations between Council, the Vice-Chancellor and his representatives on the U.I. side, and the National Universities Commission, and the Ministry of Finance on the outside. Irrespective of the total size of the cake, there is the second and even more painful problem of how to cut it between the various departments and faculties. This part of the exercise is an almost pure example of what game theorists call a zero-sum game (i.e. one in which A wins as much as B loses or vice versa). As such it brings out in its most pristine form the individualistic competitiveness between deans and department heads. During the period of field work, the exercise was more than averagely fierce because, in view of a general budget cut, departments had to demonstrate not why they should get a budget increase, but rather why their budget should not be retrenched from the previous year.

Briefly, the procedure is for each Department Head to prepare budget estimates, based on the previous years but higher, in full expectation that the allocation will be lower than the request. The departmental estimates are then collated into a faculty package by the Dean and his Department Heads. Armed with the estimates for the various departments of his faculty, the Dean pleads his case with the Finance Sub-Committee of the D.C., each Department Head having the option to appear in front of the sub-committee to defend his estimates. In practice, three main considerations determine the cutting of the cake. First, established positions are taken as the baseline unless the quinquennial development plan has clearly foreseen the foundation or expansion of new departments. (The Civil War put a moratorium on such expansion.) Privileged departments and faculties, by and larger, remain so, and vice versa. Second the aggressiveness and political aptitude of the individual Department Head determine his competitive ability to press his claims against those of colleagues. Third, the persuasiveness of the Head or Dean in convincing the sub-committee of his needs and of the value of his contribution to the University also determines the outcome. Thus, even an aggressive Professor of Classics may have difficulty holding his own against a meek Professor of Preventive and Social Medicine, for example. In 1969, the object of the game was not to maximize gains but to minimize losses in view of the anticipated budget retrenchment as compared to previous years.

The A.P.C. is perhaps the most controversial committee of Senate. Under the Chairmanship of the Vice-Chancellor, it is composed of the Deputy Vice-Chancellor, all Deans, two representatives of Council, four Professors elected by Senate, and the head of the department concerned. Being in effect the all-powerful body determining recruitment to and promotion of the teaching staff, A.P.C. members are subjected to intense pressures from individuals and interest groups, and to numerous allegations of nepotism, favoritism and "tribalism." Internally, A.P.C. is ridden with factionalism, and during the period of field work at least half-a-dozen bitter clashes occurred over both appointments and promotions. To defend itself against allegations of partiality, the A.P.C. operates within a system of universalistic rules involving public advertisements for vacancies in the press, letters of recommendations, an external evaluation by the Inter-University Council in London, and a special internal evaluation committee for each case. The "proper procedures" are, however, so dilatory and cumbersome as to be often self-defeating. If anybody is to be appointed at all, rules often have to be bent, or the Vice-Chancellor has to exercise his prerogative of appointing teachers on temporary status for one year. In any case, directly or indirectly, and whether the rules have been violated or scrupulously followed, numerous particularistic prejudices enter into the collective decisions of the A.P.C., and the opportunities for clashes of personality and interests are endless. The previous Vice-Chancellor was generally able to impose his will on A.P.C., but during the field work there were numerous conflicts between the Vice-Chancellor and several members of A.P.C.; several expatriate Professors resigned, at least in part, as a result of these clashes over appointments or promotions. In the past, the A.P.C. has tried to operate on a "consensual" basis, i.e. without formal voting. When votes are taken, decisions to appoint or promote must carry a three-quarters majority, and some recent crises have resulted from the inability of the Vice-Chancellor to impose his will and create the illusion of "consensus" as his predecessor had done. When a formal vote is taken, three or four votes are sufficient to block an appointment or promotion.

COUNCIL

The Council is the supreme governing body of the University, subject to the prerogatives of the Senate in the academic sphere. The University of Ilosho Act simply states that the Council "shall have the general management of the affairs of the university and in particular the control of the property and expenditure of the university." The Council does have precedence over the Senate. It is much the smaller body; the Senate elects four Professors as its representatives in the Council, while the Council does not elect representatives to the Senate; the Chairman of the Council who is the Pro-Chancellor of the University takes precedence over the Chairman of the Senate who is the Vice-Chancellor, and, even though the recruitment and promotion of teachers is specified as a Senate function, the official nominations are made by the Council. By convention the Council has never challenged the jurisdiction of the Senate over academic affairs (though it has on occasion raised questions about them), and, in that sense, the Senate and Council are "nearly equal" bodies, each with its well-defined sphere of authority. This near-equality is symbolized in the fact that the Joint Committee that selects the Vice-Chancellor consists of an equal number of Senate and Council members, but the precedence of the Council is reestablished by the fact that the Chairman of this Joint Committee is the Chairman of the Council.

The Council is a body of 19 voting members, plus the Registrar as Secretary. Besides the Chairman who is appointed by the Chancellor (an honorific functionary himself appointed by the Head of State who is officially the Visitor of the University), the Council consists of the Vice-Chancellor and his Deputy who are *ex-officio* members, ten members appointed by the Federal Government (including, *ex officio*, the Permanent Secretaries of the Ministries of Education and Finance), four Professors elected by the Senate, one member elected by Congregation, and one member elected by Convocation. Altogether, there are seven academic members of the Council and twelve non-academic members, ten of whom are political appointees. As of 1968, all but four of the Council members were Nigerians. The quorum used to be eight, but was reduced to six, i.e. less than one-third, in 1968.

The functional division between the Senate and Council is that the Senate is concerned with the academic side of the University while the Council is responsible for all residual functions, namely the construction and maintenance of the physical plant of the campus, all University employees other than teachers and research staff, the operation of the International School and the Staff School, the University Bookshop, the University finances, and the allocation of housing.

The Council normally meets twice a year, in November and May. Special meetings are sometimes called when crises occur, but more routine problems are handled by the principal committee of the Council, the Finance and General Purposes Committee (F.G.P.C.) Eight other committees and boards of the Council, all with academic representation, divide between themselves the other tasks of the Council, such as the appointment and promotion of non-academic staff, road repairs, primary and secondary school management, and building contracts.

The Senate is represented not only on the Council itself, but also, through the Vice-Chancellor and individual Professors, on all of its committees and boards. Indeed, except for the F.G.P.C., none of these committees and boards is chaired by the Chairman of the Council; the Vice-Chancellor chairs four, his Deputy one, and other academics the remaining three. Conversely, the Council is represented on only one committee of the Senate, the A.P.C., and then by only two members.

On the Council itself, non-academics are in majority, but this does not mean that the academic minority is not dominant. When the Council assembles, its meetings are lengthy, typically lasting at least a full day and often two or three successive days; however, the Council meets at too infrequent intervals for its members to develop an effective working relationship. Of the non-academic members, some are respectable elderly gentlemen whose appointment to Council was purely honorific, but who are no longer in any position to make any intellectual contribution. Others are traditional Northern Muslims who are learned men in the Islamic tradition, but have little conception of what a Western-style university is. Others yet are high-ranking civil servants or jurists who are fully acquainted with complex bureaucratic structures, but have no specialized knowledge about universities. In short, the non-academic members of Council are amateurs while the academics have the immense advantage of being intimately acquainted with the institution, its traditions, its power structure, its conflicts and its problems. Only they have a realistic idea of the possible, and, in addition, they have much discretionary power to implement or to ignore policies passed by Council.

Two examples will show the nature of the "communication gap" between the academic and the non-academic members of Council. The first was the attempt by the Chairman of Council, a conservative Victorian gentleman and a medical bureaucrat in the Public Health Service by prior career, to introduce the practice of opening Council meetings with a prayer. His main support came from the Northern Muslims who were also non-academics, and considerable embarrassment resulted as the academics, who argued that it was not traditional for a body of that type to open with prayers, caused the proposal to be shelved. The second instance is even more characteristic. A judge on the Council, partly under pressure from the Registrar who would have liked more disciplinary powers to deal with his subordinates, drafted a series of proposals for the disciplining of Senior Staff modelled after Civil Service regulations but totally out of keeping with academic practice. When the document came up for discussion in the Senate, the Vice-Chancellor, with his usual suave wit, said he trusted the Senate had read the proposals before it, and that it found them entirely acceptable. His remark was greeted with an instantaneous outburst of laughter, ending all discussion on the issue.

There is no fundamental basis of group conflict between the academics and the non-academics on the Council. They all belong to the ruling class which runs Nigeria, and they share broadly the same interest in the *status quo*. The Council certainly does not serve the function of an external check on the Senate to defend the interests of the Nigerian people. In effect, Council runs the physical plant of the University, and the Intermediate and Subordinate Staff through the Registrar. Even there, the interests of the Senior Staff are well protected and represented on the standing committees, and only the Senior Staff are close enough to the day-to-day running of the University to know what is really happening. Under the civilian regime, the Council was one more avenue of political patronage and graft for the political class which plundered the public treasury; but, even then, it was not an effective check on the power of the academic establishment.

NOTES

[1] Unfortunately the term "estate" is itself not free of multiple connotations. Max Weber used the term in German (*Stand*) to stress the prestige and life-style components of differential status as distinguished from both the power and the economic aspects of invidious distinctions. Here, we shall not impose that restriction on the term, and we shall be concerned with differentials in power, wealth and prestige. Other sociologists have meant by an "estate" a hierarchized social group of an intermediate degree of "openness" between a theoretically closed *caste* and a theoretically open *class*. In the present study, it is clear that the groups we call "estates" are in fact more widely open to social mobility than groups that have commonly been called "classes." But our "estates," though widely open, are nevertheless very sharply drawn both in the sense that membership is unambiguous and that the scale of differential rewards between "estates" is very wide. In these respects, then, our "estates" resemble the stratified societies of medieval Europe or Japan, or, indeed, those of several parts of pre-colonial Africa, notably the Western Sudan. This is the main justification for using the term here, but, of course, I do not mean to imply that the system I am describing is similar to these societies in most or even any other basic respect. Discussions on what to call the ruling stratum of the "new nations" of the Third World can be found in Bottomore (1966), Southall (1961), Shils (1961), Nadel (1956) and Lloyd (1966), many of these authors opting for the term "elite."

[2] I have dealt at greater length elsewhere with the social implications of the use of English and French in Africa (van den Berghe, 1968a).

[3] Virilocal residence exists when the bride upon marriage goes and lives with her husband and his relatives. Neolocal residence is practiced when husband and wife establish a new household separate from that of both spouses' relatives.

[4] There was a delicate case, for example, where an expatriate intervened in what he thought was barbarous disciplining of a servant by a Nigerian neighbor. An adolescent girl who had gotten pregnant was given a severe and prolonged beating by her employers who were also senior kinsmen, and, by European middle-class standards, the disciplining was excessive, not to say sadistic. The case was hushed up, and some Nigerians agreed that the Senior Staff person involved should be asked to resign, but other Nigerians were indignant at what they saw as unwarranted interference by a stranger into the affairs of a senior kinsman acting *in loco parentis*.

[5] Many of the traditional societies of Nigeria were of course quite elaborately and clearly stratified, but the transfer of the traditional status system into the modern one has been relatively minimal.

[6] Despite its name, the N.A.U.T. is open to Nigerians and non-Nigerians alike. The membership criterion is the holding of a teaching post at any of the Nigerian Universities. At Ilosho, a number of the younger expatriates as well as Nigerians of all ranks were active in the N.A.U.T. which functioned as a sort of opposition to Nwanneh and the "bar establishment."

[7] This is a salary bar which constitutes in fact a promotion, rather than an automatic yearly salary increment.

[8] An Associate Professorship at Ilosho is the equivalent of a Readership in the British system while a Senior Lectureship at Ilosho is roughly equivalent to an American Associate Professorship.

[9] Paragraph 11 of the preamble of the University of Ilosho Act, 1962, reads: "No person shall be required to satisfy requirements as to any of the following matters, that is to say, race (including ethnic grouping), sex, place of birth or of family origin, or religious or political persuasion, as a condition of becoming or continuing to be a student at the university, the holder of any degree of the university or of any appointment or employment at the university, or a member of any body established by virtue of this Act; and no person shall be subjected to any disadvantage or accorded any advantage, in relation to the university, by reference to any of those matters." The semi-official policy of Nigerianization of staff, however flexibly it is implemented, can be regarded as a clear violation of that clause, as it does discriminate on the basis of "place of birth or of family origin," and, indirectly, of race and ethnicity. Nationality as such is not explicitly mentioned in the act, however. There is also some discrimination by sex in the conditions of employment of the Senior Staff in that the Staff Information Handbook specifies that a female employee of the University must make a medical case for entitling her husband to the benefits of a dependent, while it is automatically assumed that the wife of a male employee is his dependent. Furthermore, an expatriate woman employee married to a Nigerian is treated as a Nigerian (and thus does not qualify for a yearly passage to Europe), whereas this clause would not apply to the reciprocal case of a male expatriate employee married to a Nigerian woman. Compared to most other universities which I have known, however, U.I. displays comparatively little anti-feminism. Several women have been Department Heads, for example, and there are no rules to prevent husbands and wives from being both employed within the same faculty or even department.

[10] During the Nwanneh era, the power distribution was not nearly as diffuse. In the early years of it, the expatriate "bar establishment" was a cohesive power bloc, and, in the later years, there was a discernible and stable Ibo ruling clique around Nwanneh. The present diffuse situation developed during the Akinode era, as the result partly of complex Yoruba factionalism and partly of the departure of a number of previously powerful expatriates.

CHAPTER FIVE

The Second Estate: Students

African universities being, to an even greater extent than those of industrial countries, the breeding ground of the fraction of one per cent which rules the continent, the question of the social, geographic, religious, and ethnic origins of African students is of great practical relevance. Fortunately, at U.I., the admission records provide fairly accurate information.[1] Of 6,130 students who matriculated for a degree course at U.I. between 1948 and 1966–67, a random sample of 3,167 was chosen, i.e. slightly over half of the total. In addition, data were obtained from 32 life histories written by students in a sociology course in 1968–69.

Nigeria's educational system, like that of all African states, is highly pyramidal and unevenly distributed.[2] Perhaps half of the population currently of school age never attend any school at all, although lower primary education is becoming increasingly widespread, and is already reaching some three quarters of the children in the Southern states. In the North, however, more than 90 per cent of the total population are still illiterate, and at most one-fifth of the children of primary school age are enrolled in Western-style schools. There also exist Muslim schools (*madrassa*), where children learn to decipher the Arabic script and to memorize the Koran, but that education is of little if any value in the "modern" sector. In the Southern third of Nigeria, 40 to 50 per cent of the total population in the more urbanized areas, and perhaps 75 per cent of the people under 30 years of age, are literate. Thus, while literacy certainly does not exceed 15 per cent for the country as a whole, some parts of Southern Nigeria have among the highest rates in Africa. Geographical disparities in levels of education between different regions are common in Africa, but Nigeria is an extreme case, having within its boundaries some of the educationally most "backward" and some of the most "advanced" areas of Africa. These internal disparities create a host of social, economic and political problems which often take the form of ethnic conflicts, since geography frequently coincides with ethnicity.[3]

Not only is the internal distribution of educational opportunities affected by geography, religion, ethnicity, and indeed by sex and social class, but the absolute amount of available resources is extremely limited, though steadily growing. Every step up the educational ladder is drastically narrower than the one below it. Only a minority of the children who enter primary school complete it; of that minority, only a tenth or so *enter* secondary school, and of that tenth only a tenth get the matriculation certificate which allows them entry into a university. Roughly, the average chance of a Nigerian child gaining admission to a university is of the order of one in a thousand. In some parts of Nigeria, it is of the order of one in a hundred thousand, in other parts of one in a hundred, but even in the relatively privileged regions the odds are extremely slim.

Selective Factors in Education

The first and most obvious selective factor in education is regional. Over the years, 53.3 per cent of all students came from Lagos and the former Western Region which make up 22.0 per cent of Nigeria's total population. The former Eastern Region with 27.5 per cent of the population produced 38.6 per cent of U.I. students, while the Northern Region with slightly over half (50.5 per cent) of all Nigerians only gave the University 6.1 per cent of its students. (Table 7) Except for the fact that the opening of a university in the East in 1960, and in the North in 1962 has somewhat re-

TABLE 7 / PERCENTAGES OF ILOSHO STUDENTS COMING FROM THE MAIN REGIONS OF NIGERIA (1948–1966)

Main Regions	YEARS				
	1948–52	1953–57	1958–62	1963–66	All Years
Lagos, West and Midwest	49.9%	53.4%	53.2%	64.6%	53.3%
East	47.1	41.6	35.8*	33.0	38.6
North	3.0	5.0	11.1	2.4**	6.1
Total	100.0	100.0	100.1	100.0	100.0***
	(N=499)	(N=813)	(N=1001)	(N=702)	(N=3015)

* Part of this drop is attributable to the opening of the University of Nigeria at Nsukka in 1960.

** Most of that drop is due to the opening of Ahmadu Bello University at Zaria in 1962.

*** "No reply's" were not included in the computation of percentages.

duced the Eastern and Northern contingents at Ilosho in recent years, the situation has not changed much in twenty years. The North is bridging the educational gap between itself and the South with agonizing slowness, despite government efforts to achieve a more even balance through scholarships and educational investments in new secondary schools.

The geographical breakdown by province (the former administrative sub-divisions of the old regions) shows in more detail the regional disparities, as well as some intra-regional ones. In the North, the only provinces which produced numbers of students approaching those from the West and East, are Ilorin and Kabba, both with large Yoruba populations, and thus culturally more akin to the West than to the North. All of the non-Yoruba Northern provinces had rates of entry into U.I. that were from 5 to 110 times lower than all but one (Ogoja) of the Western and Eastern provinces. Within the South (meaning East and West combined), except again for Ogoja Province, discrepancies were of the order of one to seven, with Ijebu Province leading by far, followed by Ondo, Oyo, Benin, Delta and Onitsha. Just as significant as the relative rates are the absolute ones. The most privileged province (Ijebu) only had a cumulative entry rate for the 1948–1966 period of 1,460 students per million population (using the 1952–53 Census as the basis). Five of the 12 Northern provinces produced under 10 students per million of population during that same period.

Closely related to regional and provincial distribution, but giving a more detailed picture of internal inequalities is ethnicity as shown in Table 8. These figures illustrate what is perhaps the most fundamental element of ethnic rivalries in Nigeria. Since control of all branches of the modern sector is almost exclusively in the hands of university graduates, ethnic groups with the educational headstart get a greatly disproportionate share of the "national" cake. Or, more precisely, the new Nigerian "elite" (as distinguished from the traditional rulers and aristocracies which are rapidly losing ground, especially since the military coups of 1966) is almost entirely Southern in origin, with Yoruba and Ibo as the two main antagonistic groups in the competition for the spoils of office. As Table 8 shows, all ethnic groups with rates exceeding 200 per million are from the South. Among the Southern groups, the Yoruba and Ibo do not have the highest rates, but their sheer absolute size puts them in a dominant position *vis à vis* the others. (The Civil War has, of course, meant a temporary loss in relative position for the Ibo, but they can be expected to make much of it up within the next decade, barring another major upheaval.) It is also revealing that the three largest Northern groups—Hausa, Fulani and Kanuri —who are almost solidly Muslim, have among the lowest rates even among the Northern groups. Some of the despised "pagans" of the Middle Belt have done relatively better than the Muslim groups of the far North.

TABLE 8 / Ethnic Composition of University of
Ilosho Students 1948–1966

Ethnic Group	Number of Students *	Per cent of Total	Rate per Million Total Population **
Yoruba	2,706	42.2%	537
Ibo	1,874	31.3	342
Edo-Bini-Ishan	395	6.6	848
Isoko	38	0.6	404
Urhobo	138	2.3	406
Ibibio-Efik-Anang	284	4.7	224
Ijaw-Kalabari	163	2.7	475
Itsekiri	58	1.0	2,071
Idoma-Afo-Yala-Igala	25	0.4	48
Nupe	20	0.3	56
Igbira	18	0.3	122
Hausa	31	0.5	6
Fulani	17	0.3	6
Kanuri	1	0.0	1
Tiv	6	0.1	8
Other Bantu and Bantoid groups	26	0.5	53
Other Northern Minorities	10	0.2	3
Non-Nigerian Africans ***	125	2.1	—
Non-Africans	59	1.0	—
No Reply ****	136	—	—
Total	6,130	100.1	194

* This table includes the total universe of students, not just the sample.

** Rate is computed on the basis of the 1952–53 Population Census. While that census was probably an underestimate, demographers agree that it was not subject to the politically-motivated distortions of the 1963 Census, and hence that the *relative* figures between the various ethnic groups and provinces are more accurate. As a rough estimate, the actual population today (1970) must be approximately twice as high as that given in the 1953 Census so that the rates in the last column of the table should be divided by two to give a better idea of *absolute* rates based on the present population. The main concern here, however, is with relative, not absolute rates.

*** Cameroonians were treated as "non-Nigerians" for the entire period.

**** Not included in computation of percentages.

This leads us to the religious factor of selection which in the last analysis is the most important causal one. Christians have a much better chance than Muslims, and traditionalists are scarcely represented at all. This is not to say that Islam is intrinsically "backward," "stagnant," or "obscur-antist" as many members of the Christian elite stereotypically believe. The situation grew, rather, out of the colonial era when Britain decided for its administrative convenience to rule the North "indirectly" through its tra-ditional aristocracy and to leave Islam unchallenged by Christian mission-aries. The "heathen" South and Middle Belt, on the other hand, were thrown open to the competitive conquest of souls by various missionary bodies. This meant Western-style schools teaching literacy in the Roman script and the language of the colonial power. Since the British controlled the apex of the pyramid, they also defined the educational skills needed to occupy those positions which they did not want for themselves. This meant that wage employment in clerical, semi-professional and professional occu-pations in the civil service presupposed attendance at mission schools, and this in turn meant adoption of the particular brand of Christianity connected with the missionary body which controlled the local school.

In Yoruba country which was already partly Islamized when the British established their control, the Muslims tried to develop a competing system of modernized Muslim schools, but, at the secondary school level, the Christian schools continued to dominate the educational scene, along with the technically non-sectarian but *de-facto* Christian-influenced elite state schools of King's and Queen's College, Lagos, and Government College, Ilosho. Generally speaking, the coastal parts of the country, and especially the Lagos-Abeokuta section of Yoruba country were missionized first, and hence got an educational headstart compared to the more remote parts of the interior.

At U.I., 91.9 per cent of the students describe themselves as Christians, some three-fourths of whom belong to "regular" Protestant denominations (mostly of British or American origin such as Anglican, Methodist, or Baptist), and one-fourth of whom are Roman Catholics, mostly from the Mid-West and Eastern Regions. Only 1.0 per cent declare allegiance to African "separatist" churches. The remaining 8.1 per cent are mostly Muslims (5.7 per cent) or students who failed to reply to the question (2.3 per cent). Only 0.1 per cent describe themselves as traditionalists, i.e. practitioners of indigenous African religions, and not a single student in the sample of over 3,000 calls himself an agnostic or atheist. Even if leaving the space on the form blank can be interpreted as rejection of organized religion, it is significant that only some two per cent did so. Con-sidering that some 45 per cent of all Nigerians are Muslims, 35 per cent Christians and perhaps 20 per cent traditionalists, it is clear that Christians are overrepresented among students by a factor of about three, that Muslims are only about one-eighth as numerous as could be expected, and that tra-ditionalists have virtually no chance of getting a university education.

The religious factor of selection holds true even within ethnic groups. The Yoruba, for example, are about 60 per cent Muslims, and 40 per cent Christians, some degree of traditional religious practice being incompatible with neither of the two major religions. Yet, despite the fact that Yoruba Muslims are in majority, the educated elite is some 90 to 95 per cent Christian, and there is a general negative correlation between the degree to which a Yoruba district is Muslim and the proportion of students it sends to university.

As might be expected not only in Nigeria but indeed in most countries, there is a distinct bias in favor of educating boys, rather than girls. During the 1948–1966 period, women students have only made up 11.0 per cent of the total, but this percentage has risen from less than 5 per cent up to 1955 to between 5 and 10 per cent from 1956 to 1961, to over 10 per cent thereafter. In 1965, a record 21.8 per cent women were matriculated. The relatively few women who do make it to university tend to come disproportionately from the more privileged groups, i.e., they tend to be even more overwhelmingly Christian, and from the Southern ethnic groups than the male students, and to be children of professional or semi-professional fathers.

The last important selective factor is parental class status, as measured by father's and mother's occupation. It might be expected that, given a fiercely competitive struggle for education, and given the great economic bottleneck of the secondary school, social class selectivity would be great. Primary education is now free, at least in theory, in many Nigerian schools; but parents do have to pay for school uniforms, books, school taxes and special levies, and these costs, while nominal by European or American standards are quite substantial in a country with a per capita income of £25 to £30 a year. The great economic hurdle, however, comes with secondary schools, nearly all of which are boarding schools with fees of some £50 to £100 a year. Since secondary "grammar" schools (i.e. the ones that train pupils for university entrance as distinguished from secondary "modern" schools that do not) are still few and far between, most pupils have to come from afar and be boarders, a factor which makes secondary schooling beyond the means of the vast majority of Nigerians.

Despite these staggering economic handicaps, class selectivity in education, while clearly present, is probably not as pronounced as in many countries with a more developed class system. Table 9 shows that a third of the students are children of professional or semi-professional fathers, and this is at least ten times as many as in the population at large. But close to a third also come from farming families. As there are practically no large landowners in Nigeria, these students are typically children of small and often illiterate farmers. It is true that these farmers tend to come more from the cash crop sector (mostly cocoa, palm oil and groundnuts) than from the subsistence sector, and to be of slightly above average income, but few of them could be called wealthy, even by Nigerian standards. Similarly, the relatively large category of "traders" suggests greater wealth than is in fact the case; most of these traders deal on a very small scale, and are worse off than many artisans or clerks on a regular salary.

TABLE 9 / Percentages of Fathers of Ilosho Students in Various Occupational Categories (1948–1966)

Occupation	1948–52	1953–57	1958–62	1962–66	All Years
1. Farmers	29.2	26.1	31.1	38.0	30.8
2. Traders	12.9	19.7	16.3	14.6	16.4
3. Traditional Chiefs	1.2	1.1	1.7	4.0	1.9
4. Unskilled Workers	0.2	0.5	0.8	1.3	0.7
5. Artisans	7.7	8.7	8.2	4.0	7.4
6. Clerical and Sales	8.6	7.7	6.3	2.3	6.2
7. Semi-professionals	23.0	22.0	25.4	18.2	22.6
8. Professional	13.6	11.3	7.3	15.5	11.2
9. Others	3.6	2.9	3.0	2.3	2.9
Total	100.0	100.0	100.1*	100.2*	100.1*
	(N=418)	(N=804)	(N=933)	(N=556)	(N=2711)**

* Percentages do not add up to 100.0 because of rounding errors.
** 'No reply's' were not included in the computation of percentages.

As a rough estimate, something like half of the students come from "common" Nigerian families, i.e. are the children of illiterate or barely literate parents with a social background of small-scale farming, petty trade or manual work. They come from large and often polygynous families of which they are frequently the best educated member. Economically, these families are probably slightly above the mass of subsistence peasants, but they are not "elite," nor do they even belong to the salaried, urban petty middle-class of secretaries, clerks and sales personnel. The other half of the students come from literate, urban, frequently monogamous families with post-primary education and with fathers on a salary, most often as artisans, teachers, clerks, civil servants, or independent professionals. The "elite" in the restricted sense of university educated professionals only accounts for 11.2 per cent of the students. This is at least twenty or thirty times their representation in the total population; however, collectively, the elite is still small enough and young enough for their children to account for only a little over one-tenth of the student population.[4]

Also of interest in Table 9 is the relatively small contingent of children of "traditional chiefs." There are several reasons for this. Some traditional societies, notably in the East, such as the Ibo, are unstratified beyond age and sex and have no "chiefs" in the sense of executive power holders. The Northern Muslim societies, on the other hand, are highly stratified and politically centralized. They are ruled by an aristocracy of political office holders under the authority of Emirs. But the Muslim aristocrats in the North resisted for the most part Western education which they regarded with mistrust on both religious and political grounds. Of the stratified societies, this left those of the West, mostly the Yoruba and Bini, and indeed a number of Obas (kings) did send their children to mission schools. Overall, however, the "carry-over" of the traditional system of stratification, where such existed, into the modern one was relatively small. The "modern" system is simply not a modification of the traditional order; it is based on totally different criteria, and is made up of an almost totally new personnel.

Table 9 indicates that, as yet, there is no tendency toward "elite closure." There is no consistent trend toward increasing representation of children of professionals and semi-professionals, and if anything the proportion of farmers' children has increased somewhat in the 1960's. The continued relative openness of the top stratum is undoubtedly due to the rapid expansion of that stratum, especially since Independence, to replace departing expatriates and to staff the openings created by a growing state bureaucracy, a rapidly expanding secondary school system, developing petroleum and manufacturing industries, and the proliferating management of state and private enterprises in banking, commerce, and transport. Nevertheless, the present rate of expansion of the top stratum cannot be maintained for much longer. There is a limit to the top-heaviness of the government bureaucracy and to a still undeveloped economy's ability to absorb technical and managerial personnel. Only the educational system can be expected to maintain its rapid rate of expansion, thereby eventually creating a grave problem of educated unemployment such as faced by countries like India and Pakistan. When the saturation point will have been reached—and there are indications that this will happen in the early 1970's—it seems probable that class selectivity in education will increase, and that the market value of a university degree will decline steeply. On the other hand, the expansion of secondary schools in the North will probably reduce ethnic, regional and religious disparities to some extent.

In several respects, however, class selectivity is already noticeable. Female students tend to come from much higher status families than male students. Throughout the world, educational opportunities for women relative to men are inversely proportional to the degree of development of the given country, and to the degree of privilege of a given group within a country. Of the men, 31.5 per cent are sons of professionals and semi-professionals; nearly twice as many women (58.4 per cent) have fathers in those categories.

Students from "elite" families matriculate much younger than children of farmers. Of the students who are less than 20 years old when they enter university, 45.5 per cent are children of professionals and semi-professionals and only 18.2 per cent are children of farmers. For students over 30 at matriculation, the respective percentages are 16.0 and 54.7. The explanation is obvious: children from educated, salaried parents have typically gone straight to secondary grammar schools and pursued their studies without interruptions. Children from impecunious and uneducated families have, for the most part, had to interrupt their secondary schooling one or more time to earn money, frequently as primary school teachers, in order to pay their fees and continue their secondary education. The great majority of those never reach university, and the lucky few with sufficient stamina and perseverance make it but at a rather late age. Only 13.5 per cent of all students entered at U.I. before age 20, and 22.5 per cent were 25 years or older. Furthermore, the age of entry has risen over time. In the early 1950's the modal year at admission was 19, while in the early 1960's it had risen to 22. One of the factors for this rising age of the student population has been the sharp decline in the percentage of students on scholarships, and hence, the need for students to interrupt their secondary studies in order to earn their school fees.

Finally, parental status is a factor in determining into which faculty a student will enroll. Children of professionals and semi-professionals make up 43.8 per cent of the prestigious, expensive, and potentially most remunerative Faculty of Medicine, and only 12.8 per cent of the low-prestige Faculty of Education; children of farmers, on the other hand constitute only 18.0 per cent of the medical students and 59.0 per cent of the education students. The other faculties fall in-between, in order of their respective status, with Science near the Medicine end of the continuum and Social Sciences second to bottom before Education.

Life Histories

These statistical data from admission records were supplemented by 32 life histories. The conclusions to be drawn from them either support or complement the statistical results. Before analyzing them, excerpts from six rather diverse cases will give the reader an idea of the wide range of family background and life experience of students.[5]

CASE 1

"It is very difficult to say with accuracy the exact date of my birth since there was no written record by my illiterate parents. But according to the information given by my sister I was born around 1943. . . . My father whose income from farming is not up to £60 a year, has two wives and six children. Both wives depend on him for maintenance and there is no work which they are capable of doing. From the time of my birth to 1948 when I entered primary school, the difficulties I encountered were so numerous that I cannot give details in an essay of this sort. . . . My father instead of sending me to the farm as other people did to their own children sent me to school in 1948 when I was very young. . . . At times I did not have a single exercise book from January to June. He could not afford to buy textbooks but managed to get exercise books and pencils. My mother gave occasional assistance by giving me one penny for my lunch in the school and by buying some exercise books and school uniforms whenever my father refused to buy them. My attendance in the school meant a lot to the class teacher since, in spite of obvious handicaps, I showed brilliant performances in any examination. . . . Most of my days in the primary school I took my breakfast at 2:00 p.m. . . . I gave up any hope of continuing my education after primary six. Irrespective of financial difficulties, my father decided that I should go to the modern school which was five miles away from our town. This was a praiseworthy decision as most of my mates started to go to the farm. . . . We spent about £20 per annum. How my father maintained me for two years in this school was a magic to me. My academic performance was unparalleled and I was made the school librarian.

"By my final year in the school my father could not go further. Previous debt had accumulated with an exorbitant rate of interest. My eyes were hollowed with hunger, clothes torn like that of a beggar; there was no help except that from God. With confidence I attended the school. At times I was driven back. . . . Eventually December came and I was allowed to take the exam by the kind permission of the headmaster.[6] I passed the exam with distinction.

"With my modern three certificate I went to Lagos . . . to look for jobs. All efforts proved abortive throughout the six months stay in Lagos.[7] I could remember one day I trekked . . . a distance of eight miles because there was no money. I worked with local building contractors for some weeks at a rate of 2s 6d a day. . . . I decided to go in 1960 on a job-finding tour of Ilorin. However I was lucky to be employed by one bookseller on a salary of £2 5s per month. I managed this throughout 1960 and I nearly read all the books in the bookshop.

"That year I took an entrance examination to teacher training college.

. . . By October I was able to collect £10 from my meagre salary which I paid as deposit. . . . I was able to finish my first year with success. During my second year one tribal association in Lagos lent me the sum of £25 which covered my debt for the whole year. I was then left without books and college uniforms. Poverty was seen daily at my face but it did not move me. I completed my Grade III (Teacher Certificate) course in December, 1962.

"In 1963 I was given automatic employment in one school in Ogbomosho. I started to balance previous debts and maintain a kind of status similar to that of a Grade III teacher. Since I had got no money to go for further studies, I decided to tackle various examinations as an external candidate. Hence . . . between 1963 and 1967, I was able to pass six subjects at the ordinary level . . . and three subjects at the advanced level.

"Should I apply for admission to any of our universities? How shall I get money? How many people can afford to help me? Who will take care of my poor parents at home? These and many other questions came to me last year . . . I was given a direct admission to this university.

"The life of an indigent student is full of ups and downs. Many of these difficulties are inescapable. No hunger can frighten me. Lack of clothes, money, and books can no longer have effect on me. That one's destination cannot be changed is an indisputable fact . . . I am still looking at God for help. Most of my previous classmates are now farmers, carpenters, blacksmiths, traders, and so forth. They all look at me as if I am God. Great thanks to God and my father who, in spite of poverty, insisted that I shall go to school."

CASE 2

"I was born into a polygamous home—very polygamous in the real sense of it because my grandfather had over fifteen wives and over a hundred children and grandchildren. But my father being a Christian had only two wives and fourteen children before he died. . . . My grandfather . . . was a warrior who took part in the [Yoruba civil wars] towards the end of the last century. . . . Because he was proud and fairly rich then, he thought that no one could treat his daughters as well as he. To give out the daughters for marriage was to him a necessary evil. His daughters when married were not allowed to live with their husbands. They only went to cohabit with their husbands whenever they wanted to be pregnant. This eventually led to the family expansion. Today there is a quarter [of the town] called Chief X's quarter. . . . The quarter of the great warrior.

"I could not guess how old my father was when he died because I was only ten years old. . . . He was the first born of Chief X, and . . . he was so intelligent, or probably talented with statesmanship . . . that he became one of the King's Council members at about 30. Till today . . . nobody younger than he has ever been selected. My father became a Christian (Anglican denomination) . . . and decided to send many of his children to school. . . . Virtually today, I am the first son of my father who is doing a degree course in a university. There are some working in various offices and schools. . . . His death so hit his family in a bad way that everybody was left to fend for himself and this actually retarded our educational progress. . . . Those of us who were young when he died had to wait for a few years after our primary school education before going to any college because of financial difficulties. . . . His death made me realize that the world is not a bed of roses and I still carry the belief that God has not been fair to me. So instead of growing up to embrace any religion I became a free-thinker. . . .

"I started schooling at the age of five and I was doing very well. From class 1 to 6 in the primary school I was always one of the best three pupils in the class. . . . My class teacher selected me to be his class monitor. . . . It was an enviable school office, because any pupil holding this office was granted all due respects. . . . I was the youngest pupil to hold that office . . . when I was only 12½ years old. . . .

"My family was not financially strong enough to send me to a Grammar School. . . . The only help the school could render me was to employ me as a teacher. . . . The public sensation then was about my age. I used to be called the 'tiny teacher,' a term I did not like then. I was in the school for some years trying to save up some amount, and with the help of benevolent gentlemen, I entered . . . a Grade Two Teachers' Training College in December 1962. . . . I have already become cynical, pessimistic about life. . . . I grew up by not trusting anybody and by relying solely on myself. By and large sentiments became killed in me. What I dislike in the world is more than what I like. . . . It is just the result of many years of suffering and endurance and feeling of insecurity. . . .

"I gained admission to the University in 1964 by direct entry. . . . My first session in the University was a failure. . . . Apart from spending all the money I saved for a year and a half, I failed my Part I B.A. Degree Examination. It was the greatest blow and shock I have ever received apart from that of the death of my father. . . . It was then I decided to change my course and see what I can do in the Department of Modern Languages, particularly French. . . . Luckily or miraculously enough, I was awarded a scholarship in March 1966. . . . I still have great belief in this French philosophical saying: 'Il n'y a ni de providence, ni de destin, toutes les choses sont le produit de la chance.' "

CASE 3

"Sometimes between 1935 and 1937 I was born into the household of a very wealthy farmer-trader. . . . To be connected in any way to this man meant a lot to the [X ethnic group]. He descended directly from one of the [chiefs] who ruled before the present [town] was founded. My mother descends from a middle class farmer, the first child of her parents.

"Having come from a well placed Christian family, daddy indulged himself in excessive polygyny. My mother could not have been higher than the twelfth out of a numberless collection of wives. (I tried to find out the exact number from my father before his death; he himself did not know). . . .

"We needed no incentive for education. My father read standard two before he joined the army. . . . And in those days, he was looked upon as one of the enlightened members of the X community. He even sat on the X Native Authority Council. But unfortunately for those of us who are his children, he saw no reason why we should go beyond Standard Six, i.e. the top class of the elementary school. Every child, including myself, was educated up to this class, after which we had to look after ourselves. Out of the twenty of us, I happen to be the fourteenth.

"I was put to school in 1942, and left the primary school in 1950. I became a pupil teacher in 1951 and in 1953 I gained admission into a college. . . . From 1954 to 1957, my education was affected by my inability to pay school fees. My brother, the only other child of my mother, was a Grade III teacher then, and he had to pay part of the fees. Our father would not hear of it at all.

"After passing the Teachers' Grade II Examination, I started teaching again in 1958. My brother had then entered the College for his Grade II certification, and so it was my turn to support his education. In 1959, I gained admission to the then Nigerian College of Technology, Ilosho, but financial problems stopped any move. I then decided to do another teachers course. So, in 1963, I again entered a teachers' college where I qualified in 1965. I again went back to teaching. . . . And after a spell of time, I decided to come and risk University education knowing full well that age may count against me in the consideration for the award of any scholarship."

CASE 4

"I was born into a polygynous family. My father, a farmer by vocation, has three wives including my mother. . . . Also he is the head of our lineage group. I am the eldest son of the family.

"It was not my father's intention to send me to school. But with constant pressure from my father's sister's son, he eventually saw the necessity of sending me to school in February, 1947, at a village three miles from my home town.

"The question of funds did not constitute a problem initially as it was possible to make a successful school career with a few school materials— a wooden slate, pieces of chalk, a pair of shorts and a shirt. . . . With time and progress in educational career, the question of school fees became a problem as my father's financial resources could no longer support the expanding family.

"To relieve him of some burden, my father asked me to go and stay with his brother who was in a relatively stable financial position. I started school [there] in 1949. . . . A part of the school fees came from my father. The cost of school materials and part of the school fees was met by my father's brother. This is not to say that I was not always engaged in income generating activities after school hours. . . . Such as making mud-blocks, weaving of baskets, fetching and selling of fire wood. I was in the regular service of my father's brother's wife on Sundays—selling oranges, fish, and locally manufactured soap.

"The observation made during my petty financial activities on Sundays made me alive to the fact that the children of those whose parents were permanent residents in the city . . . would always dress in beautiful clothes, . . . go to Sunday School . . . [or to] different social meetings where they collected money in pence against Christmas and the New Year festivities. The idea of working hard to be exactly like these permanent city boys and girls convinced me as early as 1957 to decide to live permanently in the city. This, I believed, would call for a high educational attainment. . . .

"I struggled frantically to top the class in any of the examinations we did. I always did it and the pride and price often came to me. . . . I sat for my first school leaving certificate in 1955 . . . I passed. It was not easy in those days for one to get employment with such a low level of education. Had I but the money, I would go to the Grammar School. The old story had to repeat itself. I stayed with my father's brother as a house boy. This time there was no link whatsoever with the school. There was no room for me to assert some forms of superiority.

"With time, I squeezed some few shillings which I paid as the Entrance Examination fees at a Teachers' Training College. I survived the examination and interview. I was written to come and resume school in January 1960. I kept this secret because if my father had been aware of it, he would have not allowed me to take what he would regard a risk. . . . The question of how to get money to finance my education at that time was easily answered by the free primary school scheme that was launched. More trained teachers were needed. The Divisional Council did not hesitate in sponsoring me. . . . After the course I was sent to a village school twenty miles from [the city]. It has always been my ambition to live and work in the city, but with my location . . . to such a remote area, I felt I had achieved nothing to warrant a prestigious position in the town.

"The only way available to advance my education was to take to private tuition. This I did for a year. In January 1965 I had six papers in the General Certificate of Education. . . . The following year, I put in for three subjects at the Advanced Level. I was again lucky to pass all the papers. I did cogitate on how to get money to finance my university education. I later decided to take a risk. . . . I have always believed that things will work themselves out in one way or the other. Presently nobody pays my school fees; my father is now in his dotage."

Case 5

"I was born in 1947 to an average Nigerian family. I am the only child in a monogamous family and I am female. My mother is a teacher and at the time my father was a teacher too. Both are from well-known families. My father is from the X family which is famous in Y. He went to Grammar School, passed his Cambridge [secondary school] exams and then went to a teachers training college. He taught until around 1950. He then went into the transport business. He ran some taxis and buses. In addition to this, he has some farms. Later, he went into politics and became a member of the House of Assembly.

"My mother attended Queen's College, Lagos. Her father was treasurer of the City Council and the family was very rich. After her Cambridge exams she went to Teachers' Training College. She then became a teacher and is still in the teaching profession. . . .

"Our house was surrounded by beautiful hedges, flowers and there were several fruit trees. . . .

"Since my parents and grandparents were educated, there was no decision to be made about my going to school. It was considered the normal thing. At about 7, I started schooling. . . . Before I started schooling my parents had spent their evenings teaching me the alphabet and numbers and a few other things. So I did not have any difficulty in Primary One. I passed without any effort on my own side. I had to repeat class two because I am a daydreamer and I hadn't learnt to control myself then. . . . I did not improve until I was in primary five. . . . From then, I started doing well. . . . I took my first school leaving certificate examination and had a grade 'A' pass. . . . I was admitted to Grammar School. I did well in the exam and I was offered a scholarship . . . [and] there was no difficulty about my fees. . . . We just had to pay the ten pounds a year. I lived on the school compound, in the boarding house. I found my subjects easy, and . . .

I came third and received a prize. . . . In form two, I did well too, though, at this time, I developed a hatred for mathematics. . . . In form three, I came first. . . . From this time, I maintained that position. . . . My school life was quite enjoyable and peaceful except that some were jealous of my success. I finished my school certificate examination in December 1965. . . . I decided I would work for the concessional examination for admission to the University of Ilosho . . . and I was admitted. . . . I came to U.I. took my examination at the end of the session and passed. . . . Though my parents had paid my fees for the 1966–67 session, I knew it was not very convenient for them. They had to go on strict budget to pay my fees so I decided to look for a scholarship as no member of the extended family was helping to maintain me. . . . I got the scholarship to read English and I am now using the scholarship."

CASE 6

"My father was born late in the last century. He had a mission education. He can rightly be described as one of the best educated in his time. He went as far as London Matriculation. Before he left the Government Service, he rose to the post of an Executive Officer, which very few Africans held at the time (1948). He attended a Secondary Grammar School. During the colonial days, he felt humiliated in many ways. He soon discovered that to rival the White man, one simply had to be educated enough. Highly influenced by the political activities of a host of African nationalists of high educational repute, he determined to train his children to an equal educational level. He read the work of Marcus Garvey and Dr. Du Bois.

"My mother [is] a third descendant of a Brazilian slave-merchant. She came from a respectable re-settled [Afro] Brazilian family in Lagos. She had a lady education mainly in the mission. She too believed in the education of her children as a worthwhile investment.

"I happen to be the second to last child in the family. The first son is an engineer. The second holds a doctorate in French and [is] at present a Research Fellow at [a foreign university]. He is the most brilliant in the family. The others who happen to be female are also not doing badly. Two of them are in Britain, one already a qualified secretary-typist, and the other reading banking.

"I can only say I am just one of the lucky ones of my generation to have been born into my family. From the beginning, I have had parents who know the importance of education and who are ready to sacrifice much. This came from their determination to see their sons occupy the 'white man's positions.'

"Of equal inspiration to me were my already successful brothers who are already academics. They have been helpful indeed, in not only defining the goal but as well backing me both financially and morally."

BACKGROUNDS

These six cases, while not representative of all students, do cover a wide range of social backgrounds and personal experiences, all the way from the desperate destitution of cases 1 and 4 to the relatively well-to-do but very traditional families of cases 2 and 3, to the smooth, easy and worry-free educational careers of cases 5 and 6. The latter two cases are clearly in the minority. Some four-fifths of the students experienced serious financial difficulties, facing the perennial problem of paying their secondary school fees. The combination of fierce scholastic competition and economic insecurity has made the educational experience of most students an extremely difficult one, temporarily relieved in some cases by scholarships, but seldom unproblematic. Academic ability is obviously a necessary but not a sufficient condition for success, for many able children never get a chance to get into a secondary school, much less a university.

The life histories represent, broadly speaking, three kinds of background. The privileged few come from monogamous, Christian families with parents who are at least secondary-school educated and hold regular salaried jobs in the "modern" sector. These students typically enter straight into a Secondary Grammar School which provides the surest and fastest preparation for the requisite university entrance standards. Their fees are paid by their parents, sometimes with the assistance of an older established brother or uncle, and they do not have to interrupt their studies to earn money. Their parents' social and political connections, and their academic know-how often make these students nearly as likely to receive scholarships as indigent students who need them. For example, in our Ilosho sample, 33.8 per cent of children of professionals received government stipends compared to 37.7 per cent of farmers' children. Such students also benefit enormously, of course, from their parents' intimate understanding of the school system and its demands, from supplementary tuition in the home, and from an acutely education-conscious environment full of books and other intellectual stimuli.

Some two-thirds of the students fall into one of the other two main types of social background. The most disadvantaged are children of small farmers with little cash income who have to struggle not only against overwhelming economic odds, but often against family values which do not favor Western-style education, at least not beyond primary school. For such children, the odds against success are literally less than one in a thousand, even if they are gifted.

The children of traditionally-oriented and lowly-educated but prominent and moderately well-off families make up the third category, represented by cases two and three. Such students are in a somewhat better position than those from ordinary farming backgrounds, but not very much better. The family incentive for schooling and understanding of the educational system are frequently not much greater than in the poorer families, and the greater economic resources of traditional chiefs, traders and the like are typically dissipated between a much larger number of children, as such "big men" are usually large-scale polygynists, compared to the small-scale polygyny (2 or at most 3 wives) or enforced monogamy of the ordinary farmer.

In both types of traditional families, then, children often have to fend for themselves and draw support from wider circles of relatives to pay their way through secondary schooling. Instead of taking the easy road of the Grammar School, they go to Secondary Modern Schools and Teachers' Training Colleges, which are cheaper and which offer certificates after two or three years of training (instead of the five or six year program of the Grammar Schools). The typical pattern, for the few who succeed, is a desperate scraping together of fees from year to year in order to make it to the next certificate, and two or three periods of several years' employment as a clerk, or most often, as a primary school teacher in order to raise the funds for the next step up the long educational ladder. The vast majority, of course, never make it, and the struggle is all the harder as accumulated debts have to be repaid, directly or indirectly. This means, for example, that if your father's brother paid part of your fees in Secondary Modern School, he will expect you to reciprocate when you start earning £200 a year as a teacher, and to help with your nephew's school expenses. Thus, it will take you twice as long to save enough for your next move up. Meanwhile, while teaching, you also try to pass examinations externally through correspondence schools, but these are also expensive and the chances of success are much smaller than in a regular Grammar School. These experiences, by the way, are one of the main reasons why most Nigerian university graduates regard secondary school teaching as the least desirable of jobs which a university degree can command. Most of them have already had three to five years of teaching experience under the most frustrating of conditions.

The life histories also clearly indicate the preference given to educating boys over girls, and, consequently, the fact that the few women who make it to university tend to come from high status families which alone can afford to educate all their children. At all levels except the top-most, great educational disparities between siblings are the rule rather than the exception. This is true not only between brothers and sisters, but also among brothers. Sometimes, the influence of the mother who pushes for the education of her own children makes for great differences between half-siblings. Nearly all students except a few who are second or third generation educated, have close relatives who are illiterate or barely literate, others who have completed primary school only, and perhaps one or two fortunate ones like themselves who have gone beyond that level.

Birth order seems also to be a factor in educational success. Both the oldest and the youngest boys seem to have a better chance than those in between. The oldest boy is often supported by a father or paternal uncle, while the youngest tends to get help from senior brothers.

The life histories also reveal a wide variety of motivating factors for education. In the "elite," higher education is taken for granted, and needs no other motivation than that it is the obvious thing to do. Desire for self-improvement and individual ambition are often consuming forces, and so are the desire to outshine age mates and to gain their respect and admiration. Envy or admiration of an older child or of a more successful relative is also mentioned by several students. A man reports how, as a small boy, he was impressed by the school uniform of a friend. A woman speaks of how, as a girl, she witnessed an elaborate Christian wedding and was told by her mother that, if she wanted such a wedding herself, she must go to school. Sibling rivalry, and especially half-sibling rivalry is also a motivating factor in some cases, and one often activated by competing wives of the same husband, each trying to push her own progeny. Some parents see in education of their children a long-range investment in old-age security. One student mentions his father's nationalist aspirations as a driving force for the education of his children, and another relates his illiterate father's annoyance at having to pay strangers to have letters written and read for him, and his determination that his sons should get educated to save him that expense and humiliating dependency. Others mention the desire to live in towns and to leave dull village life.

Whatever the initial motivations for education, most students are at university because a degree is their passport to economic security and professional success. Education is practically the only way to escape life-long poverty, or to stay at the top as the case might be. The odds of success are slim; the struggle is fearful; the stakes are enormous. Education is simply a grim business. Not unexpectedly, most students, when they reach university, are relatively old, mature, highly motivated, desperately earnest, and often cynical and embittered as well.

Financial Support

Once the student has been accepted into U.I. and matriculated his worries are far from over, but at least he is within sight of the summit which he now has a better than even chance of reaching three or four years later when he receives his B.A. or B.S. Financially, however his predicament is more serious than ever because his education is more expensive than at any stage of his past experience. The cost of tuition, room and board, books and incidentals adds up to some £200 to £300 a year, depending on faculties, i.e. about 7 to 10 times the Nigerian per capita income. A three-year degree course will cost some £600 to £900, a sum which would take a student some 8 to 10 years to save on a teacher's or clerk's salary, assuming that he had no family obligations. Some students are, of course, on various private and government scholarships, but there has been a decline in the number of these scholarships as the supply of university graduates in various fields came closer to meeting the demand. Between 1948 and 1966, 38.6 per cent of all students were supported by government bursaries or loans, 25.2 per cent by private institutions (such as foundations, churches and business firms), and 36.2 per cent by friends and relatives.[8] But, the percentage of government support declined from 45.0 per cent in 1948–52 to 17.0 per cent in 1963–66, while support by relatives and friends increased from 19.8 per cent to 70.7 per cent. The Civil War saw a slight increase in government scholarships to meet the special duress of students from war-affected areas, i.e. the East. Nevertheless in 1968, 64.6 per cent of all students were un-sponsored by either government or private sources, and the Vice-Chancellor listed 15.1 per cent as "genuine indigent students." This was probably a conservative estimate.[9]

The great majority of students thus have to rely on their own resources, and on those of their families to get through university. Needless to say, very few come to U.I. with sufficient funds to carry them through their degree program. Typically, students barely manage to meet their fees and room and board from term to term, and a large percentage are in arrears, with the constant threat of having their studies interrupted by indigence. Their predicament is aggravated by the extreme scarcity of summer jobs or part-time jobs during the year. Unike an American or European student who can find a wide variety of casual jobs paying substantial wages, Nigerian students must either interrupt their studies for a year or more at a time to work as a teacher or clerk, or waste time in menial odd jobs with extremely low rates of pay which many of them would not want to take for reasons of social prestige alone. Financing one's studies thus often means discontinuing them for long periods.

Scholarships are supplemented by a government loan program, and, during the Civil War, students from the war-affected areas who were often cut off from their families and suffered severe hardships qualified for government assistance. However, year after year, hundreds of students fail to pay their fees on schedule, are turned out of the halls of residence, and are threatened with being debarred from taking their examinations. Usually, the state or federal government, to avoid student unrest, comes through at the last moment with emergency loans, but perpetual financial worry is a very unsettling influence on many students. Each year, hundreds of indigent students must fend as best they can by rooming with relatives or friends in town, eating cheap, ill-balanced meals in canteens outside the main gate of the University, or illicitly scrounging and swapping meal tickets with other students, and slipping back into the halls with the tolerant complicity of friends and porters.

Such conditions are not conducive to intellectual effort. Not only do indigent students living off campus often suffer from malnutrition (especially protein and vitamin deficiencies), but their lodgings are so crowded and noisy as to make studying nearly impossible. There is practically no suitable housing for students in Ilosho where typically five or more persons share a small 10 x 12 feet room without electricity or running water facilities. Thus, except for a few students who have relatives living in Ilosho in more adequate housing, there is no practical alternative to living in university halls. Although the room and board fees of £90 to £120 per academic year (depending on faculty) barely cover the recurrent expenditures of the University, they make up half of the students' expenses and are considerably higher than what it costs to subsist on the indigenous economy as a member of an extended family.

At present, the financial situation at University maximizes the worst of both worlds. On the one hand, the tuition fees (£70 to £130 depending on faculty, Medicine being the most expensive) cover only 11.8 per cent of the total cost of university education. The operating expenses of Nigerian universities average approximately £1100 per student per year, not counting board and lodging. In some faculties, especially Medicine and Science, costs are much higher yet. In effect, this means that, subtracting the contribution of the foundations, some two-thirds of the cost of university education, even for the fee-paying students, are borne by a desperately poor citizenry. Taxpayers thus heavily subsidize the schooling of the future elite who after graduation will earn life-long incomes of 25 to 100 times the per capita average of their country.

Yet, despite this highly elitist and regressive subsidization of higher education, the students do not materially begin to benefit from the system until after graduation. Low though the fees are in relation to total costs, they are staggering in relation to the financial resources of the vast majority of students and their families for whom a stay at university means a continuous chain of material crises.

The solution to this dilemma is disarmingly simple, at least in theory, if one could discount the political problems of implementing it. Students could be made to bear the full cost of their university education to the extent of £1200 or so a year, in form of a government low-interest or no-interest loan which would be repaid after graduation by, say, a 10 per cent automatic salary deduction. Thus, the cost of university education would be transferred to its beneficiaries, and the student would be free of financial worries during his studies, and forced to live a little more parsimoniously but without serious deprivations after graduation. The main argument against such a blanket loan scheme is that previous and much more limited loan schemes have been characterized by extremely high rates of defaulting on repayment. Of a total of 427 students who had received state loans and graduated between 1964 and 1967, 85.7 per cent were in arrears in their repayments, and 40 per cent had not made any repayments at all. Previous loan schemes failed largely because of the lack of an effective machinery for collecting debts, and thus their failure is not a convincing argument against the principle of a loan scheme. In a country where the majority of graduates enter the service of the federal, state or local government, a state-enforced "pay-as-you-go" scheme presents in principle no difficulty, other than the political one that the ruling stratum is reluctant to tax itself.

For example, as of 1968, the income tax rate for persons earning £1000 a year (roughly 40 times the per capita income of Nigeria) was 7.8 per cent. Incomes of £2000 were taxed at 13.9 per cent, and £3000 (a sum earned by perhaps 0.01% of the population) at 19.6 per cent. These figures were *after* a tax increase of about 10 per cent that year.

In the paradoxical situation which now exists, most students have to struggle against overwhelming financial odds, and some are desperately indigent, but, at the same time, the even poorer citizenry gives them a nearly free ride and subsidizes their future affluence. Students are frustrated and embittered, and feel that their future salaries are a just compensation for their present and past deprivations, yet their education is in fact largely a gift from their even much more hard-pressed fellow citizens.

Admissions and Examinations

Students enter the university at two different levels. Depending on their secondary school qualifications, they are admitted either straight into the regular three-year degree curriculum or, in some faculties, they do a pre-liminary year, which lengthens their stay at U.I. to four years. In addition to the basic B.A. and B.S. programs, all faculties offer post-graduate degrees and the Faculty of Medicine gives as it basic qualifying degree a Bachelor of Medicine and Bachelor of Surgery (M.B., B.S.), following the British practice. The Faculty of Medicine also grants B.S. degrees in Nursing,

Laboratory Technology, and Radiography. The Faculties of Arts, Science, Agriculture, Social Sciences, and Education also grant a variety of professional diplomas and certificates usually requiring one year of study, either at the pre- or postgraduate levels.

Applications for admission are processed through an office of the Registry, and passed on to the relevant faculty to which the student hopes to be admitted. The Faculty Board, through a complex point system based on the marks received by the student in his various secondary school-leaving examinations, decides to admit or not to admit the candidates who are then notified.

Requirements for degrees vary from faculty to faculty, each Faculty Board setting its curricula, examinations, and required courses, subject to Senate approval, and the use of external examiners in the final examinations. The typical pattern for the B.A. or B.S. degree is for a first-year student to take three subjects (usually corresponding to the academic departments, such as History, Economics or Chemistry), at least two of which are in the faculty which admitted him. At the end of his first year, the student takes his "Part I Examination" in those subjects. If he passes them, he becomes a candidate for the Part II Examination; if he fails, he may be allowed to repeat his Part I once. Starting in his second year, the curriculum is even more specialized than in the first year. He then prepares himself for four to six specialized "papers" within a single discipline, plus one or two subsidiary subjects in other departments. In some faculties, all of the Part II examination "papers" are taken at one sitting at the end of the third year, with no examinations at the end of the second year, or indeed at any time between the end of the first and third years. In other faculties, the half-dozen or more papers are divided between examinations at the end of both the second and third year.

Examinations are thus few and far between, being held at most once a year, and the student is evaluated overwhelmingly on the basis of his performance in his various Part II papers. Depending on his results, he will be granted "first-class honours," "second-class honours, upper division," "second-class honours, lower division," "third-class honours," or a "pass" degree. First-class degrees are granted very seldom, to perhaps one or two per cent of the students. Second-class, upper division degrees, or "upper seconds" for short, are granted to 15 to 25 per cent of the students depending on the faculties, and are considered the minimum performance acceptable for the pursuit of advanced degrees, or indeed for the topmost positions in the Senior Civil Service. "Lower seconds" are the modal category in most faculties and account for half- to two-thirds of the candidates. Third-class honours and pass degrees are regarded as mediocre. The failure rate is fairly high in the Part I examinations, some faculties and departments failing up to 40 to 50 per cent of the students on their first try, but most of those pass on the second round, and in the Part II examinations, the failure rate seldom exceeds 10 per cent.

Undergraduate examinations are written and follow a highly formal and ritualized pattern. The questions are set months in advance, mailed for comments to the external examiner which each department invites from another university (very frequently from Britain, but increasingly from other Nigerian universities as well), and printed in Lagos under conditions of great secrecy to avoid "leaks." On the day of the examination, the papers are delivered in sealed packets by the Examinations Office of the Registry, administered under a rigid time schedule, "invigilated" by specially appointed lecturers to prevent cheating, collected, checked against a list of candidates, returned against receipt to the Examinations Office, checked again, returned to the internal examiners (i.e. the teaching staff at U.I.), read by at least two internal examiners, and passed on to the external examiner who is usually physically present on campus at this time. After both internal and external examiners have read the scripts, they resolve any disagreements they might have, the external examiner having the final word, and pass their recommendations to the Faculty Board. The latter does not question the judgment of the departments, but it collates the individual results of the various papers, and, after considerable discussion, decides on the overall class of the degree to be awarded to each student. The procedure is repeated in the Senate, but in a much more perfunctory way.

As can be seen, the examination procedure builds in elaborate safeguards against favoritism. Each student is assigned a number by the Registry, and identifies his papers only by that number, so that the entire procedure is anonymous, though in small departments, teachers can sometimes make informed guesses as to the identity of the candidate. The examination system is extremely cumbersome and time-consuming, but the precautions "pay off" in the sense that the integrity of the procedure has never been seriously challenged, and that examinations are one of the few aspects of University life which have remained, by and large, outside the political arena. The only aspect of it which is open to possible favoritism is the pleading of "special cases" in Faculty Board or the Senate, e.g. when a student petitions to retake an examination, or to have some regulation relaxed for his benefit, but the Senate as a body is reluctant to create precedents, and keeps "exceptions" under close check.

Especially in faculties which do not hold examinations in the second year, the middle of a student's university career is a period of relative relaxation, but in the third year, the tension mounts throughout the year, the noise level in the halls abates, seating in the reading room of the library becomes fully occupied, and the entire life of the student revolves around passing that set of examinations which will decide his entire future. If he fails, he will have to return to a mediocre clerical or teaching job at about one-third the salary he could command as a graduate. If he passes but without luster, his entry into the upper-income stratum is assured, but he will have to be content with a mastership in a provincial grammar school, an unexciting post in the Senior Civil Service, or a junior executive position in commerce. If he gets an "upper second" or by some miracle a "first," he may get an overseas scholarship for postgraduate work and return three or four years later to an academic sinecure at one of the Nigerian universities, or to a high policy-making post in government. In any case, his success is virtually assured. So important do the final examinations loom in students' lives that they even take precedence, temporarily, over family obligations and filial piety. One student, for example, was not told about the death of his father which had occurred some two weeks before the examinations so as not to upset him.

Instruction

The main features of the U.I. curriculum which were patterned almost entirely on the British system, are its highly specialized nature, and the "tutorial" style of instruction. The "3–1–1" system described above (i.e. that in which a student reads three subjects in his first year, and then specializes almost exclusively in one of the three for his remaining two years) makes for a high degree of competence and depth in one discipline, the assumption being that scope was achieved in the last years of secondary school. The latter assumption is frequently incorrect, and the system essentially trains specialists who can be quite ignorant of vast fields of knowledge, but then this is certainly not unique to Nigeria.

The "tutorial system" is another British, and indeed Oxbridge legacy, and one which pressures of time and numbers of students undermine a little more each year. In its original form, each teacher would take a small number of students, ideally no more than a dozen, and give them highly individualized instruction taking the form of weekly or fortnightly meetings in groups of two or three wherein written papers on specific topics would be assigned, verbally presented by the students, and discussed and criticized in informal exchange. While a student would also take some lecture courses, especially introductory ones in his first year, most of his work in his second and third year would take the form of these supervised discussions and individual library work based on an intimate student-teacher relationship.

A number of factors have little by little transformed this Oxbridge model into something much closer to an American-style system of lecture courses broken into discussion groups of up to twenty students each. The most obvious factor was that the tutorial system while very rewarding with small numbers of highly gifted students, is very time-consuming for the teacher, requires from him a dedication to teaching which receives scant recognition in the academic world, and is very expensive as it requires low student-teacher ratios. Ilosho, with a ratio of some 6 to 1, still spends a lavish amount of scholarly resources on its students compared to large universities in Europe or America, but that overall ratio is misleading because some faculties, especially those of Arts and Social Sciences, are in a much less favorable situation, while Medicine with its clinical mode of instruction is highly privileged in this, as indeed in many other respects.

Other pressures against the tutorial system have come from American-trained teachers who as a rule do not like it, and from the incentive for the staff to devote their energies to research and publication rather than teaching. Printed output much more than classroom dedication has been the key to promotions, and, in circular fashion, to opportunities to get away from teaching, and thus to do even more research and publication. The introduction of a "course system" proposal discussed in faculty boards and the Senate for several years and already implemented in some faculties marks the recognition that the University has gradually moved away from the Oxbridge tradition, and more toward an American or indeed a redbrick British model.

Academic life puts students in a double prestige hierarchy *vis à vis* one another. The first is, of course, based on the year at university. It is not surprising that academic seniority should have been seized as a hierarchical principle since British tradition was in this case reinforced by the strong Nigerian principle of stressing seniority in every aspect of social life. Interestingly, through the vagaries of past experiences, chronological age frequently does not correspond to seniority at University, a fact of which students are very aware. Most students are cognizant of their educational advancement in comparison with age mates and seniors, especially those who come from the same home town, and, while the younger but more advanced student takes pride in that fact, the reverse situation causes embarrassment. In the academic context, scholarly standing generally takes precedence over birth order, but students who know each other intimately, e.g. through prior schooling at home, and whose relative seniority status has been made ambiguous through the disparity between chronology of birth and of university entry, may find the situation embarrassing enough to make them avoid each other.

The other hierarchical factor within the University is the relative prestige of the faculties. The three "foundation faculties" of Arts, Science and Medicine are always listed first in the U.I. catalogue and documents, and enjoy higher status. By comparison, the faculties of Agriculture, Social Sciences and Education, in that descending order, are in a much inferior position, a fact reflected in the more lowly class origins of their students. Furthermore, as a result of a deliberate government policy of encouraging the "hard sciences," the faculties of Social Sciences and Education have received proportionately about half as many scholarships as those of Medicine, Science and Agriculture, with the result that the mass of indigent students are found in Education and Social Sciences.

Residential Halls

The material life of students revolves around the halls of residence. These were originally conceived as autonomous entities, each with their Master and tutors, their dining rituals, their servant staff and so on. Rooms were planned for single occupancy, and the common room and other facilities were lavish by Nigerian standards, and comfortable by any standards. Here again is an instance of a colonial power transplanting a set of institutions into a cultural context where it was totally alien, and expecting it to work in Africa when it had already proven archaic in Britain. The halls were to be breeding grounds for young gentlemen, where students would acquire wisdom and social graces, and learn their place in society by being relieved of all demeaning manual labor and being waited upon by a small army of servants.[10] The success with which these attitudes of snobbery have been implanted can be measured by the fact that when students leave campus or return from vacation, the vast majority do not carry their own luggage to or from the taxi stand in front of Congregation Hall to their respective rooms. On the day prior to the resumption of classes, the taxi stand is surrounded by twenty or thirty boys aged 10 to 14 who hussle with one another to earn sixpence by carrying the students' suitcases to and from the halls. When a cafeteria self-service system was introduced in one of the dining halls a few years ago, some students stoned a warden's car in protest, and, in 1969, students at a neighboring university rioted and attacked members of the teaching staff in protest against being asked to take their dirty dishes back from the dining room tables to the kitchen.

In 1968, U.I. students in one of the halls staged a vociferous demonstration against "poor conditions" in their hall: they wanted chairs instead of benches in the dining hall, more easy chairs, newspapers, periodicals and games equipment in the Junior Common Room, the television set repaired, better food, and better service from the kitchen and cleaning staff. Infuriated students threw out their wooden benches, refused to eat dinner, packed their belongings, and moved out of the hall; they then marched to the houses of the Deputy Vice-Chancellor and of the Master at 11:30 p.m., and presented petitions stating their grievances. In the end, chairs were purchased and other grievances were met, but students were forced to apologize to the Deputy Vice-Chancellor for disturbing his sleep.

These demonstrations are indicative of the view which students have of their position in society. In the words of one of the Masters, a Nigerian: "Even though students get butter, jam and all kinds of foods they never tasted before in their little villages, they still complain. They think that they belong to a certain level in society. In their families, they are kings. This is not so much the case here in the West, but in the East the educated man is God. This is an Ibo characteristic to follow educated leaders, for example, Ojukwu who brags about his Oxford degree even though he only got a third class pass."

Student grievances, however, are not entirely unjustified, and, in many ways, the halls are badly designed and represent the worst of both worlds. The individual rooms, planned for single occupancy, would have been quite adequate, even though they constituted an expensive solution to student housing. However, as they were just large enough to squeeze in two beds side by side, and as the need for housing always outpaced the construction program, most rooms were converted in short order for double occupancy. This not only resulted in overcrowding in the rooms and in all the other dining, bathroom and recreational facilities which had been planned for half their present population, but it also rendered the rooms virtually unusable for study purposes. In a tropical climate where all doors and windows are kept wide open most of the time, the noise level in the overcrowded halls makes intellectual concentration almost impossible. Added to this are the chronic breakdowns and shortages in the water and electricity supplies with their malodorous consequences in the sanitary facilities.

Virtually the only indoor amenities with sufficient quiet for studying are the reading rooms of the library, and, in the evening, the empty class-rooms. During the brief dry season, students can work outdoors under the shade of trees, but the wet climate frequently does not make that possible. In short, the halls are both needlessly expensive in design and badly suited to their purposes. Much cheaper and more suitable accommodations could have been built along communal dormitory lines, but with ample study rooms. As they stand, the halls have an opulent outward shell, and inside appearance of a noisy, overcrowded semi-slum. They are genuine white elephants, as different from the cloistered gothic quietude of the Oxford and Cambridge colleges they were supposed to emulate as Victoria Station is from Westminster Abbey.

Gradually, the British-style ceremonial of "high-table" dinners, the saying of "grace" in Latin at meals, and the wearing of academic gowns fell into disuse as it was not only culturally exotic, but socially irksome and sartorially stifling. Practices vary from hall to hall depending on who is Master, but formal dinners seldom take place more than once every other week or even once a term, and the Master, Wardens and other teaching staff nominally attached to the halls very seldom eat in them, or even visit the halls, except for the big annual dinner party described in Chapter III. Little by little, the halls came to resemble more American-style dormitories than Oxbridge residential colleges.

The earlier pattern of students being served on at tables by stewards has been replaced by a cafeteria-style self-service whereby students go through a food line with their metal trays (which are often used as noisemaking devices as well, both in merry-making and in protest demonstrations). Students still get room service, however. The menu has become increasingly Nigerianized, with breakfast being largely Western-style, and the other two meals being a kind of least common denominator of Nigerian cooking based on the main locally-grown staples such as yams, plantain bananas, beans, rice and tropical fruits.

Academically, the halls have no autonomy since all courses are given within the departmental and faculty structure of the University, and are taken by students irrespective of their hall of residence, except that the Clinical Students' Hostel in the Hospital compound caters to the Medical students.

The halls do serve several extra-curricular functions, however. First, they organize a number of formal "social" activities such as "open houses," dances, and dinner parties, as we saw earlier. Second, the halls constitute the main basis of intra-mural sports competition. In particular, each hall has its soccer team, and spirited matches take place on weekends between the hall teams. Third, as a result of communal living and the spirit of competition between the halls, patterns of friendship develop along hall lines, and certain aspects of student culture are linked with the halls. Various nicknames are given to the halls. Sometimes the halls are referred to by numbers indicating their order of foundation; thus, "Hall One" is the oldest and so on. The women's hall is nicknamed "Hall Zero," and also, since the Civil War, "the war front." This is in reference to the fact that, on weekends, a number of army vehicles are parked near the porter's lodge as army officers on furlough come to date women students, much to the displeasure of the male students.

A basic dichotomy exists between the older halls which are smaller and located nearer the heart of the campus, and the two larger and newer halls with their more peripheral location. The newer halls are nicknamed "Baluba" and "Katanga," in reference to the abortive secession movement in that Congo province and to one of the major ethnic groups therein. The residents of another hall named after a prominent Nigerian Muslim are jocularly referred to as "the Mallams," this being the traditional Muslim title for a teacher and a man of learning.

Finally, and perhaps most importantly, the halls are the main basis of organization and representation in student politics. Each hall annually elects both its slate of hall officials, and its representatives to the University-wide Student Representative Council. As representation on the latter body is proportional, the newer and the larger halls pull more weight than the others, and as voting preferences for the Student Union executive (President, Vice-President, Secretary, Treasurer, Public Relations Officer, Assistant Secretary, Sports Secretary and House Secretary) follow in part hall affiliation, candidates from the larger halls tend to have a better chance of being elected. Student protests and demonstrations, being so often linked with specific grievances about food, accommodations, the Domestic Warden, and the like, are also frequently organized along hall lines. We already mentioned a 1968 demonstration in a men's hall. In 1969, the female students staged a protest in the dining room of their hall over the behavior of their Domestic Warden, the issuance of meal tickets, and the 11:00 p.m. curfew which they felt was discriminatory since it was not enforced for male students.

As a matter of official University policy, each hall represents an ethnic cross-section of the University at large, and students do not have a choice of hall, though they may request a change of room assignment within halls. Inside the halls, informal groups often form along ethnic lines, e.g. in seating arrangements at dining room tables, but hall affiliation completely cuts across ethnic membership. To the extent that competition in sports and student politics is structured along hall lines, hall organization is the main counteracting factor to ethnic polarization in student life.

STUDENT POLITICS

The Student Representative Council (S.R.C.) is a deliberative body which can take stands and make recommendations to the University authorities, but which is devoid of ultimate power except with the narrow confines of running Student Union affairs, organizing sport events, and the like. Similarly the Student Union executive, while meeting in consultation with the Vice-Chancellor on a fairly regular basis, does not have any share of power in the governance of the University. Nevertheless, student politics cannot be dismissed as unimportant, because they relate to the broader Nigerian political scene.

Before the military coups, student politics tied in with the larger power game of the ethnically based parties in the Federation. Student candidates were often linked with and supported by political parties; student office-running served as an initiation to adult politics, and successful candidates frequently saw their careers advanced despite the fact that they sometimes had to neglect their studies and had academically undistinguished records. Since the establishment of the military regime, political parties have been officially abolished, but student politics are still a way of capturing the limelight, and securing better jobs after graduation.

The most prominent aspect of student politics at U.I., as well as at other Nigerian universities, is their financial dishonesty, both real and alleged. Students are organized into a National Union of Nigerian Students (N.U.N.S.) which has its secretariat at one of the universities. In addition, each university elects its own S.R.C. and slate of Student Union officials. Capture of offices on the national executive by individuals, and of the site of the secretariat by one of the universities are the main stakes of the game. Since Ilosho is the largest and oldest university, however, its own executive also plays an important role beyond the confines of the U.I. campus, whether the N.U.N.S. Secretariat is located at U.I. or not.

The details of every N.U.N.S. scandal differ, and so do the complex factional alignments based on ethnic, regional and university affiliation to mention only some of the main factors of cleavage. Nevertheless, student politics show certain cyclical regularities. Since elections are annual, the turnover of executives is rapid, making it difficult for any person to learn to do his job competently. Almost every year, usually in the second half of the academic session, a scandal hits the headlines of the main newspapers. Allegations of misappropriation of funds, incompetence, or, most frequently, both are made by student politicians whose faction hopes to gain by discrediting the incumbents. These allegations are eagerly printed in the sensationalist press, which adds fat to the fire by publishing condemnatory editorials on the time being ripe to clean up the cesspool of iniquity at the universities, and on what Nigeria is coming to if even the flower of its youth is corrupt. A new slate of student officials is elected on a platform of incorruptibility: the Secretariat of the national union is removed from the campus where it was located and transferred to another university; and a few months later, the cycle repeats itself. In recent years, the Secretariat of the national union was moved from Ilosho, to Lagos and back to Ilosho, each time after a financial scandal of much the same type.

A few students express indignation at the malpractices, especially if they have taken place at another campus, but the majority tend to take a highly cynical view of the entire process. Many students regard student politics as an apprenticeship in corruption, political office as an opportunity to make some money, and their elected representatives as self-interested rascals out to embezzle student funds. As is usually the case in situations where chronic scandals erupt, some accusations are unfounded and opportunistic, while others are richly deserved.

The two issues involved in most scandals are incompetence and dishonesty. Rapid turnover and inexperience of personnel militate against capable leadership, and the Secretariat is in a state of chronic disorganization, or, perhaps better, non-organization. One of the effects of sheer inefficiency is the failure to keep proper accounting of expenditures, even though student finances are supervised by the University Bursary (itself scarcely a model of efficiency). Inability to account for funds spent, in the prevailing climate of suspicion and cynicism, is almost automatically attributed to dishonesty rather than incompetence, although the balance between these two factors is probably close to equal. As one student put it to explain the reluctance of candidates to stand for the office of treasurer "if you buy a new shirt, people start accusing you of embezzlement."

Financial malpractices do occur, however, and in the last few years, N.U.N.S.-sponsored chartered flights to Europe have provided the organizers with the best opportunities for misappropriation of funds. Several years in succession, it turned out that many more tickets were sold than there were seats on the airplane, and that friends and mistresses of some of the organizers apparently received tickets free of charge. These factors, combined with plain inefficient organization, and an illicit second-hand traffic in tickets among Nigerians in Britain have totally disrupted several flights and left many people swindled and stranded.

Financial scandals often erupt as a consequence of personal rivalries, grudges, and ambitions which can be satisfied by discrediting opponents. Sometimes they originate from within the ruling executive, but more commonly from defeated candidates or personal foes of the elected officials. In the nature of the case, scandals lead to political polarization, and this in turn almost invariably involves an element of ethnicity, along with other factors. At the national level, the main line of cleavage is often by university: the four other universities typically "gang up" and try to discredit the institution where the N.U.N.S. secretariat happens to be located. Thus Ilosho which had been under attack in 1968 took great satisfaction in 1969 in discrediting the university where the N.U.N.S. secretariat had been moved, and where the loud protestations of integrity, austerity and efficiency reverted within months to the usual morass of corruption and incompetence.

Within U.I., political cleavages are usually a combination of ethnicity and hall affiliation, and, as the two factors are deliberately kept unrelated, the effect of each masks that of the other. In brief, some students vote on a "hall ticket" and others on an "ethnic ticket." We shall reserve, however, for Chapter VIII a more detailed account of ethnicity in student politics.

Of strikingly secondary importance in student politics are ideological issues. Occasionally an event with some ideological content takes place on campus. In 1969, there was a student demonstration against what was seen as NATO involvement on the Biafran side of the Civil War, with the hostility directed mostly at France, the Vatican and the United States. During the same year, the Student Union organized a public debate on socialism. Generally speaking, however, the political culture of students, while by no means unsophisticated, revolves around concrete practical issues and the game of factionalism. Cynicism is a substitute for idealism; pragmatism takes priority over political theory. The political game is engaged in for the material and prestige rewards it brings, but this is, of course, not unique to Africa or Nigeria. However, beyond pragmatism and self-interest, the political game is relished *as an end in itself,* not as a means of achieving a more desirable state of affairs. Politics are fun because they are a complex social game involving all kinds of intellectual skills such as deception, manipulation, and prediction of others' behavior. Ideology has little if any bearing on the game.

Extra-Curricular Activities

Aside from politics, student extra-curricular activities follow both an informal and an organized, formal pattern. In 1969, there were 24 active student clubs and voluntary associations on campus, not to mention, of course, the many organizations to which students may belong but which transcend the bounds of the campus. Of the 24 clubs, five were religious in nature (one Muslim, one Catholic and three Protestant); seven were academic or literary (e.g. the Sociological Society, Le Cercle Français); two were philanthropic (Red Cross, and the Students National Reconstruction Council); two were political (The Black Nationalist Movement, the Young Socialist Club); and the remaining eight were recreational or "social" (Gamma Club, Dancing Club, Chess Club). Of the "social" clubs, the Gamma Club has elitist pretensions, while the Pirates specialize in noisy merry-making.

The number and importance of religious associations is but one symptom of the relatively high degree of religiosity of U.I. students compared to their European or American counterparts. As we shall see in Chapter Seven, religion plays a significant role in many aspects of University life.

Athletics are of moderate importance, with soccer as the main spectator sport, and track events in second position. On most weekends, there is some kind of public event on the University sports grounds, and these are attended by students, a few members of the Senior Staff, a good many Obatala Village residents, and some visitors from town. Aside from intramural events between the halls, U.I. also competes with other universities in Nigeria and in West Africa. The international events, though often held far away, generate a good deal of excitement among students, but even soccer does not create the level of interest that football used to do at many American universities, and the status of athletes is not particularly high. Sports are a pastime and are not highly professionalized.

Student publications, mostly of the mimeographed variety, serve two principal functions: slander and politicking. We have already discussed the latter, but far and away the most influential student publications are the scandal and gossip sheets (The Bug, The Searchlight, Bleach, The Scorpion) which make their appearance once or more every term. Their contents range from the impertinent to the obscene, and consist mostly of the propagation of gossip about the behavior, mostly sexual, of transparently disguised individuals whose indiscretions, love affairs, *faux pas,* and other alleged failings are exposed to public ridicule. Next to sexual gossip, these scandal sheets also attack behavior considered as "bush" and inappropriate to a "civilized" community, such as hanging clothes to dry over balcony railings or chewing over tooth-cleaning sticks (the Nigerian toothbrush) and spitting out fragments thereof on toilet room floors. Attempts by the University authorities to put an end to this kind of defamation have failed, and these student publications are greatly feared, especially by the female students, who see in them a weapon of moral blackmail in the war of the sexes.

The main student "social" events are the dance parties held on at least half of the Saturday nights during the academic session. Some dances are organized by the halls and held on the hall premises, the dining and common rooms being converted into dance floors. The biggest dances, however, are held in Congregation Hall. These are generally sponsored by the Student Union or a social club. They charge admission and hire two or more orchestras playing within earshot of one another, usually one inside the hall and the other outside in the courtyard. Women students dress up for the occasion, either in traditional attire or in cocktail-type dresses and wigs, but men students tend to dress more informally. These dances are usually open to the public and attract a good many younger members of the Ilosho upper stratum, such as Senior Civil Servants and secondary school teachers, as well as students and a few university Senior Staff. The latter, however, prefer to attend dances at the Senior Staff Club, or at the Premier Hotel in town.

Downtown bars, dance halls and especially cinemas also play an important role in the leisure time activities of students who patronize these establishments and the prostitutes who frequent some of them, insofar as their limited budgets allow them. The five miles or so between campus and downtown Ilosho are somewhat of an obstacle, but the sixpence taxi service is relatively inexpensive, even by local standards.

Relations between the Sexes

The last topic of importance in the life of students concerns relations between the sexes which are laden with a high degree of ambivalence and conflict. Male students accuse female students of being arrogant, domineering, mercenary, vain, frivolous and too emancipated and disrespectful of their elders and of their menfolk. Female students, on the other hand, are mistrustful of men in general and male students in particular. Fully aware of the dual standard of sexual morality, they accuse men of being cynically exploitative of them, of "talking sweet" to them but being unfaithful at the first opportunity while expecting fidelity from women, of "spoiling girls" (a euphemism for impregnating them) and then abandoning them and ruining their reputations. In short, the generalized norm of mistrust which is so prevalent in many aspects of University (and, more broadly, Nigerian) life applies to relations between the sexes. The rule of thumb for men is "never trust a woman" and for women "never trust a man."

These attitudes are summed up by the President of the Student Union in a welcome address to the new incoming students: "The most *shocking* aspect of students' life on this campus is the Queens' and Adders' relationship, almost strained beyond repairs." [11] A medical student concurs: "There seems to be mutual bigotry between the few Queens on the one hand and the Adders on the other. In another University this could bring the social life to a halt. But not in Ilosho, girls are imported from other institutions to fill the vacuum."

A multiplicity of factors make for this tense situation. First, female students constitute only about one-seventh of the total, and thus the majority of the male students have to seek companions and ultimately spouses who are less educated than themselves. Second, women students, as we have seen, come from more privileged families on the whole than male students, and this class differential in favor of women is at the basis of the male criticism that U.I. women think they are "too good" for the male students. Thirdly, a series of complex changes have altered traditional sex roles without substituting a clear alternative. Polygyny is still widely practiced in Nigeria, and while actual traditional polygyny is extremely rare among university educated men, philandering and free and easy amorous adventures are neither uncommon nor frowned upon by men. Polygyny has, of course, little if anything to do with the extra-marital affairs practiced among the educated elite, except that in both cases men expect fidelity from women without feeling under any obligation to reciprocate.

Among male students there is a widespread acceptance both of traditional polygyny and of "modern" affairs, combined with an expectation of faithfulness from wives. Male students would themselves not marry polygynously because to do so is "bush," but, other than that, they see for the most part nothing wrong with it. In its most sophisticated form, the male defense of polygyny as a social institution seeks ligitimacy in anthropological relativism. Women students, on the other hand, have undergone much more complex changes in attitudes. As a result of a puritanical mission education many have acquired quasi-Victorian ideas of sexuality or at any rate have been told that if they want to be accepted as "ladies" they ought to affect an attitude of sexual reserve and to keep their affairs clandestine. Many Westernized Nigerian women have adopted the missionary view of polygyny as a barbarous and degrading custom, but they know that, even though they will enter a monogamous marriage, their husbands will not be faithful to them. The educated woman rejects the past system, and resents the present one. She almost looks on marriage as a necessary evil to provide her with material security and legitimacy for her children, but otherwise as an institution wherein she will lose her independence and be under the authority of her husband and her husband's kinsmen. And she tends to regard any associations with men before marriage as a game in which she is the sexual prey, and one which is only worth playing if the man is marriageable and in a secure economic position (which very few male students are).

Male students, on the other hand, have ambivalent attitudes toward their female counterparts. On the one hand, they want to marry an educated woman for prestige reasons, and because she will often be able to earn a second income. At the same time, many men fear that educated women will not accept their authority, and will be unwilling to fulfill traditional hospitality obligations to her husband's kinsmen. Ideally, many male students prefer an educated wife, but one less educated than themselves, i.e. a secondary-school educated girl but not a university graduate.

The one relationship which very few Nigerian students manage to establish across sex lines is one where the sexual tie is accompanied by egalitarian companionship and intellectual exchange. The more usual attitude is one of mutual predation: women seek marriage and security; men seek sexual gratification. The women accuse the men of only being interested in them as sex objects; the men accuse the women of only being interested in men who have cars and buy them expensive gifts.

This climate of mutual predation and hostility is further exacerbated by male accusations of snobbery against the "Queens," and by the anger of women students at the malicious and often slanderous scandal sheets put out by male students, often, they claim, the very ones who seek revenge at having had their sexual advances rejected by the girls they slander. Many women students feel that it is safer to avoid male students altogether and to go out with older men from town, a practice which is compatible with the large age differences between husbands and wives which are common in all highly polygynous societies.

Some students date and eventually marry each other, of course, but both sexes tend to take a cynical attitude toward the concept of romantic love as the foundation for marriage. Western education has acquainted them with the concept, but they do not expect it to become part of their own life experience as an antecedent to, much less a necessary condition for, marriage. A frequent adjustment to the war between the sexes on campus is mutual avoidance. Women students seek older and economically secure men, such as teachers, lecturers, senior civil servants, lawyers, and army officers, but, as these are often already married, a number of undergraduate women have affairs which they try to keep clandestine. The male students who see older men from town pick up their "dates" on campus in army vehicles or private cars are resentful, and say that the women are no different from prostitutes.

Most male students seek and find sexual gratification off campus. Some frequent prostitutes, and the Mokola section of Ilosho between University and downtown is reputed for this kind of service to the student population. Some male students have affairs with girls from neighboring secondary schools, but as many of them are in boarding school they are not as free as students would like. At University dances, secondary school girls come by the bus load in search of unattached student escorts; although they are expected to be back by a certain hour, many have sexual relations with students and, despite extensive use of condoms, pregnancies occur not infrequently. Perhaps the most comfortable arrangement for male students is to have as a mistress a relatively uneducated girl from town who may be employed as salesgirl, domestic servant, or petty market trader. These young women have the advantage of being much freer to visit their lovers, of sometimes contributing pocket money for the student's expenses, of being loving and undemanding, and of being of a lowly enough status to be proud of having a student as lover and not to expect him to marry them. Students are, of course, not free to keep women in their rooms overnight, but on weekends there are long visiting hours during the day when the halls are wide open to outsiders. On Saturdays and Sundays, groups of young women from town come to campus to visit their lovers. As most students double-up in their rooms, they arrange with each other to take turns in leaving their roommates undisturbed during the daytime visiting hours. Occasionally, girls stay in the rooms overnight, but when this is discovered and reported by a porter to the Warden or Master, disciplinary action is taken against the student. It is much easier and safer for the students to sleep out than to take in girls overnight in the halls. In any case, the halls are scarcely models of monastic austerity.

University students are thus in a transitional position. Many have suffered great deprivation and overcome staggering obstacles before they entered U.I., and will continue to be beset by financial worries and family obligations during their undergraduate days. Their living conditions on campus, though far above the Nigerian average and conditions in Obatala Village, are much below those of the Senior Staff and indeed far from satisfactory for the pursuit of higher learning. It is thus incorrect to refer to them as spoiled and pampered as the press sometimes does after a student protest demonstration. Yet, the students are a presumptive elite, and begin to assume at University many of the attitudes and characteristics of a privileged stratum. Elitism, which suffuses the entire conception of African universities is a highly contagious disease, and it is hardly surprising that students, who are constantly told by their teachers and their admiring kinsmen, agemates and less fortunate friends that they are the flower of the nation, should begin to behave accordingly, despite past and present hardships.

NOTES

[1] The compilation of the statistical data from the admissions records was done by Catherine Nuttney to whom I am especially indebted here. This chapter also owes a great deal to my three Nigerian assistants, Paul Alabi, Peter Olori and A. K. Sonaike, who not only interviewed a number of their fellow students, but were also valuable informants on local student culture. The conclusions and interpretations presented here are, of course, entirely my own.

[2] It is easy, when speaking of "education" in Africa, to equate that term with formal Western-style schooling in a rigid age-graded system. Even Africans have, with the exception of a few sophisticated intellectuals (among whom Jomo Kenyatta in his *Facing Mount Kenya* was perhaps one of the earliest), accepted this highly Euro-centric view of education. In all cultures, children are socialized in a more or less formalized way, and that certainly constitutes education. Many traditional African societies did have formal "initiation schools" where adolescents, prior to ritual admission into adult status, were exposed to a body of knowledge relevant to their adult roles. This period of instruction sometimes lasted for weeks or even months, and was often accompanied by physical seclusion from the rest of society. Thus, initiation schools did constitute specialized educational agencies, clearly supplementary to socialization within the kinship group. In addition, the Islamized parts of Africa have had Koranic schools (*madrassa*) which taught literacy in the Arabic script, but often failed to reach peasant masses. The only education that "counts" in terms of employment in the "modern" sector, however, is that conveyed by Western schools, in the great majority of cases founded and controlled by various Christian missionary bodies. Unless otherwise indicated, I shall, for the sake of brevity, follow the Nigerian

usage of referring to "Western-style education" simply by the term "education," but this does not mean that I regard people who are non-literate and did not attend a mission school as uneducated, "backward," or, to use the Nigerian idiom, "bush."

3 The link between geography and ethnicity is, in a sense, fortuitous. It just so happens that, as ethnic groups are localized in space, the unequal regional distribution of educational resources necessarily entails vast ethnic disproportions in the percentage of the educated who reach the upper echelons of the modern sector. But, in last analysis, the key causal factor for geographical disparities is religion. In the North, the British colonial administration, in the early years of the 20th century, found Islam as the established religion in a highly hierarchized, urbanized, and politically centralized society. Frederick Lugard applied a policy of indirect rule which consisted essentially in reserving supreme political authority for the British colonial administration and modifying certain aspects of the legal system, but otherwise leaving the established order largely untouched, and administering the vast territory through the Muslim Hausa-Fulani aristocracy. Part of the *modus vivendi* was the recognition of Islam and of Koranic law, and hence the exclusion of Christian missions. In the largely non-Muslim South, on the other hand, Christian missions began to proliferate from the mid-19th century on, and with missions came Western-style schools and literacy in both English and the mother-tongue. The much greater European influence in the South also had its economic consequences in the extension of external trade, cash crops and money circulation. Throughout the colonial period, the gap widened between a European-influenced and oriented South (meaning both the former Western and Eastern Regions) with a dynamic cash economy, a growing Western school system, and a modern communication and transport network, and a relatively static, feudal North where British indirect rule petrified Hausa, Fulani and Kanuri societies in much the condition in which it found them. This is perhaps the most fundamental strain in Nigerian social structure, a strain analogous, for example, to that which would exist if, by some miracle, Israel and Saudi Arabia were to constitute a single state.

4 While U.I. is the most prestigious *Nigerian* university, there is still a prejudice in favor of British universities, especially Oxford, Cambridge and London, among the top Nigerian elite. Many of the children of Nigerian professionals still go abroad for their education, and thus the total proportion of graduates who come from "elite" families is probably higher than the U.I. figures suggest although it almost certainly does not exceed one-fourth. For comparative data on Ghana, the Ivory Coast, and Kenya see Foster (1965), Clignet and Foster (1966), and van den Berghe (1968b).

5 References to names and places have been deleted to make the biographies unidentifiable, but otherwise the quotations are verbatim.

6 In Nigerian schools, including the universities, students who have not paid their fees are normally sent home and not allowed to take their examinations. This traumatic experience is the lot of the great majority of secondary school pupils at one time or another, and the frantic search for money with which to pay school fees is a perennial concern of the pupils and their parents. Often

more distant relatives help, such as older brothers with jobs, father's brothers, and so on. But financial worry and indigence is the lot of most children, especially when they are in secondary boarding schools.

[7] Urban unemployment is especially rampant among young people with too much education to want general laborers' or servants' jobs, and not enough to qualify for clerical work.

[8] For Nigerian students at large, the situation is not very different. Before the Civil War, the National Register of Students listed 44.3 per cent of the students as privately supported, while 35.5 per cent received financial help from government sources (including foreign governments), and the remaining 20.2 per cent were sponsored by missions, business firms and the like.

[9] In some African countries, notably in East Africa, the percentage of university students on government bursaries is much higher. In these countries, the number of university graduates is still very small compared to West Africa.

[10] The halls have approximately one servant for every three to four students. One of the newer, larger and more efficient halls had the following ancillary staff: 1 domestic warden, 1 kitchen supervisor, 1 kitchenmate, 11 porters, 23 cooks, 25 stewards, 15 cleaners, 2 gardeners, 2 stenographers, 24 washermen, and 1 messenger, a total of 106 servants for some 400 students. The older and smaller halls have an even higher ratio of servants to students. Thus, the women's hall with about 200 students has a servant staff of 84.

[11] The nickname of "Queens" for female undergraduates originates in the fact that the women's hall is called Queen Elizabeth Hall. To the potential delight of psychoanalysts, the slang term for male student is "adder." There is a whole student argot of relations between sexes. Going out with a girl is known as "driving." Stealing someone else's girl is to "de-dame" him. Patrons of prostitutes are "Mokolites" after the Mokola quarter of Ilosho famous for that kind of service (at 5 shillings a pass), and so on.

CHAPTER SIX

The Third Estate:
Intermediate and Subordinate Staff

The third estate is made up of the 6,000-odd employees who provide the infrastructure of non-academic services for the Senior Staff and students, and their dependents insofar as they live on campus. Other people who are more peripherally involved with the university—such as merchants who trade on campus but are not University employees nor live on campus—are excluded here. Except for a sprinkling of foreigners from neighboring West African countries, the third estate, like the students, but unlike the Senior Staff, is entirely Nigerian, and overwhelmingly Southern Nigerian. Beyond these broad uniformities, however, the group is highly heterogeneous in terms of ethnicity, religion, education, occupation, income, status, life style, family size, marital status, age, and sex.

No accurate census has ever been taken of the campus, but the total resident population is estimated at 18 to 20,000. Since there are some 600 Senior Staff members who with their families make up some 3,000 persons, and some 3,000 students this leaves some 12 to 14,000 members of the third estate living on the U.I. compound. A good third of that population are the 12 to 15 per cent of the University's Junior Staff of 4,000-odd employees who are provided with quarters on campus and who live mostly in Obatala Village with their families and dependents. The remainder are the 2,000-odd domestic servants of the Senior Staff and their relatives and dependents who occupy the "boys' quarters" (usually two rooms) attached to each Senior Staff house or flat. Over 3,000 University Junior Staff employees and a few hundred domestic servants live off campus in various sections of the city of Ilosho and neighboring villages. Their dependents make up another 15 to 20,000 people, but since they neither live nor work on campus, they have not been included in the third estate. Of the campus population of 18 to 20,000, some are relatively stable, having lived there for five or more years, while there is also a fluid fringe of boarders, visitors, relatives, school-age nephews and the like who may stay for weeks or even months but are not permanent residents. Domestic servants fall somewhere in-between in terms of stability; they are on the whole less stable than the University Junior Staff, but less transient than the "fluid fringe" just referred to.

Intermediate Staff

We have already described in Chapter III the general living conditions in Obatala Village. Since the third estate is, however, so heterogeneous in terms of status and life style, we should turn to a more detailed characterization of the principal sub-categories within that broad group. Among the University employees who are collectively referred to a "Junior Staff" for short, a distinction is made between the Intermediate Staff, i.e., those earning more than £458 per annum, and the Subordinate Staff below that salary level. The Intermediate Staff, who make up 10.2 per cent of the Junior Staff, constitute the white-collar elite of the third estate. They typically have at least some secondary education and have frequently matriculated. They speak fluent standard English, and occupy positions requiring great skill and responsibility, mostly in the Registry, the Bursary, the Maintenance Department, and the Library. Such positions as Executive Officer, Domestic Warden, and Personal Secretary carry salaries of over £600 a year, often involve the supervision of a dozen or more subordinates, and require considerable responsibility. Many of these high-ranking Intermediate Staff employees do in fact run the routine day-to-day business of complex administrative units of the university. Sometimes their competence exceeds that of the Senior Staff person nominally in charge of the unit, and several departments would cease to operate smoothly without their top level of clerical staff. Since these top clerical positions are so few, competition for them is very stiff, and the standard of efficiency is perhaps the highest of any level of administrative personnel including the Senior Staff.

The Intermediate Staff are typically highly capable people whom economic circumstances more than anything else have precluded from gaining a university education. A few of them (37 in U.I. history) are eventually promoted to Senior Staff, but, while the cases of such promotions are frequently cited as evidence of the possibility of upward mobility, the statistical probability is actually extremely low. In 1969, in response to a request by a group of some 20 Intermediate Staff employees to be promoted to Senior Staff, the University rejected the request but created a new "super-scale" of £1032 to £1314 to which seven of the petitioners were promoted. While, in terms of sheer salary, these jobs overlap with the lower categories of Senior Staff, when housing and other fringe benefits are taken into account, the economic gap remains.

In life-style, family composition, values and many other characteristics, the Intermediate Staff closely resemble the Senior Staff, the major difference being that their lower salaries preclude in many cases the ownership of a private motorcar, and that, not being eligible in many cases for University housing, many of them have to rent cramped and relatively expensive quarters off campus. Thus, their overall standard of living is far inferior to that of the Senior Staff, while their tastes and aspirations are very similar. They are mostly monogamists and Christians with a moderate number of children. They are regular readers of newspapers, and are well informed about national and international news; they put a high degree of stress on education for themselves and their children, many of them endeavoring to get their children a university education. Their desire for upward mobility is strong and they exhibit a high degree of what some social psychologists have called "need achievement," i.e., a drive for success and self-improvement accompanied by virtues of thrift, perseverance, and long-range planning. Their "reference group" is the elite above them, and they are on the whole very desirous of being accepted as urbane, educated people, putting great stress on "proper" dress, on the civilities of urban life, and on the grammatically "correct" use of English. Their wives are typically of a level of education similar to their own, and are not uncommonly employed as nurses, schoolteachers and other such semi-professional occupations. Some of the Intermediate Staff are women, but the great majority are men, as indeed in all major categories of University employment, including clerical and catering occupations.

Subordinate Staff

The 89.8 per cent of the Junior Staff in the Subordinate category range from junior clerks, typists and similar white-collar office workers with secondary education who will in many cases rise to the Intermediate bracket in later years, to illiterate gardeners, stewards and casual workers on the daily-paid list. Some four-fifths (80.2 per cent) of the Subordinate Staff earn less than £300 a year, and nearly three-fifths less than £200; thus, very few can even remotely approach the standard of living of the Intermediate Staff; at the same time, however, their income is much above the national average. Their position as an underclass within the University but a privileged minority in the larger society is thus somewhat paradoxical, and the paradox is only resolved by the fact that the University as a whole is such an island of privilege in the country.

It is perhaps in the upper ranks of the Subordinate Staff that dissatisfaction and "relative deprivation" are at their greatest. Those ranks are made up

TABLE 10 / Percentage of U. I. Intermediate and Subordinate Staff in Various Income Categories, 1968–1969*

Salary in £'s	Percentages	Percentages
Less than 120	21.3	
120– 139	14.0	
140– 159	7.4	58.1
160– 179	8.9	
180– 199	6.5	
200– 219	8.5	
220– 239	4.8	
240– 259	3.8	22.1
260– 279	3.5	
280– 299	1.5	
300– 319	1.5	
320– 339	1.0	
340– 359	3.4	7.4
360– 379	1.0	
380– 399	0.5	
400– 419	0.8	
420– 439	0.4	
440– 459	0.8	2.9
460– 479	0.5	
480– 499	0.4	
500– 599	1.6	1.6
600– 699	2.6	2.6
700– 799	1.5	1.5
800– 899	2.1	2.1
900– 999	0.9	0.9
1000–1099	0.4	0.4
1100+	0.2	0.2
Total	99.8**	99.8**

* Including the daily paid workers.
** Percentages do not add up to 100.0 because of rounding errors.

mainly of fairly young clerical employees who, by virtue of their non-manual occupation, regard themselves as superior to the other Subordinate Staff and try to emulate the Intermediate or even Senior Staff in their style of life without the material means to do so. The junior clerks and kindred white-collar employees are made up of young men and women who are fluent in English and have at least some secondary school education, but often lack their "matriculation" or "school certificate" which would qualify them for a better job. Many of them are consumed by a burning ambition to improve their lot, and enroll in correspondence schools to pass these examinations; if they are still young enough, a few may, with luck and perseverance, return to University as students. Many more will eventually rise into the Intermediate Staff and stay there.

The sight of a junior clerk or typist taking his exercise books to the office and devoting every spare moment during work or his lunch recess to his studies is a common one, and the difficulties are many. While some junior clerks are still unmarried, most have some kind of family obligation which makes saving difficult and retards their progress. They must support aged or disabled parents, or pay the school fees of a younger brother. If they are married, they are usually monogamous. These financial obstacles and the continuous spectacle of the University students who are on the threshold of success make the position of the junior clerk a highly frustrating one.

Also in the upper ranks of the Junior Staff, but very different from the junior white-collar workers, are the artisans (mechanics, carpenters, electricians and the like), and the more senior of the ancillary staff (head porters, head cooks, drivers and so on). In contrast to the junior clerical workers, they are much older, less educated, and less westernized in their tastes and values. In almost all cases, they have reached the top of their career, with secure employment, and, by Nigerian standards, an enviable economic position which offers some protection from want, if not by any means comfort. Typically, because of their age, their families are large; being more traditionally oriented than the clerical staff, and relatively well off by general standards, many workers in these ranks have two or three wives and half-a-dozen to a dozen children. This makes for very overcrowded housing conditions, the whole family sharing in most cases a single medium-sized room of 10 feet by 12 feet.

Large families also mean, of course, a reduction of the per capita income; but family resources are frequently supplemented by the earnings of the wife or wives, in most cases as petty retail traders. Thus, despite large numbers of children, a person with a cash income of, say, £30 a month and two enterprising wives who run a market stall and net another £15 or £20, may be able to sustain a relatively adequate level of living, at least in terms of diet and clothing, if not housing.

Educationally, the senior manual workers of the University have, in most cases, primary but not secondary schooling; they are literate in their mother tongue, have some minimum level of English literacy, and can speak both pidgin English and varying degrees of approximation to standard English. Seldom, however, is their English "correct" enough for them to be accepted as "educated" by employees in the clerical ranks. Their life style in terms

TABLE 11 / PERCENTAGE OF U. I. INTERMEDIATE AND SUBORDINATE STAFF BY YEAR OF FIRST APPOINTMENT *

Year	Percentage
Before 1950	1.4
1951	1.0
1952	0.6
1953	0.7
1954	0.9
1955	0.8
1956	1.5
1957	2.7
1958	2.3
1959	1.8
1960	2.7
1961	5.7
1962	5.8
1963	8.0
1964	5.7
1965	5.4
1966	12.9
1967	25.8
1968	13.4
Total	100.0

* Not including the daily paid workers.

of dress, diet, leisure time activities and the like can be characterized as "urban Nigerian" as distinguished from the more westernized style of the clerical group. The same is true of their values in such things as preference for polygyny, for maximum fecundity, and for a more hedonistic, "present-time" orientation to life as contrasted with the "achievement motivation," austere ambitiousness, and "delayed gratification" pattern found in the up-wardly mobile clerical stratum.

For the 58.1 per cent of the Junior Staff with incomes of less than £200 a year, material existence is difficult, especially if family obligations are heavy. Even though their cash income still puts them well above the average peasant and allows them to purchase more manufactured items, the cost of housing, the crowded and unsanitary conditions of urban living, and the higher price of food cancel much of the cash income differential, and often do not leave enough for a balanced diet. All the same, as urbanites, they have access to a number of amenities and services, especially hospitals and schools, which they value highly and which are not nearly as available to the rural population.

Among the Junior Staff, the most precariously placed are the over 1,000 daily-paid workers who have no job security, and the vast majority of whom earn less than £120 a year. Excluded from the U.I. pension plan and from other fringe benefits, these people are unskilled, casual workers paid on an hourly basis, and hired and fired by the University to fulfill the need for temporary work. Many of these, for example, are hired as grasscutters by the Maintenance Department. Those workers vary widely in age, ethnicity, and background, but for the most part they lack even the basic primary education and minimum literacy which the University normally requires of its regular staff.

The 700-odd Subordinate Staff members who cater to the students in the halls of residence belong for the most part to the regular staff, and, hence, are financially more secure than the daily paid casual workers. Nonetheless, their status is scarcely higher, the two groups together constituting the bottom half of the prestige hierarchy among the Junior Staff. The caterers, who are organized in a militant sub-group of their own within the U.I. Workers Union, suffer from the stigma attached to domestic service, and constitute a quasi-caste of their own. In theory, they are supposed to be literate and to have gone at least to primary school; but, in fact, perhaps one-fourth to one-third of them know little or no standard English (though they might speak Pidgin) and are functional illiterates even in their mother tongue. More than their relatively low degree of formal education, caterers are looked down upon by other University workers because they are regarded as servants, and servants of relatively low-status persons at that. Among the Yoruba this prejudice against domestic service is so strong that few of them are employed in the halls. The catering staff thus comes predominantly from the Mid-Western and former Eastern Region, with many Ibo, Ibibio, Ijaw, and Bini. The Ibo, in particular, have the reputation of being willing to start in the lowly position of servant in order to save money and improve themselves. The Yoruba regard this alleged Ibo trait as an explanatory factor in their success and mobility, but also as evidence of lack of pride.[1] The most deprecated University jobs are those connected with the Zoo, as those people are held to be servants of animals, the most despicable condition for a man. The caterers, in an attempt to enhance their status, stress that they are University employees and try to de-emphasize the servile aspects of their jobs. From the relative security of their University position they look down on the 2000-odd private servants employed by the Senior Staff.

Domestic Servants

The private servants have the lowest status on campus. They do not belong to the Junior Staff since they are not employed by the University. Consequently, they lack security of tenure, pension benefits and minimum wage protection that the regular University employees enjoy. Materially, their position is comparable to that of the daily paid University workers. They can and often do lose their jobs when they incur the displeasure of their "master" or "mistress,"[2] or when their employers leave Nigeria, as expatriates frequently do. As is not uncommon among low-status groups, domestic servants are themselves organized in an elaborate hierarchy with many fine distinctions based on their position in the household where they serve, and the status and nationality of their employers.

Within a given household, the cook has the highest status and usually has authority over the other servants, who typically include a gardener and a "small boy," sometimes also called "steward" when his age makes the other designation appear more than averagely inappropriate. The steward is usually an adolescent or a young man who does the house cleaning, laundering and some kitchen chores, and who is in effect almost as much a servant of the cook as of his employers. The gardener is usually not under the direct authority of the cook; even though his status is lower, there is a clear division of labor and jurisdiction between the two. When the household employs a driver, he usually claims a status superior to that of the other household servants, a claim which he can vindicate because of his skills and because his tasks are least onerous. The bulk of the work is done by the "small boy" who gets the least pay.

The other main factors affecting the status of servants are the nationality and position of their employers. Servants of Americans constitute an aristocracy, followed in descending order by servants of Europeans, of other expatriates (mostly Asians), and of Nigerians (unless they occupy an exalted position such as Vice-Chancellor). What on first glance looks like a peculiarly twisted form of racialism among servants does in fact correspond to important differences in work conditions. The hierarchy follows rather closely the cash wages. Servants of Americans earn roughly from £10 to £15 a month; of Europeans from £8 to £12; and of Nigerians £5 to £7 on the average. In Nigerian families, servants are normally fed, since they eat much the same staple foods as their masters, and this adds some £3 to their real wages, but they are often expected to work harder and longer than in expatriate families. The typical pattern in Nigerian Senior Staff families is for the housewife to cook, often assisted by one or more younger relatives who board with the family. A single paid servant, unrelated to the family, is often expected to do all or most of the heavy work in the household and garden.

Servants of expatriates, though not normally fed, not only get higher wages and usually share the workload with more fellow servants, but they frequently also receive a variety of informal fringe benefits such as discarded clothes and empty bottles which are resold to itinerant traders, and, for cooks, "chiseling" on the price of food if they are sent to do the buying themselves. Nigerians, who know the prices better, are not as readily "taken," and the pickings for their servants are generally much less. The higher wages of servants of expatriates also reflect the fact that they are expected to be literate, to speak and understand standard English (as hardly any expatriates in Ilosho make an effort to learn Yoruba or any other Nigerian language),[3] and to cater to culinary and other tastes which, being alien to Nigerian culture, require a greater amount of learning and experience for Nigerian servants.

The various groups of servants employed by these respective nationalities each constitute something close to an occupational sub-caste. When expatriates are about to leave, they either pass their servant staff directly on to their replacement as in the case of Americans on Ford or Rockefeller appointments, or they try to place them by word of mouth or through the Senior Staff Club bulletin board. The servants themselves are organized in efficient networks of friends and relatives placing each other in expatriate households and providing replacements for each other when they go on leave. Expatriates of the same social clique (which in most cases are mono-ethnic or close to it) also "borrow" each others' servants for parties, another fact which consolidates those informal networks. Thus it is not uncommon to find that a certain group of Americans, for example, will all have Ibo servants who come from the same area and are sometimes even related to one another.

Obatala Village

An important distinction within the third estate is between those who live on campus with their families, and those who simply work at the University but live in town or in one of the satellite villages around the campus. Despite its severe shortcomings and its enormous overcrowding, Obatala still offers amenities far superior to those in most of the city of Ilosho and its surrounding villages. Furthermore, it does so at controlled and relatively low rents which make Obatala economically attractive as well. In short, compared to Senior Staff housing, Obatala Village is an appalling slum; compared to much of the city of Ilosho, it is almost a model community.

Obatala is truly a community within a community. Through its density of settlement, it is turned inwardly and it displays some of the characteristics of a traditional African village after one has learned to overlook the monotonous regularity of its aligned, row-type dwellings. Obatala is also physically and socially segregated within the campus from both students and Senior Staff, with the two churches, the mosque, and a large vacant space known as Morgan Field (which serves as a meeting place for the U.I. Workers

Union in times of crisis) as both a "buffer zone" and a place where the three estates fleetingly meet on Sunday mornings.

Unlike the non-resident Junior Staff for whom the University is mainly a place of work, the residents of Obatala partake much more fully of U.I. life, albeit not on equal terms with the students or the Senior Staff. They have relatively easy access to medical facilities and to the primary school, far inferior and overcrowded though these facilities are compared to those for the Senior Staff. On weekends they can enjoy, as spectators if not as participants, the student sports events. Their religious life centers for the most part around the adjacent mosque and the Catholic and Protestant chapels and their respective congregations. Most importantly, perhaps, the inhabitants of Obatala engage in a wide variety of social activities together, as indeed sheer propinquity forces them to do.

Where there are no permanent structures provided by the University, Obatala residents have created their own makeshift arrangements. The amenity most widely criticized for its absence, and without which any Nigerian community is incomplete, is a public marketplace. In one area, there is concentration of wooden tables used by women traders as makeshift stalls, but there is no planned marketplace. The result is a dispersal of commercial activities throughout the village, every third or fourth dwelling using its little porch to sell a small stock of £2 to £5 worth of wares, much the same all over, for a fractional profit. Thus, the original planners who, by not providing a marketplace, probably hoped to avoid what they regarded as the unsightly disorder of an African market, had their aims defeated by the irrepressible Nigerian spirit of free enterprise and penny capitalism.

Similarly, attempts to bannish poultry and control their movements meet at best with very partial success, and, were it not for the three speed bumps on the main street (which also leads to the Farm, the Arboretum, and the Motor Transport yard with its petrol pump), the rate of feathered casualties would be much higher than it is.

The primary school with its population of some 1000 pupils and its adjacent playground and soccer field is another bustling center of noisy activities which contrasts sharply with the sedate, dormant appearance of the Senior Staff residential areas. The Obatala School is reputed to be scholastically one of the best in the Western State, and the pressure to get into the badly overcrowded facilities is great. In the words of one report, "Not only are parents trying to register their under-age children, they also smuggle in children of their extended families as their own children."

Though superior in physical terms to much of Ilosho, Obatala Village nevertheless remains a lower-class ghetto within the University community. A Nigerian member of the Senior Staff who produced a report on "Social Life and Amenities in Obatala" writes:

With the congestion that is so evident everywhere in the village, it is quite surprising that the population is still relatively happy, peaceful and neighborly. This can probably be explained by the fact that almost all legitimate members of the society have various duties, official or unofficial, to perform at all times. This reduces the tension and there is very little risk of the devil finding work for the empty hand.[4]

A long-time resident in the village and a teacher in the Obatala school gives a rather different picture from the "happy singing natives" perspective gained from the top of the social pyramid. Interviewed by one of the research assistants, he stated:

> Tell whoever is in charge of this research that we are suffering silently here. I have been in this place for the past ten years and the University neglects this school just as it has neglected the welfare of junior workers living in Obatala. I have only a room and nine live in it. . . . We don't force parents of pupils to pay [a special £2 school levy] . . . they have decided to do so since they know that is the only way by which they can help their children.

On another occasion, when one of my research assistants was observing the proceedings of the Obatala Council, a member turned to him and asked him to report their complaints about the school and the clinic to me with hope that I would present their case to the University authorities who seemed to care less about the Junior Staff than about the Senior Staff. What purpose, he asked, did the Obatala Council serve if its recommendations were not paid attention to?

Administrative Control

The administrative office concerned with the personnel side of the Intermediate and Subordinate Staff is the Establishment and Labour Office (E.L.O.) of the Registry, while the running of Obatala falls within the tasks of the Estate Office, also within the Registry. Ultimately, since the Junior Staff is entirely non-academic, its control falls squarely within the jurisdiction of Council, and more specifically of the Intermediate and Subordinate Staff Sub-Committee of the Finance and General Purposes Committee thereof. That sub-committee consists of 13 voting members and the Assistant Registrar for E.L.O. as Secretary. There is no Junior Staff representation whatsoever on it, despite U.I.W.U. demands to that effect. The Registrar is Chairman and the members are mostly heads of administrative departments who belong to it *ex officio,* or heads of academic departments elected by their respective Faculty Board. Although this is a sub-committee of Council dealing with exclusively non-academic affairs, seven of the thirteen voting members are academics, and six are heads of academic departments.

Council has the ultimate power to appoint and dismiss persons to the Junior Staff, but except in the rare case of a disciplinary dismissal, Council deals with most Junior Staff matters in the most routine fashion, and the actual power resides at lower levels. In effect, power over Junior Staff is shared by the Registrar and his subordinate, the Assistant Registrar of E.L.O. on the one hand, and the various Department Heads, administrative and academic, and the Masters and Wardens of halls on the other. Heads of departments exercise day-to-day authority over their subordinates; their preferences and desires carry disproportionate weight in the hiring of Junior Staff; Department Heads recommend their subordinates for promotion and salary increments, and after three warnings, they can recommend dismissal to the Disciplinary Committee, and thence to the Registrar and to Council. Within any department, then, the fate of a Junior Staff member is primarily determined by the Department Head; arbitrary power of the Department Head is, however, circumscribed by the employee's right to request a transfer, and by the necessity on the part of the University to show cause for dismissal after an employee's probationary period is over, and after his appointment has been confirmed. Like civil servants, U.I. employees on the permanent staff with "confirmed" appointments are effectively protected against unemployment and dismissal, barring gross misconduct, incompetence or neglect of duty.

The E.L.O. and the Assistant Registrar at its head exercise overall administrative supervision over the entire Junior Staff. They must see to it that vacancies are advertised and filled according to the elaborate procedures provided therefor; they deal with the U.I.W.U. and its secretariat on a day-to-day basis, settling grievances and disagreements before they escalate into labor disputes; and they keep the personnel records for the 4,000-odd employees under their jurisdiction. Considering the scope of its tasks and the high potential for conflict in the E.L.O., that office has been run with remarkable efficiency under the present Assistant Registrar, and has managed to avoid any serious labor dispute since the major crisis of 1966 when the dismissal of an Intermediate Staff employee within that very office precipitated a general strike and the most serious ethnic and political crisis in the history of the University. In particular, the Assistant Registrar has achieved a *modus vivendi* with the Union based on informal consultation, mutual respect and accommodation. The introduction of a new and better pension plan and death benefit system in 1968 is hailed by both Union and "management" as the major benefit which grew out of this policy of amicable cooperation.

Junior Staff can be hired on two different bases. The most unskilled categories of workers are hired on a daily-paid and temporary basis, usually on the initiative of the department head and without the usual advertisement and interview procedures. All other categories of jobs are supposed to be advertised when vacancies occur. For jobs under £198 a year, the advertisement is internal, i.e., within the University, while for jobs above that salary level, ads are placed in Nigerian newspapers as well. The E.L.O. normally collects all job applications with supporting letters of reference, school certificates and other necessary documents; it then sorts applications into those which meet the minimum educational qualifications for the job and those which do not, passes the file on to the Department Head for his consideration, and, after establishing a short list of eligible candidates, sets up an interview panel consisting of the Assistant Registrar of E.L.O., the Department Head or his representative, one or two persons nominated by the Department Head, and some person with technical expertise relevant to the candidate's qualification if appropriate.

Each member of the interview panel rates candidates after a verbal interview, using a mimeographed sheet which includes such attributes as "Personality—Physique, Grooming, Agreeableness, Confidence, Frankness etc."; and "Ability to Communicate—Fluency, correct English usage, clarity of speech, comprehension." As the interviews are conducted in English, the linguistic factor and the amount of formal schooling are paramount considerations, even in the most menial job categories where the relevance of English fluency and of formal education is questionable. Scores from the ratings are then added, and a discussion between panel members follows wherein the Department Head's wishes often carry more than proportional weight, so that the candidate with the highest numerical score is not necessarily appointed.

This elaborate and universalistic procedure is intended, of course, to circumvent favoritism and the operation of the patron-client system described earlier. But a number of factors defeat, at least in part, the intent of this complex system of safeguards. First, as already suggested, the interview routine itself is contaminated by particularistic factors which are not demonstrably related to job competence. Second, the Department Head can (and occasionally does) use his power to push the claims of his clients and impose his will over the other members of the interview panel. This disproportionate weight given to the opinion of the department head is justified on the grounds that he is the person who has to work with whomever is appointed, and, hence, that he should have a powerful say in the matter. However, in the Nigerian context, this results in an open door to the clientage system. Third, the universalistic system, as for Senior Staff appointments, is extremely cumbersome, time-consuming, and dilatory. Even the lowliest of Junior Staff appointments consume twenty or more hours of

Senior Staff time, and between advertisement and the filling of a vacancy through the regular procedure just described, a minimum of six to eight weeks elapse.

The net result is that the universalistic system is so unwieldy that it breaks down under its own weight. It would simply be impossible to fill vacancies if the "regular" procedure were applied in every case. Therefore, built into the procedure is a provision for "temporary" appointments, usually for a period of one year. These are supposed to be used only in exceptional cases, but the clause is so convenient that it is in fact resorted to in the great majority of cases. During the period of September, 1967 to June, 1968, for example, a total of 942 persons were hired by the University in the Junior Staff ranks (*not* including the daily paid workers); of these, only a little over one-third (35.6 per cent) were appointed according to the "regular" procedure of advertisement and interviews, and nearly two-thirds (64.4 per cent) were appointed to "temporary" jobs.

"Temporary" appointments are not part of the regular "establishment," can be hired much more expeditiously (in effect, on request by the Department Head and without advertisement and competitive interviews), and can be fired without cause on 30-day notice. In practice, temporary appointments are nothing of the sort. The vast majority of them are absorbed into the University "establishment" after a year or so of service, and thus enter the permanent staff without having had to undergo the competitive procedure. In the few departments where the head is notorious for his resort to nepotism and ethnic favoritism, this creates, of course, the rankest type of inefficiency. Some academic departments, for example, have typists with a speed of twelve or fifteen words a minute, and who are incapable of typing a sheet with less than ten to fifteen mistakes.

As all Junior Staff are first appointed on a probationary basis, and have to be confirmed after one or two years of service before they achieve security of tenure, there is in actual practice no meaningful difference of status between "temporary" and "permanent" employees on their first appointment. The "temporary" procedure has become almost purely a method of circumventing the regular one, both for "legitimate" reasons of necessity and urgency, and for "illegitimate" reasons of nepotism and favoritism. The fiction that temporary appointments are only resorted to in exceptional circumstances is easily preserved, however. At any given time, only 7 to 10 per cent of the Junior Staff appear on temporary status (not including the daily-paid workers). The reason for this relatively low percentage is that the vast majority of the temporary appointees are absorbed into the establishment after a year of service, and thereafter vanish from the category. In fact, some two-thirds of the *new* appointments follow the "exceptional" procedure.

Labor Union

Far and away the most important representative organ of the Junior Staff is the U.I. Workers Union. First organized in 1951 and constitutionally established in 1952, the U.I.W.U. is almost as old as the University itself. It has an active list of some 2,000 dues-paying members, i.e., approximately 50 per cent of the Junior Staff, and probably some two-thirds of the "established" or permanent staff. Membership is voluntary, and dues, relative to wages, are high: daily paid workers pay one shilling a month while members on salaries pay two shillings. The University Bursary has agreed with the Union to deduct dues from the wages, with the worker's consent of course. This greatly facilitates dues collection for the Union, but, on the other hand, increases its dependency on the University.

Union officers and an Executive Committee are supposed to be elected annually by a general meeting of the membership, but between 1966 and 1969 there were no elections because of the bitter ethnic strife which split the organization. The Executive Committee consists of a President General, two Vice-Presidents, a General Secretary and two Assistant Secretaries, a Treasurer, an Organizing Secretary, a Publicity Secretary and twenty unofficial members elected on a roughly proportional basis by the various branches organized by major University departments. The political life of the Union thus closely parallels the organizational structure of the University, with the additional characteristics that, within the Union, the catering and other non-academic departments which are also the larger ones play the most important role, while in the University at large the academic departments take precedence.

The day-to-day running of Union affairs is in the hands of the General Secretary who is a salaried employee of the Union and an experienced professional union organizer. He receives a salary of some £700, and runs an office just outside the main gate of the University. The office consists of two rooms, and the staff besides the General Secretary and his Assistants includes two typists and a messenger.

A 1969 draft constitution framed by the Caretaker Committee established after the 1966 crisis also provides for a Delegate Conference to meet annually and to hold supreme authority. The draft provides for the dissolution of the Executive Committee by a two-thirds vote of no confidence at a General Meeting; it excludes illiterates from the offices of President, Secretary, Assistant Secretary and Treasurer; and it states that "when acts of treachery, espionage or sabotage have been proved against a member, such a member shall lose his seat in [the Executive] Committee."

The Union has had, like the University, a stormy history. At some periods, it has been a militant and effective body resorting to strikes. In the June

1964 General Strike, the U.I.W.U. played an important role in a nation-wide protest against the Government's dilatoriness in publishing the findings of the Morgan Commission Report on wages; it joined the national strike movement, and since then the customary assembly field for U.I.W.U. members on campus has been known as Morgan Field. During that strike minor clashes ocurred between students, Senior Staff and workers. On other occasions, the U.I.W.U., or the Caterers' Association within it, have struck against the University to demand better wages and conditions of service.

There are several lines of political cleavage within the U.I.W.U. and the Junior Staff in general. All of these tend to weaken Union solidarity and effectiveness. The first issue is one of class. Many Intermediate Staff members, and indeed more broadly much of the clerical staff, identify more with the Senior Staff above them than with the manual workers, and hence their solidarity with, and interest in, the Union are limited. There is a general negative correlation between Union militancy and activity on the one hand, and social status on the other. The low-status caterers in the halls of residence are especially class-conscious, and constitute a well-orga-nized pressure group within the U.I.W.U. as they demonstrated in the 1969 elections, when, through block-voting, they managed to get virtually all their candidates elected to the new Executive Committee. This outcome was widely criticized, especially among the clerical staff and among the Yoruba who are greatly under-represented among the caterers. Many workers thought that the elected Union officials were too uneducated to be able to run Union affairs and to carry any weight with the University authorities.

Besides class, the Union is also split along ideological lines of right and left, each wing wanting to affiliate with a different world labor organization. Ideology, however, only concerns a few of the more educated Union mem-bers, and is not an issue of general importance. Of greater concern to most members is departmental affiliation, since the representative structure of the Union is on a departmental basis. Members are thus concerned about the departmental affiliation of the elected officials. As some departments (e.g., the Bursary and Registry) consist predominantly of clerical personnel and others (e.g., the halls and Maintenance) are made up mostly of manual workers, departmental affiliation is often closely related to the class cleav-ages just mentioned.

Most divisive of all, however, have been the ethnic cleavages within the Union. These came to a violent climax in the 1966 crisis which shook the entire University and nearly wrecked the U.I.W.U. Reserving a more detailed discussion of these events for Chapter 8, we should mention here that the Union was split largely along Yoruba-non-Yoruba lines; that two rival Executive Committees claimed exclusive legitimacy over what was left of the running of Union affairs; that several members were severely beaten in fist fights between rival factions and that one prominent Yoruba Union leader had to be hospitalized; that the Union lost virtually all effectiveness as a bargaining body *vis à vis* the University because it became deeply imbroiled in a much wider political conflict; and that total disintegration was only narrowly averted by the establishment of a Caretaker Committee which held office for three years.

During the 1966–69 period, the old wounds were still festering, and dissatisfaction of the Yoruba with the Union remained high, as both the President and the Secretary were Mid-Westerners. The Union limped along, but was in no position to be militant *vis à vis* the University. The non-Yoruba—mostly Mid-Westerners and non-Ibo Easterners during my period of field work—accused the Yoruba of being disinterested in Union affairs because they could get what they wanted through their clientage ties with well-placed fellow ethnics in the University Senior Staff. The Yoruba, on the other hand, accused the Union Executive of running Union affairs as a Mid-Western interest group. The result was that the U.I.W.U. established an amicable, cooperative *modus vivendi* with the University administration. There were no work stoppages, and the Union gained representation on three non-statutory bodies regulating its relations with the administration. These are the Joint Negotiating Committee, the Joint Conciliation Committee, and the Joint Disciplinary Committee. The last one is particularly sensitive, since it was the disciplining of a Union member by the Registrar in 1966 which unleashed the strike and the great crisis. The Joint Disciplinary Committee consisting of three Senior Staff and two Junior Staff members with the Union Secretary in attendance makes recommendations to the Registrar. All three committees are consultative and advisory in nature, and ultimate power resides with Council.

The deducting of Union dues by the Bursary is also part of the *modus vivendi* with the University. So is the fact that, in order to insure that the 1969 Union elections would be fair and peaceful, a five-member committee consisting entirely of Senior Staff and under the Chairmanship of the Union's patron, a senior, knowledgeable and powerful Nigerian professor, was called upon to supervise them. Supporters of the policy of cooperation with the University administration point to the new pension plan and death benefit system (reinstituted by the University in 1968 after a lapse of six years when no plan was in effect) as a major achievement of the system. Whatever the benefits, it is clear that, during the 1966–69 period, the U.I.W.U. had in fact become something very close to a "company union," so ridden with

internal class and ethnic divisions as to render it nearly impotent as a negotiating force. Whether the situation will continue now that the more militant
caterers won most Union Executive positions remains an open question.

NOTES

[1] The Ibo, on the other hand, who come from a traditionally lowly stratified
society, regard the elaborate Yoruba etiquette of age deference (including complete prostration for men and kneeling down for women) as evidence that the
Yoruba are cringing and submissive. Thus, each group, seizing on different
criteria which are interpreted out of their cultural context, believes that the
other shows a despicable lack of pride.

[2] These terms are normally used by domestic servants when they speak English,
both to address and to refer to their employers. In colonial practice, the domestic
servant was referred to as "boy" or "girl," a terminology which still survives in
the term "boys' quarters," but which educated Nigerians increasingly avoid and
which many servants deeply resent.

[3] In Northern Nigeria, where Hausa is a widespread *lingua franca,* a number
of foreigners speak the pidgin variety of that language. Unlike in the South,
very few Northern Nigerians speak English.

[4] It is interesting to note the attitude of colonial paternalism which the University administration takes *vis à vis* Obatala Village. While the Vice-Chancellor
and other members of the Senior Staff describe the situation as deplorable and
in need of drastic improvement, they blame residents for many of the conditions,
and conceive of remedial action in administrative as distinguished from community participation terms. Thus, an *ad hoc* committee to study the situation in
Obatala was appointed by the Vice-Chancellor in 1968, and consisted of six
members of the Senior Staff and only one member from the Obatala Council.
Typical of this quasicolonial attitude toward Obatala are the following comments by a Nigerian member of the Senior administrative staff:

> People there live just like animals. . . . Some 200 litter bins have been distributed
> in the village but people still throw their refuse everywhere. They go and relieve
> themselves in the bush instead of using the latrines. They expect the University
> to do everything for them, even sweep their own rooms, instead of helping them-
> selves. If you sent a detail of men to clean the place at 2 p.m., at 2:10 p.m. the
> place would look like a shambles again. . . . If one asked me what to do about
> Obatala, I would suggest razing the place to the ground because it is a potential
> source of epidemics and an eyesore in an academic community. You drive past the
> beautiful grounds and the Chapel of Resurrection, and all of a sudden you see
> this place in shambles. . . . Yet until an epidemic of smallpox or some other dread-
> ful disease breaks out, nothing will be done. In town, if people violate sanitary
> regulations, they can be taken to court after a warning, but here no sanctions are
> taken and the people themselves do not care.

CHAPTER SEVEN
Religion: Christianity and Islam

For the last half-millennium, West Africa has been the theater of competition between two of the "world religions," Islam and Christianity, spreading respectively from the north and from the south at the expense of traditional religions. The number of traditionalists (contemptuously referred to as "pagans" by both Muslims and Christians) is hard to evaluate with any degree of precision because traditional practices are by no means incompatible with more or less nominal membership in one of the two major faiths. But at most 20 per cent of all Nigerians could be termed traditionalists in the stricter sense of claiming no affiliation to either of the large monotheistic religions. Of the remainder, Muslims constitute close to two-thirds and Christians a little over one-third. In Yoruba country where Islam has made in-roads all the way south to Lagos, Muslims slightly outnumber Christians, and the city of Ilosho is said to be approximately three-fourths Muslim.

Hierarchy of Religions

Yet, these population figures do not accurately represent the socio-political situation of the country; indeed the various religions are in a clear hierarchical order. At the bottom of the social pyramid are the "pagans" found in greatest concentration in the Middle Belt of Nigeria sandwiched between the large Muslim emirates of the north and the christianized population of the rain forest zone to the south. Next in the prestige order come Muslims whose religion was long associated with the large empire of Kanem-Bornu, and the Sultanate of Sokoto and its vassal emirates among the Hausa, Fulani, Nupe and Northern Yoruba. There is a substantial Muslim aristocracy and literati class in the north whose traditional status is very high, but, having failed for the most part to acquire Western-style education, this Muslim elite is scarcely represented in the new ruling class which runs the modern sector of Nigeria, and hence its importance is rapidly declining, especially since the advent of the military regimes in 1966. Since most "modern" schools during and even before the British colonial period were operated by Christian missionaries, Western education and conversion to Christianity became nearly synonymous. Thus, there has developed a situation where a predominantly Muslim country is dominated by an overwhelmingly Christian bureaucratic mandarinate.

Among Nigerian Christians, there are further status distinctions. The most prestigious denomination is the established Church of England to which most of the oldest Lagosian elite belongs. Of distinctly lower status are other denominations spread largely by non-English missionaries, such as Baptism, an American-dominated sect, and Roman Catholicism. Lowest among Christians and indeed of no higher status than Muslims are various syncretistic sects that have incorporated both Christian and traditional elements.

This rough hierarchy of religions does not preclude a wide status spectrum within each of the two main faiths. It is quite possible for a Muslim to reach the top of the modern sector, and the reason why relatively few have is not religious prejudice as such, but rather the result of the historical factors just mentioned. Conversely, while most of the modern elite are Christians, most Christians do not belong to the elite or even to the clerical and semi-professional sub-elite. Only among traditionalists, is there practically no class differentiation. A "pagan" has virtually no chance of becoming anything but a farmer because the acquisition of the necessary skills to be anything else would involve his incorporation into either a Christian- or a Muslim-dominated environment, and, hence, in the long run his conversion. Indeed, migration to a city means in effect entering either a Muslim or a Christian world. The urban world is monotheist, at least in theory; "paganism" has become largely a rural phenomenon, though by no means all, or even most, peasants are traditionalists. Today even the Yoruba and Bini cities which antedate by several centuries any contact with either Islam or Christendom have become absorbed by the two "world religions."

Christianity

Not surprisingly, U.I., which was patterned strictly on the Western model of the university, is an overwhelmingly Christian (as distinguished from either Muslim or traditionalist) organization. *De jure,* the University is secular, as indeed most of the modern European universities are. *De facto,* however, the concept of a secular university in Nigeria is almost a contradiction in terms because the larger society, and even its Western-educated elite, have undergone almost none of the process of secularization that Europe has experienced in the last two or three centuries. What little anti-clericalism was shown in U.I. history has come almost exclusively from expatriates, and found little support among Nigerians. It was mostly Nigerians who wanted a Department of Religious Studies established, which, under a Nigerian Professor, became in effect a Department of Protestant Studies. Muslims, who could not find a congenial home in the misnamed Department of Religious Studies, sought refuge in a Department of Arabic and Islamic Studies which combined the disciplines of linguistics, history and theology. Thus the University now finds itself saddled with two religiously-inspired academic departments, although the Department of Arabic and Islamic Studies is more secularized than its Christian counterpart.

As the University was to be a self-sufficient residential community, places of religious worship were incorporated in the plans. The Chapel of Resurrection, by far the largest caters to the Protestants, with pastors from the main orthodox denominations alternating in officiating at the Sunday services. A Catholic Church of more modest size is located nearby. Not until in 1963, was a Mosque (by far the smallest house of worship on campus) also built in the same vicinity, between Obatala Village, the student halls and the Senior Staff housing.[1] The University has no official pastor, but since several members of its teaching staff are clerics, they take turns in leading their respective congregations. Attendance at religious services is optional but widespread among both staff and students.

U.I. also falls short of being completely secular in that it gives official recognition to religious holidays. The terms of the academic year are simply called "first," "second," and "third" instead of the religious labels (Lent Term, etc.) used in the Oxbridge tradition, and the vacations are also non-sectarian, except that the recess between the first and second terms coincides with Christmas and the Christian New Year. However, U.I., like the Federal Government, recognizes a similar number of both Christian and Muslim festivities as official holidays. The heavy preponderance of Christians among Senior Staff and students lends the Christian holidays much greater luster. For example, Christmas services are followed by a reception for the Senior Staff at the Vice Chancellor's lodge, a function which has no counterpart on Muslim holidays.

In theory, the Senior Staff School and the International School, operated on behalf of University Council, are non-sectarian, but, in fact, the children pray every morning at "assembly." Furthermore, as the teachers are nearly all Christians, the religious atmosphere of the school is decidedly Christian, and indeed Protestant, not to say high-church Anglican. Many school activities, such as nativity plays, hymn singing sessions and the like, precede

Christian holidays, while Muslim and Jewish holidays are largely ignored.

Religion is one of the main bases of solidarity across social strata and ethnic groups. Both major monotheistic faiths have among their campus congregations some members of all three estates. This is true even of Muslims, although they constitute only 5 to 6 per cent of the student population and an even lower percentage of the Senior Staff. Muslims are somewhat more numerous among the Junior Staff, but a majority of all three estates are Christians. Some 95 per cent of Senior Staff and students are Christians, but at least half of the Christians belong to the Junior Staff.

TABLE 12 / RELIGIOUS AFFILIATION OF U. I. STUDENTS*

Religion	Per Cent of All Students
Roman Catholics	17.9
Main Protestant Churches	44.5
Christian, unspecified	28.5
African Christian Churches	1.0
Muslims	5.7
Traditionalists	0.1
No Reply	2.3
Total	100.0

* Statistical data on religious affiliation was only available for students.

Religion also cuts to some extent across ethnicity, although there is a strong correlation between the two. Some ethnic groups such as the Kanuri, Hausa and Fulani are almost entirely Muslim, but these groups from the north are scarcely represented at U.I.; other ethnic groups like the Ibo, Ibibio, and Ijaw are mostly Christians or at least non-Muslims. The Yoruba, however, who are the most numerous ethnic group on campus, are religiously split between Muslims and Christians, with further sectarian distinctions within these faiths. For example, Oyo Division is an American Baptist fief; Ilorin has been a Fulani-ruled emirate since the Jihad of the early 19th century; and Lagos and Abeokuta have an Anglican elite and a Muslim majority. Among the Yoruba masses, there is great religious tolerance, and indeed syncretism between traditional cults and the monotheistic faiths, and it is common to find both Christians and Muslims within the same extended family. The Yoruba elite, however, is overwhelmingly Christian, and looks down on both Muslims and "pagans." On campus, most members of the old Lagosian-Egba-"Brazilian" elite are Anglican, but Baptists are also strongly represented among the Yoruba Senior Staff. The most dynamic leader and organizer of the Muslim congregation is a Yoruba lecturer who also serves as Imam (prayer leader). Catholics are drawn mostly from the Bini, Ijaw, Ibo, Ibibio, Ishan and other small groups; there are also a number of Protestants from these groups, but almost no Muslims.

Expatriates, to the extent that they associate with any denomination at all, which at least half do not, are nearly all Protestants or Catholics, the former being in large majority. An American convert to Islam, who is on the permanent Senior Staff plays an active role in the Muslim congregation, and there is also a sprinkling of Muslims from Asian and other African countries, several of whom teach in the Department of Arabic and Islamic Studies. Finally, a few expatriates are Jews and Hindus. What distinguishes the expatriates most clearly from the Nigerians, however, is not their religious affiliation, but rather the lack of it for a large proportion of them. Many foreigners express surprise at the religiosity of their Nigerian colleagues and students, and, conversely, Nigerians, even intellectuals, find it difficult to accept the agnosticism, atheism or religious indifference of many expatriates.

The degree of religiosity among students is evident from responses to the request for religious affiliation or preference on admission cards. Only 2.3 per cent of a random sample of over 3,000 students failed to give a religious preference, and none described themselves as atheists or agnostics even though a blank space allowed for that response. Nor is the expression of a religious affiliation the perfunctory kind of act of, say, a British student checking "Church of England" on a questionnaire. There are five active student religious organizations out of a total of some 25 student clubs and voluntary organizations. These associations are affiliated with national organizations; one of them is Muslim, one is Catholic and three are Protestant. Informal prayer and hymn-singing groups of students form in the halls. The few expatriate students living in the halls express surprise that even in shower rooms much of the singing is religious.

Sunday and Friday services, for Christians and Muslims respectively, are well attended by Junior Staff, Senior Staff and students alike and are major social events of the week. Expatriates often attend church in light informal clothing, but most Nigerians dress formally, either in Western style (hats, stockings, horsehair wigs and even gloves for women, coat and tie for men) or, more commonly, in the full indigenous attire (*agbada*). This formal style of dress, both in its European and Nigerian variety, is all the more oppressive as the main and most fashionable services, both Catholic and Protestant, are typically held in the late morning when temperature approaches its maximum. The Senior Staff typically come in cars even though some only have a few hundred yards to walk from home to church, and the number of cars around the churches is a good index of the relative affluence as well as the size of the congregations. The Protestant Chapel attracts between 60 to 100 cars for the main service, compared to 40 to 50 for the Catholics, and at most half a dozen for the Muslims.

Islam

Mosque services on Friday are much less ostentatious than the Christian Sunday services, partly because of the lesser affluence of the worshippers, and partly because of the strong Muslim norm against distracting and flashy dress at prayer meetings, but even among Muslims the orthodox norm of simple, drab attire is not strictly observed. Attendance of women, generally characteristic of the more tolerant Yoruba Islam, also marks the campus Mosque services, as do sermons in English and Yoruba. These unorthodox practices are frowned upon by Northern Muslims (of whom there are very few on campus), and clearly indicate Christian influence on Southern Islam. The Imam at U.I., an Arabic scholar on the teaching staff, is definitely a "progressive" Muslim, and his "modernism" sets the tone for the congregation.

It is perhaps within the Muslim community that the stress on egalitarianism is strongest. For a long time, the Muslim Students' Society (M.S.S.) dominated religious affairs on campus and services at the Mosque. Obatala Muslims had their own small Mosque and Imam, and in 1969 challenged the M.S.S. leadership to account for the spending of the money contributed by the congregation. (The spending of funds is always a delicate matter which almost invariably opens the officers of student organizations to charges of embezzlement.) When the M.S.S. failed to respond to the request, a group of Obatala Muslims petitioned the Vice-Chancellor to arbitrate the dispute. A 9-member Management Committee consisting of two members of the Senior Staff (one of whom was the chairman), three students and four Junior Staff representatives was appointed, and the Muslim community was reorganized on a more democratic basis. Given, however, the importance of literacy in Arabic for religious leadership, and the scarcity of that skill in Southern Nigeria, the Arabic scholars on the Senior Staff continue to play a decisive leadership role, as well as an arbitration function between the M.S.S. and the Obatala Muslims.

Among Protestants and Catholics, religious services also draw all three estates together, and a common faith creates networks of mutual aid, notably in the search for employment; nevertheless, status distinctions within the Christian congregations remain more striking and visible than among Muslims, perhaps because students and Senior Staff are more strongly represented. Inside the church, during the Sunday services, the three status groups intermix and take their seats irrespective of rank, but once the service is over they each go their separate ways: the Senior Staff families, after exchanging greetings with friends, walk to their nearby motorcars and drive away to their homes; students walk back to their halls; and the Junior Staff streams back on foot to Obatala Village. Church affairs, among both Protestants and Catholics, involve the Junior Staff only minimally, and there is no representation system comparable to the Muslim Management Committee established in 1969.

Religious Conflicts

Whatever links religion creates between social strata and ethnic groups, it constitutes itself an important line of cleavage in Nigerian society and at University. Muslims feel very much on the defensive, not only as a minority group on campus, but also as a group which is the target of considerable prejudice. Educated Christian Nigerians tend to identify Islam with conservatism, lack of education, "backwardness," and religious intolerance. While they recognize that there are some Western-educated Muslims, they tend to regard them as anomalies who do not fit into their stereotypes of Muslims as being ignorant peasants, illiterate herdsmen, or feudal emirs. A Yoruba Christian student whom I had assigned the task of attending a Friday mosque service as training in field methodology was extremely reluctant to undertake the task, stating he would feel very ill at ease and out of place. Later, having completed the job, he reported that he had had a hard time not bursting out laughing when the worshippers "went up and down," and when prayers were recited in Arabic which to him was "pure gibberish." Another Yoruba Christian student described to me Muslims coming down on lorries from the north. They smelled like goats, she said, and were in a state of filth and degradation that she could not have imagined. "They were just like animals." [2]

While these attitudes may be extreme, most Christians who have often gone through bigoted mission schools have in most cases acquired strong anti-Muslim prejudices; they tend to find the Islamic ritual ridiculous, and to associate the lower average level of literacy and Western education among Muslims with their religion. Interestingly, it seems that anti-Muslim prejudices are much more developed among educated Nigerians than among ordinary farmers or townsmen. Among the non-literate or barely literate Yoruba, for example, there is widespread religious tolerance between Muslims and Christians who, as we have seen, often belong to the same lineages and live in the same compound. The "modern" elite, being nearly entirely Christian, on the other hand, tends to equate Islam with lower social status, and, therefore, to look down on Muslims.

Muslims, and especially educated Muslims, are resentful of those prejudices, and charge the authorities with bias against them. For example, in
1969, Muslims in Ilosho attacked the Western State Commissioner for
Education for the blatant underrepresentation of Muslims on appointed
school boards. In a city that is roughly 75 per cent Muslim, half a dozen
Christian denominations were given a seat each, as against a single Muslim
to represent his faith. Muslims also resent the near-monopoly on modern
education maintained until recently by mission schools. They have attempted
to remedy the situation by developing Muslim secondary schools, but they
still lag far behind Christian schools. In many cases, therefore, a Muslim
child is forced to go to a Christian school if he is to get any education other
than rote memorization of the Koran and Arabic transliteration which he
can get in a *madressa* (traditional Muslim school). When a Muslim child
goes to a Christian institution, social pressures and the fear of ridicule or
ostracism often incite him to convert, and, thus, the stereotype of backward,
uneducated Muslims becomes a self-fulfilling prophecy.

There are also negative stereotypes between Protestants and Catholics,
but not nearly as pronounced as between Christians and Muslims. During
the Civil War, however, what was seen as the pro-Biafran stand of the Pope
put local Catholics on the defensive, and many dissociated themselves from
Caritas, the Catholic relief agency, which was flying unauthorized missions
to the encircled remnants of Biafra. Protestants tended to associate Catholics with Biafran secession because disproportionate numbers of Ibos are
Catholics, and because of the partisan stance of the Vatican on the Nigerian
civil war. Particularly irritating to all Nigerian intellectuals irrespective
of religion was the obviously biased and false interpretation of the war in
Catholic circles in Europe as a Muslim Jihad against the Christian Ibo;
and non-Catholics criticized Catholics on the Federal side for not adequately
informing Catholic foreign opinion of the real nature of the war.

To summarize, religion at U.I. is far more important as a basis of social
solidarity than it would be at a university in a more secularized, industrial
society. The great majority of Nigerians at all class levels are active members of church groups, and religion is both a line of cleavage at U.I., and a
source of solidarity ties across class, and, to some extent, ethnic lines. Religion
both unites and divides, as indeed it does in most parts of the world. The
most invidious aspects of the religious cleavage, however, do not so much
arise from differences in beliefs. Indeed, Christianity and Islam share nearly
identical sets of basic values. Rather, religious division has become embittered
largely because the spread of Islam first, and of Christianity later, was
accompanied by a military conquest which created a hierarchy. This hierarchy still persists today in the form of a structure of greatly unequal
opportunities in the fields of education and employment, even though the

systems of political domination which were linked with Islam and Christianity, namely the quasi-feudal emirates of the north and the British colonial regime, have given way to a nominally "national" government. As with ethnic cleavages which we shall examine presently, religious sectionalism at University reflects in microcosm the rifts in the larger society.

Notes

[1] There are also some inconspicuous traditional shrines in the undeveloped, rain-forest covered parts of the campus, but most students and Senior Staff are unaware of their very existence.

[2] These are people, who for a small fee, hitch a lift on the back of a lorry, and are exposed to rain and dust for the three or four days of the journey from Kano to Lagos.

CHAPTER EIGHT

Race and Ethnicity

Race

Numerous references were made in past chapters to ethnic conflicts and to differences between Nigerians and expatriates. Now we must take a more systematic look at the factors of "race" and ethnicity. Most of whatever importance "race" had before Nigerian independence has been lost since, and this is even truer at University than in the society at large. The British colonial regime was, of course, a racist one, in that there was for a long time a specifically racial barrier to senior positions in the civil service and the army, a rigid color bar in residential areas and other public and private amenities, and a good deal of color consciousness and arrogance on the part of colonial officials. Yet, compared to other African countries like South Africa, Rhodesia and Kenya which have had substantial white settler populations intent on staying in Africa, Nigeria's sultry climate earned it the protective reputation of being a "white man's grave." Few Europeans have had a permanent stake in Nigeria; this greatly facilitated the transition to independence, and the colonial legacy itself has been much less bitter than elsewhere.

In the North, Lugard's policy of indirect rule established a *modus vivendi* between the colonial power and the local Fulani-Hausa ruling class based on grudging admiration and minimal interference. The British largely froze the *status quo,* and thereby let the North fall further and further behind the South in Western education and economic development, but there was little racial bitterness. In the Eastern Region, British policy was least successful, insofar as the colonial administration was never able effectively to cope with the politically decentralized societies it encountered there. In the stratified state societies of the Western Region, the British colonial regime had mixed success, but, there too, there was no lasting legacy of bitterness.

215

A key factor in the lack of a significant colonial "hangover" in Nigeria is the enormous resilience and vitality of indigenous civilizations. Unlike, for example, in South Africa where European conquest shattered African societies, and destroyed their political and economic basis, Nigerian cultures underwent rapid change, but remained fully vital and self-sufficient. Mission education did not appreciably destroy the self-respect and dignity of Nigerians as it did in many other parts of the continent where the European impact was more devastating, and where indigenous societies proved more brittle on contact. Nigerians, on the whole, exhibit very little "brainwashing" or "colonial mentality"; they acknowledge only the technological superiority of the West, and exhibit a tranquil, self-confident sense of cultural pride in their own traditions. The unself-conscious wearing of traditional dress among all social classes is symbolic of this self-assurance. Culture pride is perhaps most developed among the Yoruba who tend to consider themselves not only equal but superior to their fellow Nigerians and to Europeans. Although there is an ill-defined but nevertheless quite real hierarchy of ethnic groups within Nigeria, Nigerians, by and large, show a refreshing lack of inferiority complex vis à vis foreigners, and this makes for free and easy interaction across the "color line," insofar as one can speak of one at all.

Even on campus, there exists, of course, a certain amount of color consciousness. Many Nigerians still expect some racism on the part of whites, and are still sensitive to anything which might be interpreted as such. European students in the halls report that they feel "on trial" in this respect: female students, for example, find it sometimes difficult to reject the sexual advances of Nigerian men without their behavior being interpreted as racist. A few years ago, an American student posted a tactlessly phrased do-not-disturb notice on his door in a hall, and Nigerian students took offense and accused him of racial prejudice. There are also a few Nigerian members of the Senior Staff who, as a result of long residence in the United States, have been traumatized on the color issue and have to some extent become contaminated by American racism, but these cases are quite exceptional. The overwhelming majority of Nigerians have not caught the Western virus of color prejudice, and accept whites on universalistic terms. At worst, differences in cultural values, as in the cases cited above, might be interpreted as racism, but there is a freer climate of interracial tolerance in Nigeria than in many other countries of Eastern and Southern Africa, or North America.

Even interracial marriage, of which there are a score or so of prominent examples on campus, is widely accepted. There is in fact a small colony of interracially married expatriates (West Indians, Europeans and North Americans) whose stay in Nigeria is in part motivated by the climate of greater tolerance they encounter there than in their "home" countries.

Among the Nigerian elite, a number of men marry European or American wives, and while such a marriage might be a slight handicap in a political career, it is completely accepted in academic circles. The Vice-Chancellor of the University is married to a white woman, and so are several other Nigerian Senior Staff members. There is perhaps more resistance to Nigerian women marrying foreigners, and such cases are less common. The reason for the lower frequency is probably that most Nigerians who marry whites do so during their student days in Europe or America, and that the vast majority of overseas Nigerian students are men.

Interracially married couples tend to associate with each other and to form a little social group of their own, but they are not in any way ostracized or even frowned upon. Some Yoruba criticize, however, their Nigerian colleagues married to white wives who speak English at home and whose children are unable to speak any Nigerian language.

Not surprisingly, "color" is most significant among the expatriate American community, which, as elsewhere in the world, shows an uncanny ability to export its home caste system. The Americans are split between two racial groups which scarcely interact. The reason is not so much the racism of white Americans, as much as it is the sometimes studious attempt of black expatriates to dissociate themselves from everything American and to identify with Africa. This attitude is frequently frustrated by the fact that Nigerians, not being racists, find the notion that pigmentation can be a basis of solidarity rather incongruous, and regard black Americans in the same light as white ones. In a country where culture and ethnicity are the primordial criteria of group solidarity, black Americans find their racially-based attempt to solve their identity problem irrelevant.

The Yoruba word *oyimbo* is used to designate whites, but the term is neither derogatory nor specifically racial. In fact, it is often used to mean "expatriate" rather than "white," and these two categories are not coterminous. Some 90 per cent of the foreigners are white, but there is a substantial and highly heterogeneous residue of black or at least non-white foreigners as well, not to mention a few Nigerians of mixed African-European descent. The Nigerian-expatriate cleavage, then, to the extent that it is significant, is not a racial one. There are quite a few West Indians, Americans, and Africans from other countries who, though just as black as the Nigerians, are regarded and treated as foreigners.[1]

It may be argued that the Nigerian-expatriate cleavage at U.I. is, to all intents and purposes, a racial because there are no white Nigerians and so few black non-Nigerians, but even if one were to disregard the treatment of the "exceptions" and accept this superficial racial interpretation, one could not get very far with it. Indeed, even the Nigerian-expatriate cleavage is not a very important one; before independence, it was to some extent a predictor of political attitudes, if only because the vast bulk of the expatriates belonged to the nationality of the colonial power. Since independence, however, the foreigners have become an extremely heterogeneous group, and nationality is no longer an accurate predictor of anything much. Politically, some expatriates are far to the left of most Nigerians, and there are very few issues where such simple polarization takes place. There are some political conventions within the University which implicitly assume that Nigerians and expatriates on the Senior Staff represent two different interest groups, as indeed they do in terms of some fringe benefits such as "home leaves" and retirement plans. Most expatriates accept the principle of Nigerianization of the staff all the more readily as they do not, for the most part, intend to stay in Nigeria much longer than it will take to train a Nigerian to replace them. Among the old-time British staff, there is a group with a longer-time stake in the University who hold tenure headships of departments, and who tend to take a more conservative view of the qualifications and seniority needed for promotion than has become customary at U.I. over the years. In 1969, there was an important clash within the Faculty of Medicine involving the slowness of an expatriate head of department to promote younger colleagues, and the person resigned. This behavior, however, does not characterize the expatriates collectively, and Americans on the staff, for example, have tended to push hard for quick Nigerianization.[2]

In view of general lack of resistance to Nigerianization by most expatriates, Nigerians, on the other hand, do not perceive foreigners as competitors, and thus welcome them as colleagues. Especially now that Nigerianization of the Senior Staff is past the 60 per cent mark, with administration almost completely in the hands of nationals except in the Bursary, Nigerians are beginning to feel—quite rightly so—that they run the show, and that the expatriates are simply useful guests. The U.I. Council is now almost entirely Nigerian (17 out of 19), and, in the Senate, in 1969, 64 per cent of the *ex-officio* Professors and Department Heads were still expatriates, but 75 per cent of the elected Lecturers and Senior Lecturers were Nigerians, thereby giving the Nigerians an overall near-parity of 48 per cent under a Nigerian Chairman.

By unwritten convention, ever since the Vice-Chancellor has been a Nigerian, the Deputy Vice-Chancellor has been an expatriate. By a mixture of convention and voting strength, the vast majority of the members of Congregation elected to the Senate have been Nigerians. While expatriates have felt free to stand for election to Senate, there has been consensus that the contingent of elected Senate members was meant at least in part to give greater Senate representation to the Nigerians, and to compensate for the fact that most of the professorships were still held by foreign incumbents.

Until 1969, most of the elected representatives of the Senate to the Council were expatriates, thereby giving the expatriates a small but audible voice on the Council, but in the 1969 elections, two of the resigning expatriates on the Council were replaced by Nigerians. The balance of power thus continues to shift toward the Nigerians, and some of the old-time British staff feel increasingly insecure and uncomfortable in a situation which they no longer dominate; but many of the foreigners are in Nigeria to spend a few interesting years and are delighted to see their Nigerian colleagues shoulder the burden of University administration. The more conservative expatriates complain about the alleged deterioration of standards and resign to take a post in their home country. In a few cases, individual Nigerians and expatriates may engage in a power struggle over a Headship, an appointment or a promotion, but there is seldom anything like a *group* cleavage along lines of nationality. Even in voting for Deanships and other elective offices, there is considerable cross-voting and *ethnicity* is a much better (but by no means exclusive) predictor than nationality or "race."

Senior Staff Club

The closest thing to a racial cleavage on campus concerns the use of the Senior Staff Club, which, on first glance, has an almost South African atmosphere with its black servants and largely white guests. Even though expatriates make much more extensive use of the Club, make up most of its elected officers, and take a much more active interest in Club affairs than their Nigerian colleagues, this situation has nothing to do with racism. The Club has traditionally been an expatriate preserve and still remains so to a large extent, but Nigerians are, of course, free to belong and a good many do. The reasons why many Nigerian members are not active participants in Club affairs are complex, but are unrelated to any desire by the expatriates to exclude them.

First, the very conception of a recreational and social club of this type is much more European than African, and as a cultural product will naturally appeal more to expatriates (including a number of black West Indians who are among the most active Club members, perhaps because they come from a British colonial type of society where the social club is the focus of elite activities). Second, to many expatriates, the Club is the only congenial place to go to outside their own homes, while Nigerians have many more ties off campus. Third, Nigerian homes are generally much more active centers of sociability than those of expatriates. Intervisiting on weekends, for example, is much more common among Nigerians. The more gregarious expatriates tend to prefer the Club to their homes as a place to entertain guests and meet friends. Fourth, the facilities of the Club appeal more to expatriates than Nigerians. Tennis is played by both groups, but the swimming pool is used predominantly by expatriates, if only because many Nigerians cannot swim. The restaurant is relatively expensive (10s 6d per meal), and thus beyond the means of many Nigerians who have on the whole lower salaries and much heavier family responsibilities than the foreigners. As to the bar, it too is patronized primarily by non-Nigerians, to the tune of £ 15,785 worth of sales in 1967–68. Nearly all of the heavy or even regular drinkers on campus are foreigners, and Nigerians tend to be abstemious. Muslims, of course, are supposed to be complete teetotalers, but Christians too drink very moderately, and then mostly beer rather than hard liquor.

Ethnicity

This brings us to that ubiquitous factor in Nigerian affairs, namely ethnicity. The topic is as complex as it is important, and most interpretations of events by participants as well as outside observers suffer from gross oversimplification of the ethnic reality. At the same time, beliefs about the role of ethnicity in Nigeria affect the very nature of the problem, and must therefore be taken into account, though not accepted at face value.

First, although ethnicity intrudes as a relevant factor in a great many kinds of situations, it seldom accounts by itself for most, much less all, of the variance. The common situation is one in which ethnicity allows one to understand and predict events with reasonable accuracy only in combination with two or three other key variables. For example, to explain a key election, ethnicity alone might enable one to predict the *direction* of the vote, and this successful prediction might give one the impression that only ethnicity was significantly involved. But a closer look at who voted for whom will show that perhaps 50 to 60 per cent of the people did not vote as you would have expected them on the basis of ethnicity. On the other hand, if you take religion, faculty, and place of university training into account, you might be able correctly to predict 80 per cent of the individual votes. Of course, even those who *appear* to have voted along ethnic lines might often have been motivated by other factors which fortuitously coincided with ethnicity.

There is one dimension, however, in which ethnicity has a disproportionately salient place among the divisive factors in Nigerian society, namely that of *scale*. Ethnicity is more "macro-divisive" than many other bases of cleavage.[3] Thus, it has farther-reaching consequences for the society at large. The other potential sources of division that would result in cleavages of equal or greater magnitude, namely sex, class and religion, have not become as politically activated in Nigeria. The sexual cleavage is, of course, clear, profound and sharply dichotomous, but it has not become politicized to any great extent, and its significance is largely circumscribed to the sphere of family structure and of occupational specialization. The Nigerian class structure is extremely complex but rapidly changing, and, as yet, amorphous enough to minimize class polarization as a dominant source of conflict. One can only perceive the barest beginnings of a Nigeria-wide class structure with distinct, corporate, conscious class groups. Religion comes much closer to ethnicity as a macro-divisive factor, with easily identifiable communities quite conscious of their differences. But both sectarian and linguistic divisions within each of the religious communities, as well as a spirit of religious syncretism and tolerance in some groups, have generally given religion less political salience than ethnicity in Nigeria. Ethnicity, in short, is the most *salient* of the bases of cleavage that result in the formation of *relatively large antagonistic groups.*

Notwithstanding the great importance of ethnicity, the great analytical pitfall, and one to which both Nigerians and foreigners are all too prone, is to overstate and oversimplify the effect of ethnicity in explaining Nigerian events. Ethnicity is both important and pervasive enough to lend itself to a facile one-factor determinism. It is just as easy and convincing to propose a simplistic but plausible one-factor theory of human behavior based on ethnicity as, say, on economic interest. The temptation to do so in Nigeria is enhanced by extreme ethnic diversity and the as yet relatively fluid and embryonic character of class cleavages. Everything then becomes "tribalism," an epithet the content of which will be modified to suit the needs of the given situation. What makes this abuse of the term "tribalism" even worse is that the label is frequently used both as an analytical tool to explain events and as a political weapon to influence their course.

These remarks bring us to a fundamental distinction between the "objective" and the "subjective" components of ethnicity. The "objective" aspects, i.e., those that are directly observable to an outsider, are the cultural (including, prominently, the linguistic) characteristics of an ethnic group. Allowing for sub-cultural variation and indeed for a wide range of idiosyncratic behavior within an ethnic group, it remains true that the behavior of members of an ethnic group is at least *modally* distinguishable from that of other ethnic groups, and that often the distinctions are quite unambiguous. Perhaps most basic and irreducible of all forms of culture-specific behavior is *speech*. The speech community is that group sharing a "mother tongue," i.e., a medium which allows for the relatively free and easy interchange of the whole intellectual and emotional repertory of that group. Communication in the mother tongue is almost invariably much richer than through the medium of a second language. The "speech barrier" is *not* a figure of speech; it is a fundamental human reality. Man becomes human only through the acquisition of a culture which at the same time allows him to interact meaningfully and predictably with other members of that culture, and impedes such interaction with members of other cultures. Such is the nearly ineluctable "objective" side of ethnicity. Only a few exceptional individuals manage, because of very special life circumstances, to become truly bi-cultural and bi-lingual. The overwhelming majority of mankind are and will remain "ethnics." Ethnicity cannot simply be wished away.

At least as important as the objective aspect of ethnicity is the subjective side of it; that is, the attitudes, opinions, sentiments, stereotypes, and prejudices which members of an ethnic group have about themselves and about other ethnic groups. These ideational products can seldom be directly observed, and in most cases can only be inferred from behavior, such as etiquette, deference patterns and the like. While group membership, and hence the main lines of cleavage, are largely determined by the objective cultural similarities within, and differences between groups, the ideational super-structure of ethnicity is at least partially independent of it, although causation between the two aspects of ethnicity is to some extent reciprocal. Objective ethnic differences underlie the subjective perception of such differences; in turn, subjective perception underlies differential and discriminatory inter-ethnic behavior; and inter-ethnic behavior can itself attenuate or accentuate actual cultural differences between ethnic groups.

THE VICIOUS CIRCLE OF ETHNIC CONFLICT

At U.I. and indeed in Nigeria at large, ethnicity is ubiquitous in both its subjective and objective aspects, and the phenomenon is extraordinarily complex. Not only are there obvious cultural differences between the members of the many ethnic groups represented on campus, but there is a widely accepted popular theory of ethnicity. The vast majority of both Nigerians and expatriates believe that ethnicity is in fact a major determinant and predictor of social behavior, and these expectations become, at least in part, self-fulfilling, thereby "validating" the theory. As most popular theories, this one is a vast oversimplification: it attributes to ethnicity a much greater importance than it has in fact, and underrates the influence of a multiplicity of other factors. By and large, people expect members of ethnic groups other than their own to be "tribalists," i.e., to be biased in favor of their own fellow ethnics and against "strangers" to the almost complete exclusion of universalistic considerations.

The popular theory of tribalism far outstrips the actual incidence of the phenomenon, because, as we have stated, ethnicity is only one of a multiplicity of criteria affecting preferences and dislikes; nevertheless, the very existence of the folk theory enhances the actual relative importance of ethnicity, giving it far greater salience than it would otherwise have. A vicious circle is created wherein the gap between theory and reality tends to be narrowed because the two feed on each other. The operation of this vicious circle in Nigeria throughout the 1960's brought the entire Federation on the brink of collapse and cost at least half a million lives. At University, the consequences were far less disastrous and sanguinary, but quite nefarious all the same.

PARAMETERS OF ETHNIC CONFLICT

First we must define the main parameters of ethnic conflict in the University in terms of what is at stake and who is most directly involved.[4] Unlike in some multi-national states such as Canada, Belgium or India, Nigerian ethnic groups are not primarily fighting against what they perceive as a threat to their continued cultural and linguistic identity, and for what they conceive as a right to cultural distinctiveness and political autonomy based on commonality of culture and language. While common culture and language define ethnic boundaries, they are not at stake in Nigerian ethnic conflicts. The choice of English as the "national" language, whatever liabilities it has in accentuating class differences, is ethnically neutral and largely removes language use from the sphere of politics. No ethnic group attempts or is perceived as attempting to impose its way of life or language on others. Fears center rather on the capture of political power and its spoils, especially in the form of bureaucratic patronage.

In Nigeria, ethnic conflict is first and foremost an elite rather than a mass phenomenon. This point was made by the Nigerian Head of State, General Yakubu Gowon, in unusually strong terms for a ceremonial speech. At his formal address on the occasion of the installation of the new U.I. Chancellor in 1967, Gowon said:

> Unfortunately, our universities instead of playing their proper role have fallen victim of some of the evils which have plagued us in this country. Take tribalism, for instance; it is a matter for regret that the University of Ilosho, made up of eminent scholars, has not been able to set the right example for the whole country by containing the more glaring manifestations of tribal chauvinism. Far too many individuals have tried in this institution to use tribalism as an instrument for attaining personal ends.
>
> If I may take a recent example—the evidence available shows that the attempted secession of the East from the Federation was hatched mainly in the University of Nigeria, with the active assistance of some of the senior staff who were once with you on this campus.
>
> I know that the university community is also called upon to pursue the truth

at all times. The trouble in Nigeria is that most Nigerians tend to see the truth only as it affects themselves or their particular ethnic groups.

Ironically, Gowon was merely echoing the sentiments expressed in a graduation speech the previous year by a man who was himself the target of numerous accusations of tribalism, who was forced to resign a few months later as a result of ethnic conflicts, and later openly espoused the cause of Ibo nationalism and Biafran secession. On June 29, 1966, Nwanneh said:

> It must be said to our shame that the Nigerian intellectual, far from being an influence for national integration, is the greatest exploiter of parochial and clannish sentiment. . . . As you leave us, you are going into a Nigeria torn by tribal strife, a country in which deep suspicions exist between the different sections. You will be no credit to this university if you leave us to join the band of educated advocates of tribal division and strife and worshippers of tribal gods.

Superficially it may seem surprising that the Western-educated class which presumably should be most "detribalized" exhibits the most "tribalism." It may even seem doubly incongruous that a community of scholars trained in a tradition of respect for universalism, objectivity and impartiality should not be above parochialism. In fact, the paradox is only apparent. Since the main stakes of ethnic rivalry are the spoils of political power, and since the structure of privilege is highly pyramidal, it follows that competition becomes fiercest as one approaches the apex. Traditionally, the ethnic divisions were not competitive because the various groups were not incorporated in a single political structure; during the colonial period, while they became incorporated into a single polity, the elements of conflict and competition were minimized by common subordination to the colonial power. With independence, the scramble for the political kingdom was on, and the pre-existing ethnic cleavages constituted the most likely framework for playing the political game. The University, as one of the major arenas of the struggle for political control, was no more exempt than the more ostensibly political sectors of the elite, although academic norms against the naked use of violence served to cloak the conflicts in a certain amount of decorum and gentility.

The logic of "tribalism" in the context of academic competition works roughly as follows: I expect my colleague from the X group to violate the universalistic canons which are supposed to govern his behavior, and to show instead ethnic favoritism. To counteract my rival's attempts to establish his ethnic power bloc, I can resort simultaneously to two equally effective strategies. First, I can accuse my rival of tribalism in the full expectation that the charge will be found convincing enough to non-X's to mobilize an opposition constituency. In some cases, the charge may be justified; in others, it is pure moral blackmail, but the success of the strategy is quite independent of the veracity of the charge. Secondly, I may pursue a strategy of "pre-emptive tribalism"; i.e., I may myself favor fellow ethnics to redress the balance and offset the anticipated effect of my rival's bias. If my behavior is questioned, I can either deny the charge or plead self-defense.

Given this kind of situation of nearly universal expectations and accusations of "tribalism," the phenomenon itself is endemic in the system. It is at best extremely difficult for any person in authority not to respond to pressures for ethnic favoritism and nearly impossible to prove one's impartiality. So pervasive are both the reality and the expectation of tribalism that even foreigners are sucked into the vortex of Nigerian ethnic conflicts. This takes two forms: first, foreigners organize themselves into their own "tribal" cliques; and second, they are perceived as taking sides with one or another of the Nigerian ethnic factions. The final outcome is that ethnicity as a determinant of behavior is no more typical of Nigerians than of expatriates. "Tribalism," not racism, is the great Nigerian disease; it spreads by contagion among Nigerians and non-Nigerians alike.

Let us take the hypothetical case of an English Department Head, who, innocent of the complexity of Nigerian politics, decided that a few years at Ilosho would be a nice change of climate from the billowing smokestacks of Birmingham and the London smog. After a few months at U.I., he has to fill a vacancy for a Lecturership. If he is lucky, there is only one applicant; but, more probably, there are several who meet the minimum qualifications. Unless an expatriate applicant is clearly superior, he will attempt to atone for his country's past colonial guilt by pushing for the appointment of a Nigerian, who, let us say, is a Yoruba. A few weeks later, he has to reprimand a messenger who was sleeping on duty and who, unluckily, happens to be an Ibibio. After one or two more episodes of this nature, his behavior will be interpreted in an ethnic framework, e.g., that he is clearly pro-Yoruba. He may try to disprove that theory by failing to put up a Yoruba Lecturer for promotion, and thereby antagonize all major ethnic groups. In that case, he might withdraw to the bar of the Senior Staff Club, seek solace in the consumption of gin-and-tonics with fellow Englishmen, and become a stereotypical British tribalist. Alternatively, he may be tempted to maintain pleasant relations with at least one of the Nigerian factions, and thus become identified with it and model his behavior according to the very expectations of favoritism that were once unfounded. The point is that, whatever he does, he will not find it possible to stay out of ethnic politics if he is in a position of authority. Nigerians are much in the same

situation, except that their initial freedom of action is perhaps more circumscribed because initial expectations are better defined and more overtly
expressed.

RELATIVITY OF ETHNICITY

So far we have assumed that ethnic group membership is easily definable
and unambiguous. The actual situation is far more complex because there are
several levels of ethnicity which become activated in different circumstances,
and are meaningful to different people in different ways. In other words,
the Nigerian population is not clearly divided into a finite number of
distinguishable and mutually exclusive ethnic groups, but rather fragmented
into a multiplicity of groups and sub-groups that are not always mutually
exclusive, and that often have fluid boundaries between them. These groups
form ever shifting coalitions, a factor which greatly contributes to making
the Nigerian political game bewildering not only to naive outsiders but to
Nigerians themselves.

The same person may, and very often will be perceived by others and
define himself according to different ethnic labels depending on the issue
at stake, the political alignment of other groups, and the level of ethnicity
which seems most relevant in a given context. Thus, in the Nwanneh-
Babalola crisis, the issue was defined as a Yoruba-Ibo one, or even Yoruba-
non-Yoruba polarization because one of the contenders was Ibo and the
other Yoruba. Now that the Yoruba by themselves constitute roughly 75
per cent of the Nigerian staff, the main Yoruba sub-groups have become
much more significant units of ethnicity than before, and the category
"Yoruba" has lost some of its political meaning. Within the Yoruba, a
broad distinction is often made between the "Yoruba proper," i.e., the region
of the old Oyo empire, versus the "fringe" Yoruba. More often, finer distinctions between a dozen or more dialectical zones are made, e.g., the
Ondo, Ekiti, Ijebu, Egba, Owo, Egbado, Oyo and so on. At a lower level,
people often align themselves according to local cities which often correspond
to traditional city-states, e.g., Iwo, Ede, Abeokuta, Oshogbo, Ila, Ilesha,
Ilorin and so on. The level of Yoruba ethnicity or sub-ethnicity which
becomes activated is often a function of the degree of "ethnic distance"
between the contestants in a political crisis, with loose and ever-shifting
coalitions of sub-groups polarizing for the duration of a given issue around
the two main protagonists.

Often it is by no means clear whether a given group is an autonomous
ethnic entity or a sub-group of a larger one, and the definition of the
situation will often depend on whether one speaks to an insider or an outsider: e.g., do the Itsekiri belong to the Yoruba nation or is their dialect

sufficiently different to justify treating them as an altogether separate group? Are the Efik and the Ibibio two distinct ethnic groups or merely sub-groups? Even the criteria used to settle this kind of argument vary widely: they may be based on linguistic affinity, historical origin myths, or common incorporation in a now defunct traditional empire. Thus the Bini, for example, will sometimes align themselves with other Mid-Westerners against the Yoruba, and plead minority status, even though within the Mid-West they are a plurality, and on campus they are the second largest major group. But when political expediency calls for an alliance with the Yoruba, or with one of the Yoruba factions, this can easily be justified by invoking the origin of the Benin monarchy in the sacred Yoruba town of Ile Ife, or the more recent political ties between the Benin and Lagos Oba (Kings).

A further complication making for unclarity of ethnic cleavages is that in-group and out-group definitions often do not coincide. Generally, the minute differentiations made by in-group members are not meaningful to outsiders. The latter will use broad categories such as "Hausa" to mean any Northern Muslim, or "mid-Westerner," which to people from these areas have little if any meaning or may even be regarded as downright false. Thus an Efik might resent being lumped together with the Ibibio, just as a Scotsman's vehement protest that he is not an Englishman will elicit a mixture of amusement and bewilderment among the Ijaw.

Finally, it should be noted that there are many individuals who are of mixed ethnic parentage or who have become so "detribalized" that they defy any attempt to pigeonhole them. For examples, a senior Bini administrator is the son-in-law of the traditional ruler of a Yoruba city, and is sometimes regarded as a Yoruba by adoption. Among the Yoruba elite, there are many families who in previous generations had migrated, voluntarily or involuntarily, to Brazil, Sierra Leone or Ghana, and who in the process have lost any clear ties with a local Yoruba town, and thus have a kind of special status of Yoruba cosmopolites. Some of these Yoruba have married non-Yoruba wives and have become English-speaking at home.

In short, the Nigerian ethnic kaleidoscope allows for a nearly infinite number of combinations depending on the expediency of the concrete political situation. Having defined the meaning of ethnicity in Nigeria and at University, we must turn now to a description of ethnic attitudes and ethnic relations as they affect concrete situations.

One of the most pervasive characteristics of ethnic attitudes is mistrust. A common assumption about social behavior in Nigeria is that the conduct of others is primarily motivated by the ruthless pursuit of self-interest. It is generally expected that others will "cheat" one, unless they belong to a circle of close associates to whom norms of trust and reciprocity apply. Dishonesty is the normal expectation, and cynicism is a widespread philosophy, particularly among students and Senior Staff. Corruption, nepotism, and tribalism are assumed to be even more widespread than they are in actual practice.

In this atmosphere of cynicism, the "circle of trust" is limited to kinsmen and a few other intimates, and seldom extends beyond the boundaries of the ethnic group or even sub-group. People from other ethnic groups are, almost by definition, strangers, barring a few friendships or old school ties. And strangers, by definition, are not to be trusted. The malevolent interpretation cast on the use by others of a language not understood by one is symptomatic of this pervasive climate of mistrust. There is a strong norm among students, for example, to use English in a group composed of more than one ethnic group, and any deviation from that norm (beyond a few words of greetings, or an occasional colloquialism) is interpreted by the person left out of the conversation as a deliberate slight at best, or possibly even a sinister plot. Beyond the use of one's mother tongue, there exists a quasi-paranoid mistrust between ethnic groups. In periods of crisis, for instance, rumors of such and such an ethnic group holding secret nightly meetings to plot against one's own group circulate widely; indeed ethnic caucusing is part of the political game and thus provides some factual basis for these fears, but the scope and significance of the allegations and rumors frequently exceed reality.[5]

ETHNIC HIERARCHY

Beyond generalized suspicion, ethnic groups have stereotyped views of each other, and stand in a semi-hierarchical relationship to each other. There is no simple clear-cut rank order of ethnic groups so that each group could be assigned a definite position in relation to others. Nevertheless, the more "advanced" groups view themselves as at the top of a prestige order, and measure other ethnic groups by degree of "advancement" or "backwardness." This scale is probably not consensually valid, but on campus it broadly represents the views of the Southern ethnic groups which alone are significantly represented at the University. The underlying basis of this ethnic hierarchy is twofold: first, the relative complexity and differentiation of the traditional societies, with the stratified, urbanized and politically centralized ones ranking higher than the unstratified, "acephalous" societies; and second, the degree of "modernism" as measured by amount of Western education, consumption of imported manufactured goods, architecture of the cities, representation in the bureaucracy and the modern sector of the economy, and, generally, adoption of the material and intellectual products of a mechanized, industrial society.

According to that double scale of evaluation, the "naked pagans" of the Middle Belt rank lowest on both scores and are generally regarded by educated Southern Nigerians with very much the same kind of moralistic depreciation as one associates with the old-style European missionary outlook. They are viewed as backward, primitive savages living in a state of degradation unworthy of the human condition, as people who "cover the cold with their hands," and are considered a national embarrassment. Students and intellectuals, for example, are very irritated at the interest of expatriate tourists in these peoples, and resent the showing of photographs of persons in a state of near nudity. The moralistic missionary attitude to nudity as a symbol of both depravity and primitiveness has been widely accepted by educated Nigerians who often make remarks about their compatriots, which in the mouth of an expatriate, would be interpreted as the most blatant expression of Victorian racism and ethnocentric moralism.

Northern Muslim groups fall in the middle of the ethnic hierarchy as viewed by Southerners. Northern Muslims rank higher than "pagans" because they are conceded a distinguished indigenous urban civilization, but lower than Southerners because they are viewed as resistant to change, uneducated (in the Western sense), and unmodern. Many Southerners regard the North as a stagnant, feudal society, and a millstone around the neck of Nigerian economic and educational development.

Among the Southern groups themselves, further invidious distinctions are made on the same two bases of degree of modernism and of "traditional greatness." Thus, the Yoruba and the Bini regard themselves as superior to stateless, non-urban groups like the Ibo and Ibibio. The Yoruba and Bini consider themselves heirs to great indigenous urban civilizations, powerful states, distinguished art traditions that are accorded the accolade of "great art" in the world's museums, and civilizations which, unlike those of the Sudan, owed almost nothing to non-African sources. The Yoruba often claim superiority over the Bini because of the tradition which put the origin of the Benin monarchy in the sacred Yoruba city of the Ife, the navel of the Universe where Oduduwa created the earth and through his sixteen sons gave birth to mankind.[6] Finer distinctions are made between sub-groups of the same traditional nation. Thus among the Yoruba, the coastal Ijebu and Egba regard themselves as more educated and modern than the Northern and North Eastern groups such as the Ekiti, Igbomina and Yagba who are regarded as "bush." The same prejudice exists among Ibo as between Onitsha and Afikpo, for example. On the other hand, the Yoruba from Oyo and Ile Ife claim traditional superiority over the Southern sub-groups as subjects of the spiritually pre-eminent Oni (King) of Ile Ife and the powerful Alafin (King) of Oyo, the politically dominant Yoruba state in the 17th, 18th and 19th centuries. Among Senior Staff and students at University, "modern" criteria, and especially amount of Western education, are more important as criteria of ethnic hierarchization than the traditionally based claims, but among Junior Staff the latter are also significant. The Yoruba in particular are very proud of their culture and very historically oriented.

ETHNIC STEREOTYPES

In addition to notions of relative rank, ethnic attitudes are also colored by more specific stereotypes which groups and sub-groups have of each other. Thus, the Hausa are widely regarded as astute traders in the traditional sector, but unwilling to modernize and religiously intolerant, not to say fanatical. The Ibo, on the other hand, are regarded as enterprising, agressive if not downright "pushy," adaptive, innovative, willing to start in a lowly job such as domestic service if they see in it a way of improving their status, but also as clever in a deceitful way, clannish, tribalistic, and greedy for both power and wealth. The Ijaw who live in the aquatic environment of the Niger Delta regard the Ibo as dirty people who are water-shy and do not bathe. "Cold water boils them," the Ijaw say of the Ibo. Onitsha, the largest market city in Iboland, is widely regarded as the most dishonest place in the Federation. Cannibalism is also a frequent charge against the Ibo. The Yoruba are thought to be nationalistic or even chauvinistic and arrogant about their own culture, yet badly divided among themselves, politically sophisticated but ruthless, urban but effete, unwilling to fight as soldiers (despite chronic warfare among the 19th-century Yoruba states), and educated and dynamic, yet also traditionalist. These stereotypes are sometimes partly accepted by the group in question and some of them do, of course, have "grains of truth." [7]

Stereotypes also exist between ethnic sub-groups. Thus, for example, the Ijebu Yoruba, who are notoriously successful entrepreneurs, especially as urban landlords in other Yoruba cities, are ascribed much the same qualities as the Ibo: aggressiveness, cleverness, adaptability, cunning, and deceit, plus the added trait of lavish displays of wealth on ceremonial occasions. The Yoruba nickname for a counterfeit coin, for example, is "Ijebu," in reference both to alleged cunning of the group and the alleged geographical origin of the counterfeiters. [8]

As might be expected from these attitudes of mutual suspicions, ethnicity is an important determinant of interaction, but in a much more complicated way than is generally assumed. Ethnic groups are not, by any means, mutually hostile armed camps ready to jump at each other's throats. For example, there does not exist a generalized Ibophobia (similar to, say, Nazi anti-Semitism) in Nigeria, as many non-Nigerians have been misled by war propaganda to believe. A major reason why this is not the case is the extreme fluidity and relativity of ethnicity in Nigeria as we have already mentioned.

Spheres of Ethnic Interaction

One must distinguish two general spheres of interaction. In the public sphere, i.e., on the job, and at formal, protocolar, official or semi-official functions such as Graduation ceremonies, receptions at the Vice-Chancellor, hall parties, dances, sport events and the like, there is seemingly free and easy interaction across ethnic lines, unless a political crisis makes for ethnic polarization even at the official level. The common pattern then is for the party that sees itself as aggrieved by those in power to withdraw from such events altogether. One of the games of the politically conscious among the Senior Staff is to look around for who absents himself from official parties, and thereby confirm or invalidate hypotheses about current political alignments.

Public behavior is, of course, laden with symbolic significance, especially ceremonial public behavior which, to the extent that it is "beyond the call of duty," is all the more indicative of one's stance. The official norm at University being against "tribalism," public events are thus important occasions to demonstrate, often very self-consciously, that one is above petty ethnic rivalries. The official hosts such as the Chancellor or Vice-Chancellor and their wives make deliberate attempts to circulate among all groups, and so do many of the guests. In fact at such occasions groups tend to form much more on the basis of departmental or faculty affiliation than ethnicity. To the extent that these functions are official or semi-official, they are perceived as a sociable extension of the job situation, which is of course determined largely by department and faculty affiliation. Among students, there is perhaps a greater tendency for ethnic groupings at such events, but hall of residence and subjects of study are at least as important as criteria of aggregation at formal events. The norm is clearly that it is bad behavior to exhibit tribalism at such events, one of the main purposes of which is precisely to reaffirm the solidarity of the University as a community which transcends ethnicity.

Official anti-ethnicity policy at University is most clearly formulated in respect to students. From the start, there has been a policy to prevent the halls of residence from becoming ethnically segregated, and ethnic balance remains an important factor in assigning students to halls. (Students have little choice in the matter, though they may request room reassignment.) During the Civil War, of course, when Yoruba students constituted some three-fourths of the total, this policy lost much of its meaning. Student elections are closely supervised by the Senior Assistant Registrar for Students who is responsible for enforcing the University policy of banning ethnic campaigning. Explicitly ethnic student associations are forbidden, though the ones based on locality, which are in fact sub-ethnic, are not. A number of exclusive student associations based on origin in one of the "divisions" of the former regions flourish on campus. E.g., a large poster announcing a gathering read as follows: "Oyo Divisional Union of Students, Annual Get-Together Party, Sat. March 18. All sons and daughters of Oyo Division cordially invited. Admission: Strictly by invitation." That these unions are in fact ethnic in nature is shown by the fact that current place of parental residence or even of one's birth is not the criterion of membership, but rather ancestral origin.

In the private sphere of leisure and sociability, there is a distinct preference for interaction with fellow ethnics, a tendency which is fully as pronounced among expatriates as among Nigerians. Among Junior Staff, students, and Senior Staff alike, the campus consists of vast numbers of small cliques of friends drawn mostly, though not exclusively, on the basis of ethnicity. Inter-visiting, commensality and other forms of intimate association largely take place between groups of friends belonging not only to the same ethnic group, but frequently to the same locality as well, though friendships made at secondary school sometimes transcend these lines. The actual unit of social intimacy is thus frequently much smaller than ethnicity, especially for the larger groups that are widely represented on campus. The smaller ethnic or nationality groups like Poles, Czechs, Indians, West Indians among expatriates, or Idoma, Gwari, or Igala among Nigerians, who may be represented by only half-a-dozen individuals, or three or four families on campus, tend to be more closely knit than the large groups, even though they may come from relatively distant areas of their home territory.

Among the Yoruba, Bini, Ibo, English and Americans, on the other hand, circles of intimates are typically based, beyond ethnicity, on a number of further criteria. The Americans on campus are split between whites and blacks as already mentioned, but also according to whether they belong to the Ford Foundation or Rockefeller Foundation staff, each of these constituting a close interacting clique. Among the British, university ties are often important; for example, there has been a Cambridge group which played an important role in the early development of U.I. Among the Yoruba, home town is the key factor. Friendship circles among Yoruba are also formed on the basis of having gone to the same secondary school, but as every Yoruba town of any size has at least one such school, these ties overlap greatly with locality ties. At the other extreme, among the smallest groups, there may even be regroupings of several distinct but related ethnic groups. For example, the Poles, Czechs and Slovaks during the period of my field work met regularly at the house of a senior Polish professor, as an informal Ilosho pan-Slavic union.[9]

Cultural Barriers

Language, as already noted, is one of the most important barriers to inter-ethnic communication. This is especially true among the Subordinate Staff where fluency in English is frequently insufficient to allow for the transmission of complex thoughts across ethnic lines. Language barriers are, of course, less important among Senior Staff and students where fluency in English is a common denominator; but, nevertheless, the pleasure and satisfaction of being able to speak one's mother tongue to communicate feelings and experiences which cannot as readily be transmitted through a second language are often sufficient incentives for preferential ethnic association. Though fluent in English, educated Nigerians are far from being fully Anglicized in their culture. With few exceptions, they remain culturally very un-European, and the English language, however adequate as a medium of intellectual communication, operates, as it were, in a cultural semi-vacuum. Except for Nigerians who have spent years in Europe or America, Western culture is something learned through books or marginally experienced in contact with expatriates, but not a living reality like their own culture. Despite many years spent in primary and secondary schools where they were often punished and reprimanded for speaking their own language instead of English, most Nigerians continue to prefer their mother tongue with intimates, and conversely find it difficult to become intimate with someone whose first language they do not share.

Other aspects of culture also act as powerful barriers to inter-ethnic association. Value systems may be so different as to strain relationships; norms of reciprocity, concepts of privacy, standards of sexual behavior are often so much at variance as to maximize the probability of inter-ethnic friction. Even more touchy are norms of honesty and expectations of generosity and reimbursement of loans. The dictum that strangers (i.e., in the first instance, non-fellow ethnics) cannot be trusted expresses both *bona fide* differences in norms prevailing between groups, but also frequently norms that standards of honesty and solidarity which apply within the in-group do not extend beyond it. Thus, the same person who may scrupulously reimburse a loan from fellow townsmen will disappear without a trace to avoid repaying a loan from, say, an expatriate. In one case, the interaction is regulated by norms of reciprocity; in the other it is based on a predatory confidence game. The main norm of interaction between ethnic groups, or indeed persons beyond the sphere of kinsmen and intimates, is protective mistrust.

Another seemingly trivial but nevertheless significant barrier to inter-ethnic association is cuisine. Diet and style of cooking vary enormously, and food constitutes a deeply symbolic and internalized part of every culture, as shown by its universal role in religious and social ritual. On campus, the importance of food manifests itself, among other things, in the frequency of student complaints and even organized protest over their diet in the halls. Although there are underlying similarities in staple foods and even styles of cooking between the various Southern Nigerian ethnic groups who constitute the vast majority of students, there is sufficient diversity to make it extremely difficult to cook to everybody's taste, not to mention the problems of maintaining the quality of food preparation under conditions of mass production. The biggest "food barrier" exists, of course, between Nigerians and expatriates. Southern Nigerian cuisine is much spicier, especially in the use of pepper, than European or North American cooking, and most staples of the Nigerian diet are unknown in non-tropical countries. The sight of a watery-eyed Englishman or American trying to be polite while bravely downing a Yoruba stew cooked in a rich red pepper sauce is a highly amusing spectacle for many Nigerians. Yams, cassava, kola nuts (a bitter and astringent nut which has become the symbol of hospitality in traditional cultures of West Africa, and which cannot politely be refused), mangoes, passion fruit, paw-paws, not to mention certain animal delicacies such as bush rats and enormous snails, are all strange if not repulsive to the untrained European palate.

To mitigate the effect of the "food barrier" at all formal University functions where expatriates constitute a substantial proportion of the guests, both indigenous and some local approximation of "English" food are served, and even Nigerian dishes are often in "watered-down" form. Indeed, in the Nigerian elite, the diet has become strongly Europeanized, even to the extent of spending much money to buy expensive imported tins, though unlike many expatriates who never touch local staples, Nigerian Senior Staff members typically eat a mixed diet.[10]

INTERMARRIAGE

Interestingly, the ethnic barrier in the field of sexual relations and even marriage is not very strong. In the words of an informant, "the bed is the great equalizer." Pre- or extra-marital affairs between students, or between male students and town girls, or between female students and Senior Staff men frequently cut across ethnic lines, although male students sometimes express hostility against women students from their ethnic group dating outsiders.

Even intermarriage is not subjected to powerful taboos; and, while inter-ethnic marriages are much less common than one would expect by chance alone, they are by no means exceptional, nor are they frowned upon, at least not in academic circles. In other words, ethnic groups tend to be statistically endogamous, but there is no prescriptive rule of ethnic endogamy as would be found in a caste system. Most traditional African systems of marriage are based on explicit prescriptive rules of lineage and class exogamy, but seldom are there any rules of prescriptive endogamy. Insofar as endogamy is a statistical tendency, ethnicity is only one of several operative principles, along with religion and social status. Among Western-educated Nigerians, there is a strong tendency for spouses to have a not-too-disparate level of formal schooling, even though husbands tend to prefer wives who are slightly less educated than themselves. Among many students and Senior Staff, educational endogamy would be viewed as more important than common ethnicity, even though their choice might be viewed critically by less educated relatives. Among both Christians and Muslims, religious endogamy is in theory more important than the ethnic factor, although religious endogamy is also far from absolute or prescriptive since both faiths welcome conversions.

In any case, the tendency toward ethnic endogamy operates in competition with class and religious endogamy, and there is no concensus about the order of importance between these principles. Traditionalists might tend to rank ethnicity first, while the educated elite would tend to give more weight to social status, and very devout Christians and Muslims might regard religion as most important. In the end, ethnic endogamy frequently loses out to the other two main factors, and this entails no strong ostracism. A number of prominent members of the University are either married to persons of other groups or are themselves of mixed ethnic parentage, and the situation is common enough not to attract a large amount of attention or adverse comment. At the national level, one of the war heroes, Brigadier Adekunle, is of mixed parentage; and the inter-ethnic marriage of the Head of State, General Gowon, attracted nothing but favorable comments.

The Politics of Ethnicity

In last analysis, the prime significance of ethnicity, and certainly its more disruptive consequences, lie in the political arena. In any given conflict situation involving competition over scarce resources, the probability of ethnic polarization is high, even though ethnicity seldom provides an anywhere near complete explanation of the conflict. At the University, as indeed in the country at large, several of the most severe crises have been, at least in part, ethnic conflicts, or they have become so defined even when they did not begin as such.

Two important areas of decision-making are relatively free of open imputations of "tribalism," namely the grading of examinations and the admission of students. The latter process is regulated by an elaborate point system based on results obtained in the West African School Certificate or equivalent secondary school examinations. These examinations, under the control of an international commission, have been the object of some scandals because of "leaks" in the question papers, but tribalism has not been the issue there. Within U.I., the routine part of admission procedures and examination is administered in two special offices of the Registry, and although these offices and their Assistant Registrars have been under attack for making clerical errors, their good faith has not been openly questioned, even during the War when one of these offices was headed by an Ibo. These offices have no discretionary or decision-making powers; their job is purely to process applications, distribute and collect examination papers, keep student records, and the like.

The final decision-making power for both admissions and examinations lies entirely within the jurisdiction of Senate which jealously guards its prerogatives. The bulk of the actual decision-making takes place, however, at the departmental level for examinations, and at the faculty level for admissions. Any departure from the elaborate established procedures, or any petition for "special cases" is debated at length by the various faculties and further scrutinized in Senate. Examinations are a collective process involving the entire department staff and an external examiner from another university as well. This applies to every step of the process from the drafting of questions to the final mark, each question being read by at least two and often three teachers. The external examiners, who in most cases still come from foreign countries, especially Britain, have the final word in cases of disagreements, and the marking of examinations is done "blindly," each student being assigned a number not known to the teachers.

These rigorous safeguards for impartiality have thus been largely successful in minimizing allegations of favoritism, nepotism and "tribalism." Newspapers occasionally attack the University for "irregularities" in admissions and hint at favoritism or tribalism, but insofar as these irregularities are established they are generally attributable to clerical errors in the Registry which, like most university administrations, operates well below optimum efficiency. Within departments, there are sometimes internal conflicts, especially on the granting of "upper-seconds," as this is the level of performance which normally qualifies one for post-graduate work and eventual entry into the academic profession; but, even when allegations of ethnic partiality are made between teachers in the same department, these allegations are kept at that level and seldom transpire at Faculty Board or Senate meetings.

Almost any other aspect of University life is rife with accusations and counter-accusations of "tribalism," the major arenas of conflict centering around appointments and promotions, especially of Senior Staff; disciplinary actions against students and Junior Staff; elections at all levels (U.I. Workers' Union, Student Union, elective academic positions); internal struggles for power between individual members of the University; and, of course, campus repercussions of ethnic conflicts in Nigeria at large or in the Western State.

Appointments and promotions are perhaps the most chronic bases of ethnic conflicts. Decisions of this nature are made by the relevant committees at frequent intervals during the academic year; and the process of job-seeking and status enhancement is, of course, continuous and fiercely competitive, given the extreme scarcity of posts in relation to at least minimally and formally qualified applicants, and the steeply hierarchical nature of the University. From the lowliest to the most exalted positions, there are several times as many applicants who possess the minimum paper qualifications than there are positions available; furthermore, the ladder narrows rapidly with every step.

The modalities of the process vary somewhat depending on the level of appointment. For Junior Staff, the office of the Assistant Registrar for Establishments and Labour processes applications; recommendations for appointments and promotions are made by the Intermediate and Subordinate Staff Sub-Committee of the Finance and General Purposes Committee of Council, and these recommendations are formally approved by Council. Competition for jobs in terms of ratio of qualified applicants to jobs is most intense in the unskilled and semi-skilled categories, which in effect means that such jobs are most frequently allocated by patronage according to the system of patron-client ties already described. The key role of department heads in this recruitment process is formally recognized by the fact that each Faculty Board nominates one of its academic department heads to sit on that sub-committee; collectively these heads make up nearly half of the sub-committee, even though its jurisdiction is entirely non-academic.

The head of the hiring department can often exert sufficient influence in the job interview to get his way, and as these jobs do not appreciably affect the structure of the University, junior appointments seldom generate much controversy, except among the Junior Staff of the relevant department and, of course, among the unsuccessful candidates.

The more common form of particularism in the allocation of such jobs is frequently based on kinship, locality or obligation networks between patrons and clients rather than ethnicity as such; but as these criteria overlap in the majority of cases with ethnicity, outsiders tend to view the process as an expression of "tribalism." Here again we observe the tendency by persons not directly involved to jump to the simple interpretation of "tribalism" when the motivations involved are in fact much more complex.

Appointments and promotions of Senior non-teaching Staff are handled by the Appointments Committee for Administrative and Technical Officers and Technicians, a committee of Council. As this is a largely non-academic committee, it is outside the mainstream of University politics. During the period of field work, there were allegations of tribalism in the promotion of a senior administrator, but that case was the aftermath of a long-standing conflict which was linked with the Babalola controversy.

More than any others, promotions and appointments of the teaching staff constitute one of the main centers of political conflict at University. Both within and outside U.I., notably in the press, accusations of tribalism are rampant, and candidates and decisions are almost invariably evaluated at least in part in terms of ethnicity. These decisions are ultimately confirmed by the Council which does not, however, challenge the recommendations of the Senate. Within the Senate itself, appointments and promotions are seldom debated, the very touchiness of the issue precluding open discussion in a body of 100-odd members. The effective decisions are made in the powerful Appointments and Promotions Committee (A.P.C.) of Senate which presents its recommendations for virtually routine endorsement by the parent body. Many of the ethnic conflicts revolve, thus, around the A.P.C. and its members, prominent among whom is the Vice-Chancellor who is also ex-officio chairman of the A.P.C. Under Nwanneh, although accusations of tribalism against him were common, open ethnic clashes within A.P.C. were kept in check by the fact that Nwanneh was powerful enough to impose his will on the Committee, and astute enough to play a game of ethnic balance whereby on key appointments to professorships and department headships he typically paired off his favorite Ibo candidate with a Yoruba and got A.P.C. to approve both. (He did this, for example, in History and in Agriculture.)

During the Akinode era, the situation changed drastically. The sudden departure of most Ibo and some expatriates during the war made it imperative to replace the vacancies quickly, and, in the nature of the case, the great majority of qualified applicants were, by default, Yoruba. Inevitably, Akinode was accused, like Nwanneh, of tribalism. Many of the remaining expatriates were strongly anti-Yoruba from the start, and saw Akinode as following a systematic policy of Yorubaizing the University as quickly as possible to make the most of the war-time opportunity to fill vacancies. Several interrelated crises developed during 1969 over appointments and promotions, as well as over one of the deanships and several department headships. What to most non-Yoruba on the Senior Staff looked like a clear pattern of ethnic favoritism on Akinode's part involved, in fact, a far more complicated set of issues in which Akinode encountered bitter opposition from several prominent Yoruba professors and department heads locked in Byzantine factionalism bearing no clear relationship to ethnicity or even locality.

Akinode did not have sufficient support to impose his will on the A.P.C. as Nwanneh had done before, and the A.P.C. itself became the theater of open conflicts, with complex plays of influence brought to bear on A.P.C. members by contending candidates and factions. The procedures of the Committee were questioned more than ever before, and allegations of procedural irregularities and unfairness of outside referees proliferated, as was indeed inevitable in a system of rules so complex and dilatory that unless violations occurred no appointments could ever be made.

Several related issues which initially had little to do with ethnicity became ethnicized in the heat of the power plays. Underlying several of these was the feeling shared by Akinode and many other Yoruba that some old-time British heads of department were blocking the appointment and promotion of Nigerians. They felt this obstructionism resulted from favoring fellow Britons (sometimes from the same home university as themselves), from adhering to antiquated criteria of seniority and achievement that had been discarded in the process of accelerated promotions initiated during the Nwanneh era, or from exerting undue influence on British friends who were called upon to act as supposedly impartial referees for Nigerian candidates by the Inter-University Council (I.U.C.) in London. The I.U.C. in particular was widely resented as a neo-colonial institution, and, indeed several letters by British referees displayed a very irritating tone of condescension, suggesting, for example, that a candidate would be good enough for an African university, or that so-and-so was among the best *African* students they had ever had. The Faculties of Science and Medicine in particular were regarded as strongholds of reaction.

When Akinode and his supporters launched an attack on some department heads by trying to force the promotion of their junior colleagues over their opposition, enemies of Akinode accused him of tribalism and nepotism, as some of the persons involved had ties of locality and political loyalty to him, and as some expatriates were felt to be equally if not more worthy of promotion. In the end, one of the main crises was solved by promoting both the Yoruba and the expatriate candidates, and by the resignation of the expatriate department head who was obstructing both promotions. This resignation provoked press attacks against Akinode and was also queried in the Council, a relatively rare occurrence.

The anti-Akinode faction also accused Akinode of exercising with ethnic partiality his discretionary power to rotate or not to rotate the full professors of a department into the headship. It was felt that Akinode applied the rotation rule when the old head was a non-Yoruba and the other professor a Yoruba, but that in the reverse case, he found rationalizations for not rotating the headship. In one such department, internal factionalism split the Yoruba themselves, a common situation, and Akinode by not rotating an expatriate professor into the headship occupied by a Yoruba earned the bitter enmity or another Yoruba, who, as Western State Commissioner for Education, lost no opportunity to attack Akinode on the issue of the International School as we saw earlier.

Linked with these other issues was the question of one of the Deanships. The incumbent Dean, a West Indian of long standing at Ilosho, had already resigned from U.I. to accept the Vice-Chancellorship of a South American university. He decided, however, to resign from his Deanship before the end of the academic year. A complicated wrangle over whether and how he had resigned from his Deanship ensued between him, Akinode and the entire faculty in question. Akinode was accused by that faculty of misrepresenting the facts of the case, and of attempting to interfere with that faculty's procedure for electing a new Dean for fear that one of his enemies, a very prominent, powerful and senior Yoruba, would get elected. In the end, Akinode alienated the vast majority of that faculty, Yoruba and expatriates alike. Once more, the simple theory of ethnic alignment did not hold, although many non-Yoruba looked at the case as part of Akinode's master plot for a Yoruba takeover of the University, because the candidate for the deanship allegedly supported by Akinode was also a Yoruba. The complicated issue came up for a full-scale Senate debate at which Akinode, who found it better to absent himself as Chairman, was attacked in more or less veiled terms by most members of the faculty concerned, including all but one of the Yoruba, and indeed by several prominent Yoruba in other faculties. The fundamental issue in the minds of many members of the Senate was faculty autonomy rather than ethnicity in this instance.

All these cases point out the extreme complexity of ethnicity at U.I., and the differential perception of its effects, depending on one's position in the system. The Akinode administration was perceived by most expatriates and non-Yoruba as following a policy of capture of the University by the Yoruba and for the Yoruba. In fact, the Yoruba were split into at least four or five major factions, each led by a powerful figure, and all in varying degrees of opposition to the Vice-Chancellor, albeit on different issues and for different reasons, many of them quite unrelated to ethnicity. That the net result was indeed the appointment and promotion of several Yoruba in key positions, and the resignation of a number of senior expatriates was more the fortuitous consequence of the Civil War and the vacancies it left in the ranks of the teaching staff than of any master plan of Yorubaization, although, no doubt, the latter motivation was not altogether absent in some instances.

The most severe ethnic conflicts within the University have been unleashed by disciplinary actions, especially suspensions of administrative personnel. The power struggle between Nwanneh and Babalola has already been described. It just happened that Nwanneh was Ibo and Babalola Yoruba, but the dispute was a personal one complicated by clashing political loyalties, allegations of incompetence, and different conceptions of the functions of their respective offices. Support for Babalola among many Yoruba was at best lukewarm to start with, and did not much improve even after ethnic polarization had taken place. As time went on, however, and as the political crisis in Nigeria went from bad to worse, the University was increasingly split along ethnic lines, most Ibo and expatriates siding with Nwanneh, and most Yoruba, however reluctantly, with Babalola.

ETHNICITY IN THE WORKERS' UNION

The precipitating incident of the suspension of an Intermediate Staff member mobilized the U.I.W.U. against Babalola. The Junior Workers initially responded on the basis of class solidarity, demanding the suspension of the Registrar as responsible representative of the University authorities. It happened, however, that the worker in question was non-Yoruba, and that both the Assistant Registrar above him and the Registrar were Yoruba. Quickly, therefore, the situation became reinterpreted in ethnic terms. The disciplinary action was part of a Yoruba plot, thought the non-Yoruba. The Yoruba junior workers on the other hand, became for the most part convinced that they were being manipulated by the Union leadership to take action against their own ethnic interests. In a matter of days, a profound ethnic rift split the U.I.W.U. The non-Yoruba workers proceeded with a mass strike and demonstration in May 1966, on the day of a Council meeting, demanding the dismissal of the Registrar, and thus reinforced Nwanneh's stance in recommending and obtaining Babalola's suspension at the Council meeting. The Yoruba junior workers refused for the most part to join in a demonstration which they saw as supporting Nwanneh against the Yoruba. Violent clashes between the ethnic factions of the U.I.W.U. occurred, and a prominent Yoruba Intermediate Staff member was seriously beaten and injured and had to be hospitalized.

The rift lasted for several months, with two rival Union executives claiming legitimacy. In part as a result of the mediating skill of the Union's Patron who, although a Yoruba, is married to an expatriate and is himself of Sierra Leonean origin, and is thus widely regarded as above ethnic politics, some of the U.I.W.U. membership realized that they were destroying themselves as a bargaining body, and that their effectiveness was contingent on their maintaining class rather than ethnic solidarity. A caretaker committee with equal representation from both factions was established, and the Union limped along, but three years later, the wounds were still unhealed. In 1968–69, there was a steady trickle of Yoruba resignations from the Union, and the Yoruba membership generally viewed the Union executive as dominated by Mid-Westerners and unrepresentative.

Finally, in May, 1969, Union elections were held, the first ones since the 1966 crisis, and ethnic suspicions were still so prevalent that a supervisory committee of five Senior Staff persons under the chairmanship of the Union's Patron was set up to insure the fairness of the exercise. The election was contested along both ethnic and departmental lines, with the more militant and better organized catering staff of the student halls of residence dominating the field. Because few Yoruba are willing to hold jobs as domestic servants, the catering staff consists predominantly of Mid-Westerners and Easterners. A Mid-Westerner won the presidency, narrowly defeating his Yoruba opponent. At this point many Yoruba left Congregation Hall where the elections were being conducted, and left the field open for the non-Yoruba drawn disproportionately from the catering staff of student halls. The well-organized caterers won most positions in the Union executive, a result which will almost certainly fail to satisfy the Yoruba who constitute an over-all majority of the Junior Staff.

Indirectly linked with the Babalola crisis was a disciplinary action taken by G. Hickerson as Acting Vice-Chancellor against a Yoruba accountant in the Bursary. That department was the last major administrative unit to be headed by an expatriate, a fact which did not prevent its being in a state of disarray. A British accountant was brought in as a consultant under Rockefeller Foundation auspices to reorganize the Bursary and improve the accounting system, apparently without much success. A conflict developed over whether or not that consultant had any executive authority over the Bursar's subordinates. The matter seems to have been complicated by lack of tact. The Yoruba accountant accused the consultant of having a "colonial attitude," and another expatriate superior of not treating "even his house boy in this manner . . . humiliating orders may not be obeyed." The crisis escalated to charges of "a formidable catalogue of insubordination" and "efforts to sabotage the discipline of the Department" on the one side, and of colonial mentality, incompetence and unethical behavior on the other. A further trivial dispute developed over the Nigerian accountant's right to park his car in a given spot, which brought him in conflict with another Englishman, and when Hickerson, a New Zealander but, to all Nigerian intents and purposes, an Englishman, took the action of suspending the Yoruba accountant from duty, the crisis had developed into a full-blown British-Yoruba ethnic conflict with charges of colonialism flying about freely.

To complicate matters further, the accountant had been a supporter of the Registrar in the fight against Nwanneh, and, thus, the two cases were linked in the minds of most Yoruba as facets of the anti-Yoruba master plan by the Ibo-British faction. The fact that a distinguished Yoruba professor was one of Hickerson's two direct assistants did not alter that interpretation, and the close association of that person with Hickerson (and Nwanneh before) still makes him a widely mistrusted person among Yoruba. When the accountant's case came up to Council, that body did not uphold Hickerson's disciplinary action and it reinstated the accountant, a decision which was, of course, viewed as a Yoruba victory and undermined Hickerson's position.

With the reinstatement of Babalola after the dramatic episodes recounted earlier, there was an extensive reshuffle of personnel in the Registry as well as a wave of promotions. This reorganization was officially described as a routine reassignment of duties. Established procedures would have made any formal demotions impossible. The general pattern seemed, at least to Babalola's opponents who were mostly non-Yoruba, to be one in which the pro-Registrar Yoruba were either rewarded with a formal promotion or reassigned to a more responsible and important branch of the Registry, while his non-Yoruba opponents were, if not formally demoted, reassigned to less important jobs. Thus, this complicated chain of events which began some five or six years earlier with a largely personal clash between the Registrar and the Vice-Chancellor snowballed in the ethnic climate of Nigeria into a succession of major ethnic crises involving virtually every segment of the University including the Junior Staff. The very basis of the University's authority structure was threatened in a flurry of mutually countermanding official memoranda issued respectively from the Registrar's and the Acting Vice-Chancellor's office, and, as we have seen, the supreme authority of the Head of State had to intercede to resolve the *impasse*.

We have already noted the importance of ethnicity in U.I.W.U. elections. As might be expected, ethnicity plays a key, though never an exclusive, role in all levels of elections from the selection of the Vice-Chancellor to student body officers. This is almost inevitable since elections are formal processes of political polarization, and since ethnicity is the most fundamental and pervasive cleavage in Nigerian society. Most Nigerians recognize the nefarious effect of "tribalism" on politics, and there are norms at U.I. which make ethnicity illegitimate as a basis for overt political appeal. The effect of these norms, however, is not to eliminate the effect of ethnicity, but simply to make its verbal manifestations less open and explicit. Everybody is against "tribalism" but, since nearly all expect everybody else to be "tribalistic," everyone can justify his own prejudices on grounds of self-defense. This vicious circle is almost impossible to break.

ETHNICITY IN STUDENT POLITICS

In student elections, the two major determining factors accounting for political alignment are ethnicity and membership in halls of residence. And, as it is University policy to achieve ethnic balance in all halls, the two principles have countervailing effects which blur and mitigate the impact of ethnicity. Overt appeals to ethnic loyalties during electoral campaigns are forbidden by University regulation, and student elections are supervised by the Students' Affairs Office of the Registry to insure fairness. Nevertheless, ethnicity is covertly a factor, and defeated candidates commonly level accusations of "tribalism" at their victorious opponents, ascribing the results to unfair and irregular practices. Before the Civil War, there was a balance of Yoruba and Ibo plus a sprinkling of minority students on the Student Representative Council and among the elected officials. During the Civil War, the Yoruba by virtue of making up approximately three-fourths of all students dominated the elections, but, as among Senior Staff, the micro-politics of Yoruba localism gained in relative salience as the Yoruba collectively no longer faced a numerically significant ethnic group.

Sometimes these allegations of tribalism are linked with accusations of corruption and inefficiency as well. This happened in 1969 when a Student Congress (i.e., a mass meeting of students which can be assembled by petition to unseat a student union executive) was convened by an opponent of the incumbent U.I. Student Union President whom he accused of having misappropriated travel expenses to an international student congress which (through no fault of the President) did not take place. Although the alignment split the Yoruba internally as usual, the opposition to the Yoruba president was disproportionately recruited among the "minority" (i.e., mostly Mid-Western and Eastern) students, and the President successfully weathered the storm, only to be accused by the unsuccessful challengers of intimidating his opponents at the Student Congress. A few minor scuffles did develop at the Congress, but usually student elections and politics are non-violent, the controversies remaining at the level of libelous insinuations and scurrilous invectives circulated through mimeographed sheets in the halls.

The issue of ethnicity in student politics is further complicated by the fact that there are numerous unions of students from a given locality, often based on the Divisions of the old Regions. These unions are recognized by the University and hold social functions. Given the close link between geography and ethnicity, many of these unions are sub-ethnic (and hence internally mono-ethnic) in character. For example, among Yoruba students, there are student unions from Oyo, Ekiti, Ondo, Ijebu and so on. In regions that are ethnically quite fragmented, these regional unions are in fact ethnic conglomerates, e.g., the Midwest Students' Union; but, despite their internal heterogeneity they are often regarded as "tribal unions" by outsiders. Through a common urban phenomenon referred to by some anthropologists as "supertribalization," several ethnic groups are fused into a single larger identity. At Ilosho, for example, since the separation of the Mid-Western Region (and later State) from the old Western Region, the Yoruba often refer collectively to "Midwesterners" as a kind of super-ethnicity, and have only the fuzziest conception of linguistic and cultural differences between the Edo, Ishan, Ibo and many other peoples of the region.

In effect, then, these regional student unions, while they do not present slates of candidates at elections, do provide a quasi-ethnic organizational structure at University, but being ostensibly based on locality they are not outlawed. It is interesting to note that, in the Nigerian context, locality almost invariably means "place of origin of one's parents or grand-parents," and not place of birth or present geographical location. Thus, an "Ekiti man" is not a person who happens to live in Ekiti Division of the Western State, but a person of Ekiti origin whose family may, for example, have been living in Lagos for 50 years. This loyalty to the place of origin of one's ancestors is so strong that some people will go through the trouble of registering their motorcar in their ancestral home far from their present place of residence, so that the letters on their registration plate will identify their origin.

ETHNICITY AMONG SENIOR STAFF

Among the Senior Staff, ethnicity also plays an important role in elections, but the alignments tend to be much more complex. Aside from ethnicity and localism (or sub-ethnicity), departmental and faculty membership, place of university training (British *versus* American), past political party affiliation, and personal patron-client ties all influence to a greater or lesser degree the outcome of elections. The major elective academic offices are the thirty-odd Congregation seats on the Senate, the one Congregation and the four Senate seats on the Council, the faculty deanships, and the non-*ex-officio* seats on Senate committees, especially on the crucial Development Committee and Appointments and Promotions Committee. Capture of these elective offices, particularly of the deanships, constitutes in fact the very core of University politics, and determines the composition of the ruling oligarchy of senior professors, as we have seen in Chapter IV. To the extent that U.I. politics generally have polarized along lines of ethnicity, so have these elections, candidates to offices being broadly identified with the administration or the opposition.

Thus, in the latter years of the Nwanneh era, his power basis rested in good part on the support of two Ibo deans. By contrast, one of the weaknesses of the Akinode administration was that, even though several of the faculty deans were Yoruba in 1969, Akinode could reliably count on the support of only one of them, while several others were leaders of rival Yoruba factions. One dean in particular was closely associated with a powerful political party and with a leading member of the Federal Military Government, and had made an unsuccessful bid for the Vice-Chancellorship against Akinode. The Civil War brought a major shift from an over-riding bi-ethnic conflict to a more diffuse, complex and shifting pattern of Yoruba factionalism based partly on locality and partly on political party alignments during the First Republic.

The political contest for the succession to Nwanneh in the Vice-Chancellorship highlighted this shift in the ethnic situation. In his letter of resignation in December 1966, Nwanneh hinted that his successor would have to be acceptable to the people of the region where U.I. was located, i.e., by implication be a Yoruba.[11] The Council, when accepting Nwanneh's resignation, expressed regret at that imputation that ethnic considerations would enter into the choice. The resentment was all the more intense as Nwanneh was, in the end, correct in his prediction. A Joint Committee consisting of five members of Senate and five members of the Council was set up by the Council under the Chairmanship of the Chairman of the Council, and entrusted with the task of seeking a new Vice-Chancellor. Little transpired of the deliberations of that first Committee, but although its choice was a Yoruba, several non-Nigerians were seriously considered for the job.

When that person, after first accepting the post, declined it to accept a United Nations job, allegedly under pressure from the Federal Government, the succession crisis became much more politicized and ethnicized. A second Joint Committee was appointed, and the process took the form of a political campaign. The press got into the act with alacrity, mentioning names of several alleged contenders, all Yoruba.

The climate of opinion crystallized in the direction predicted by Nwanneh, namely that the new Vice-Chancellor should be a Yoruba, and this immediately opened the Pandora's box of Yoruba factionalism. Two closed Yoruba caucuses involving the top political, professional, and academic elite both within and outside University met as an informal body of kingmakers to discuss strategy and if possible exert pressure on the Joint Committee. After lengthy and allegedly stormy deliberations, Akinode emerged as the narrow victor, and indeed that choice was confirmed by the Joint Committee, even though the Yoruba were not in majority on the latter. There is, of course, no firm evidence that the Yoruba members of the Joint Committee voted as a bloc under mandate from the caucus. It seems more probable that, while the caucus exerted some persuasive influence, the Yoruba vote was not unanimous. It should also be added that Akinode was strongly supported by a number of expatriates. Akinode's close rival was all the more bitter at his defeat as he was by far the more senior man, a criterion of considerable weight in Yoruba culture.

Naturally, ethnicity at U.I. does not operate in a vacuum; it is closely linked with the ethnic conflicts in the larger society. We have already dealt with the political links between individual members of the University and the political elite at the regional and federal levels. To the extent that the entire political life of Nigeria is suffused with ethnicity, these political links are often ethnic as well. Difficult though it often is to disentangle the effect of ethnicity from that of other factors, we must again stress that in the larger society as well as the University, ethnicity is never a complete explanation.

If this chapter has achieved nothing else, it should at least convince the reader that ethnicity in Nigeria is not the easily definable phenomenon that many Nigerians and non-Nigerians assume it to be. Nor is ethnicity the sole determinant of action as one-factor theorists in search of simple explanations for complex events are inclined to believe. The typical situation is one where ethnicity is only one of several important factors, where the very boundaries of ethnicity and sub-ethnicity are by no means unambiguous, where the levels of ethnicity activated in various issues may vary widely, where the ethnic alignments are fluid, and, perhaps most importantly, where the "myth" and the "reality" of ethnicity interplay so closely that it becomes impossible to distinguish the one from the other. A classical vicious circle is established: the expectation of "tribalism" calls forth its actual manifestation and the latter reinforces the expectations. Accusations of tribalism become a form of blackmail, a political weapon in the contest for power, and a defensive justification for one's own prejudices. Even at the purely intellectual level, the concept of tribalism becomes the mental wastebasket which gives one a satisfyingly simple explanation for a bewilderingly complex world.

Who can in last analysis say that the alliance of X and Y is based on their common ethnicity and the enmity of Y and Z on their lack of such a tie? The question, of course, cannot be answered *a priori*, but if enough members of the society believe that ethnicity is a determining factor, then to some extent it becomes so, quite independently of the specific motivations of individual actors. In an ethnically conscious society, it is practically impossible not to be a "tribalist," because one's behavior is always defined in good part by others. The massive tragedy of recent Nigerian history proves the point all too poignantly. And perhaps the greatest tragedy of all is that even millions of human casualties do not insure that the lesson of history has been learned.

NOTES

[1] Some Nigerian colleagues even told me that the word "oyimbo" has now come to mean by extension a member of the elite, or an obviously affluent person such as the driver of a private motor car. When I mentioned that, while driving through Yoruba towns, swarms of children would greet me with friendly shouts of "oyimbo," they told me that they have had the same experience.

[2] Again this did not reflect any radicalism, but rather the fact that many of them were Rockefeller or Ford Foundation appointees on a one- or two-year tenure at U.I. who therefore had no interest in retaining their jobs. Thus they could easily afford to be liberal at no cost to themselves.

[3] For this discussion of the *scale* of cleavage and the term "macrodivisive," I am indebted to my colleague Richard Schermerhorn who gave this chapter the benefit of his sharp and constructive criticism.

[4] Much of the discussion that follows applies, *mutatis mutandis,* to the country at large, but the present account focuses on the University.

[5] The pervasive cynicism of Nigerian intellectuals is in good part a product of the corruption, kleptocracy and nepotism which flourished during the First Republic. Of course, mistrust and cynicism are not unique to Nigerian culture. Mistrust of strangers is a universal trait, and the ravages of the slave trade, civil wars, and colonial domination during the last 400 years of Nigerian history were scarcely conducive to a philanthropic view of humanity. In the recent past, the escalating political crisis of the 1960's brought anomie to its climax.

[6] According to a popular version of the Yoruba origin myth, earth itself was created by Oduduwa putting a lump of it on water, and then placing a five-toed chicken upon it which scratched the earth in all directions to the confines of the planet (Bascom, 1969, p. 10).

[7] One of the most extensive investigations of ethnic stereotypy in Africa has been done by LeVine, and his study of "achievement motivation" in Nigeria (1966) has been criticized as resulting in little more than a restatement of pre-existing ethnic stereotypes. This raises the basic question of the degree of validity which stereotypes must achieve before they can no longer be called stereotypes.

[8] The rejection rate for coins in Nigeria is quite high, and is another symptom of the climate of mistrust. Every coin exchanged on the market place is closely examined by the recipient for fear that it might be counterfeited, and a large proportion of perfectly legal coins that are accepted unquestioningly in any bank are rejected if they are slightly worn, or misshapen. Oddly, banknotes, which are much more profitable to counterfeit, are accepted with much less suspicion.

[9] The presence of a Hungarian family in that group, however, may partly invalidate this ethnic interpretation, and suggest a political basis of association, since that group was also coterminous with the contingent from the Socialist countries. But then many other ethnic cliques on campus have one or two members belonging to a different group, a condition insured alone by a substantial rate of ethnic intermarriage.

[10] Expatriates' wives spend much time around the Senior Staff swimming pool complaining about the scarcity and price of food since the Civil War, and

unavailability of such items as tomato catsup and French wines. Most Nigerians from the elite have learned to prefer bottled beer at 4s 6d a bottle to nutritionally superior palm wine at approximately one-fifth of the price. Seldom is palm wine, the most common alcoholic beverage in Southern Nigeria, even available at the Senior Staff Club. The Club restaurant does serve, however, both English and Nigerian food. European foods such as wheat bread have become a prestige symbol, even among people who can least afford them.

[11] The text of Nwanneh's letter of resignation was given in footnote 16, Chapter 1.

CHAPTER NINE

Cooperation and Conflict
in Heterogeneous Social Systems

Conflict and Consensus Theories of the Social Order

The ultimate question about all social systems is what holds them together. Several types of answers have been suggested to this "Hobbesian problem." The consensus school of functionalism considers that commonality of basic values is the most fundamental integrative force. At the other extreme of the theoretical spectrum are those theorists who believe that societies are held together by the coercive force wielded by those who have an interest in maintaining the status quo. Others yet have suggested that economic exchange relations make for interdependence and hence for social stability; people stick together because it is mutually beneficial to do so. Some conflict theorists have argued that social systems are integrated through criss-crossing lines of conflict; differences of values and interests are inevitable, they hold, but so long as the alignments shift with the issues, no overall polarization can take place and the system is not threatened. (Coser, 1956; Dahrendorf, 1959) And, of course, the easiest "solution" of all has been advanced by those who do not regard stability as problematic at all, and postulate instead that all social systems are characterized by an inherent tendency toward inertia which can only be disturbed by extraordinary and extraneous circumstances.

The problem of order is, of course, compounded in highly heterogeneous social systems such as the one described in this book. Whatever else holds it together, it is not consensus on basic values or norms. Any attempt to explain social integration at U.I. in terms of shared internalized values runs into serious difficulties. This is not to say that behavior is unpredictable, or that there are no role expectations, or that these role expectations are not based on norms. The difficulty lies, however, in the fact that so much normative analysis in sociology has been linked to notions of legitimacy and consensus.

251

In schematized form, the normative consensus model has been presented somewhat as follows: underlying the culture of any group are certain fundamental premises about the desirable relations between men, and between man and nature. These premises constitute the "value system" of that culture. From these general values about what is desirable, flow certain more specific norms which in turn define, within certain limits, expectations of behavior between actors in concrete situations.

Perhaps the broadest "values" on which there is consensus at U.I. are those of cynicism, mistrust, and egoism. Most people assume that all others except those in the small circle of intimates (fellow kinsmen, fellow townsmen, or persons linked by patron-client ties) will behave in a way which furthers the other person's interests at the expense of oneself. Cheating and lying are the most common behavioral expectations, and the most common accusations outside the narrowly defined solidary group. Thus, even though there is widespread consensus about these behavioral expectations, that consensus is scarcely conducive to social integration. Consensus on the primacy of self-interest leads to the acceptance of conflict as a norm. What consensus there is cannot be shown to be importantly related to holding the system together, nor, vice versa, can social integration be shown to be related to consensus in the simple and axiomatic way which the Comte-Durkheim-Parsons tradition assumes.

This system of "competitive mistrust" might be dismissed as an extreme and exceptional case brought about by great cultural heterogeneity, large status differentials, and the steeply pyramidal character of the reward structure. I am quite willing to concede that these conditions might exacerbate competition and mistrust, but the ethnographic literature is replete with cases of relatively "simple," undifferentiated, unstratified (beyond age and sex), and homogeneous societies which are ridden with accusations of witchcraft, one of the most universal expressions of mistrust. The Dobu, the Tiv, the Zulu, the Navaho, are but a few well documented and widely scattered cases of "simple" societies where mistrust is elaborately institutionalized. Certainly, whether in "simple" or "complex" societies, the amount and the relative balance of trust and mistrust, of consensus and conflict are empirical questions which cannot be answered by an *a priori* theoretical postulate.

Having observed a large amount of dissension and conflict in a given society, and having noted that such consensus as exists takes the form that "you can't trust anyone," it does not by any means follow that the social system in question is characterized by an anarchic war of all against all. No society comes even close to it, or when it does it ceases to be a society. The problem thus becomes: why are societies ordered, despite conflict. And, in seeking to answer the question, is not the whole issue of norms and values irrelevant?

Social behaviorism in an attempt to sidestep the entire problem of values and norms, makes no assumptions about legitimacy, consensus or internalization. It substitutes instead a model that social behavior is a function of rewards and punishments ("positive and negative reinforcements") meted out in the interaction process. That model is extraordinarily potent in predicting the behavior of electrically shocked rats, banana-seeking rhesus monkeys, or even poker-playing undergraduates. Even if one concedes that the model is generalizable to more complex types of interaction, and no doubt it is, the repertory of questions it can answer is both limited and unexciting.

Thus, I can predict with a fair degree of confidence that a young American male is far more likely, given a choice, to offer this fiancée a bottle of Channel No. 5 for her birthday than a bottle of deodorant. Although I will gladly concede to the behaviorist that he would be able, in a neatly controlled experiment, to reverse that pattern by having an alluring female stooge slap the subject every time he proffers the perfume and passionately kiss him when she is offered the deodorant, I would still argue that the initial behavior was learned by means other than sequences of slaps and kisses. My purpose is not to prove that American males would rather be kissed than slapped by nubile females, but rather to understand the social significance of two alternative pieces of symbolic behavior. This I can do far more parsimoniously by reference to a normative system than through a behavioristic explanation.

Analysis of Normative Systems

Normative analysis must, however, become far more sophisticated than it has been in the past, and must be stripped of gratuitous assumptions of consensus and legitimacy if complex forms of interaction between heterogeneous groups are to become explainable. Interestingly, even when faced with clear normative conflicts, sociologists have still tried to salvage the simplistic consensus model. Thus, faced with the problem of "deviant behavior," criminologists have created the notion of the deviant sub-culture with its own set of norms and values, at odds to be sure with the "straight" society, but consensually held and internalized within the deviant group. While this conception might be a slight improvement over considering the "criminal" an asocial, amoral monster, the model is still far too simple to account for reality.

Let us take our University situation and try to arrive at a slightly more adequate account of a complex situation where consensus is patently overshadowed by conflict. As appointments to the Senior Staff are such crucial decisions and are both circumscribed by elaborate formal rules and subject to acute conflicts of interests and norms, we shall construct a hypothetical but realistic case, and try to analyze the behavior of the actors. Let us say that a Lectureship in Mathematics is vacant and has been advertised as usual in the Nigerian and British press. There are three candidates on the short list, after five obviously less qualified applicants have been eliminated. A, a mid-western Ibo, is coming back from the United States with a brand-new Ph.D. in Mathematics from the University of Wisconsin; B is a Yoruba who is returning from Britain with a Ph.D. from Manchester, and C is a somewhat older Englishman who has six years of teaching experience as Junior Lecturer and Lecturer at the University of Sussex, has published five articles in respectable journals, graduated with a "first" from Cambridge, but, true to the inverted Oxbridge snobbery, never bothered to get a Ph.D.

The Head of Mathematics, a Briton, favors C whom he knew as an undergraduate at Cambridge, and regards as the most brilliant student he ever had. Both A and B have, as usual, glowing letters of recommendation pronouncing them young men of exceptional promise, but neither has published yet, and neither has taken the trouble of requesting from his university a microfilm of his thesis. Within the Mathematics Department, B has majority ethnic support among the Yoruba, while A is favored by a minority made up of most non-Yoruba and some expatriates. Except for the Professor, however, the members of the Mathematics Department carry next to no weight in the decision, and their professional evaluation of the candidates is not solicited. A also happens to be the junior brother of the Professor of English a powerful "committee professor" who, although not a member of the Appointments and Promotions Committees, can use his influence to sway at least three of the fifteen members of that body. B can expect support from five Yoruba on the Committee, but two of them are bitter enemies, and out of personal spite, they might vote on opposite sides if their egos get involved in the discussion. Seven members of the A.P.C., can be expected to be neutral; two of those are the Council representatives in A.P.C. who seldom attend the meetings; three are Deans, one of whom supports the Vice-Chancellor while the other two oppose him; they can be expected to vote for or against the V.C. rather than for or against a given candidate; and the last two are a Bini married to a Yoruba who may side either with the Yoruba or with the anti-Yoruba faction, and an apolitical Englishman who takes a very cynical and amused view of the entire exercise.

Let us imagine a typical scenario within the A.P.C. It turns out that only ten members of the Committee are present, four Yoruba, an Ibo, a Bini, an American and three Englishmen, including the Head of Mathematics. According to the three-fourths majority rule, three votes can block an appointment, but if the majority faction is on the Vice-Chancellor's side, the Vice-Chancellor as chairman of A.P.C. may attempt to avoid a vote and declare that there is a consensus in favor of the candidate he favors. Everybody on A.P.C. is aware of the universalistic rules for recruitment of staff and of the elaborate procedures to insure that the rules apply. Yet, with the exception of one or two people whose behavior appears consistently to follow universalistic norms, it is obvious that nearly everybody also operates under a multiplicity of particularistic norms involving kinship, ethnicity, sex, clientship, friendship, politics, and a variety of other prejudices that bear no relationship to the candidates' ability to perform the job. At one extreme, are the few persons who take the universalistic norms seriously and are in fact able to keep irrelevancies out of their judgment. At the other, are those cynics, who, while fully aware of the official norms, believe in consciously manipulating them for their own particularistic ends. In between, are those who, while honestly believing that they behave impartially, do little more than cloak their prejudices under universalistic rationalizations.[1]

Overtly, the entire discussion invokes universalistic criteria. Whether he believes in them or not, everybody is aware of the formal, "legitimate" rules and procedures. Any overt deviation from the formal norms is nearly always detrimental to one's position. The formal rules serve two main functions: to disguise one's own prejudices and to attack the prejudices of one's opponents. A complicated charade results in which the procedure is ostensibly universalistic (unless someone makes a blunder or indulges in an embarrassing display of cynicism), but in which nearly everybody imputes illegitimate or at least irrelevant motivations to the others. The outright cynics, i.e., those who consciously manipulate the formal rules to suit their own particularistic ends, are probably in minority, but even those who believe in their own honesty and impartiality find their colleagues wanting in these qualities. The cynics are usually the ones who relish playing the political game, which becomes their favorite intellectual pastime and the main outlet for their creativity; they frequently carry the day because of their greater expertise.

One major limiting factor in the ability of the A.P.C. to apply universalistic criteria is that typically only one or two of its members are in the same discipline as the candidates. Thus, insofar as an attempt is made at judging professional competence, it must rely largely on second-hand judgments or indirect indices. Letters of recommendation are seldom less than extremely laudatory, and, when they are, this is as likely to reflect academic feuds and other irrelevancies as objective judgments. In last analysis, members of the Committee cast a glance at the references (to which they typically refer only if the letters confirm their own prejudices), and at the *vita* of the candidate; they evaluate his degrees according to their subjective opinion of the quality of the granting universities, attempt to assess the quantity and quality of his publications according to such criteria as the respectability of journals, and endeavor to forecast his promise as a scholar by relating his past accomplishments to his age.

As each academic is reasonably familiar only with the specific academic system of which he himself is a product, he will, in most cases, be disqualified to assess the merits of somebody who comes from a different tradition; but, instead of admitting his disqualification, he will often be blindly prejudiced. He will assume that if he has not heard of a university it cannot be very good. As the British-trained dominate the scene at Ilosho, this results in a general bias against American, Continental European and Asian degrees. Even the attempt to apply universalistic criteria, then, is largely invalidated by the Committee's lack of specific expertise. The motions are gone through for the sake of appearance, but several members of A.P.C. lack confidence in the validity of the exercise. Thus, the way is open for the game of academic power politics. Formal constraints put, to be sure, some limits on this game; candidates *do* have to possess minimum paper qualifications from a "respectable" university. But the scope for particularism is still quite wide.

Let us return to our hypothetical scenario. The Head of Mathematics will brief A.P.C. on all three candidates, stating that all three look good to him, but that knowing C as he does and having read his work, he thinks that C has an edge over the other two, and has already established himself as a mathematician of repute. The Head of Mathematics, however, knows that he will have a difficult time getting the A.P.C. to vote for C, since C does not have a doctorate and since there are two qualified Nigerian applicants who do. As a graceful way out he suggests that C, considering his experience, should really get a Senior Lectureship for which there is no vacancy. As between A and B, the Head leans toward A because B is a Yoruba, and, having alienated the Yoruba in his department, he does not want to strengthen their group. On the other hand, being himself British, he naturally believes that B's Manchester degree is better than A's doctorate from Wisconsin. In the end, however, he decides to support A; and to defend his case, he finds an undergraduate award in A's *vita* that seems to give him an edge over B.

Before the meeting, A's senior brother, the Ibo Professor of English, has mustered another three votes on A.P.C., those of the Ibo, the Bini and one other Englishman. The Vice-Chancellor, a Yoruba, only votes when his vote would be decisive, but he can be expected to lean towards B, as indeed the other three Yoruba present, unless the two of them who are sworn enemies can be gotten to take opposite sides. The American can be expected to vote with the Yoruba because he is an Anthropologist who has written his *magnum opus* on the political organization of the Oyo Kingdom. The third Englishman is an Oxonian Professor of Classics, and a world authority on Juvenal. Naturally, he does not think much of those upstart colonial universities in America, but, on the other hand, he does not get along with the Yoruba, several of whom had the audacity to suggest in Senate that Latin was perhaps not all that relevant to the needs of Nigeria. He therefore quixotically decides to vote for C who does not have a ghost of a chance. In the end, the two antagonistic Yoruba professors feel constrained to disagree publicly with each other, and one of them ends up voting for A and the other for B. All candidates fall far short of the three-quarters majority and no appointment can be made for now. Two months later, however, A informs the University that he has accepted a job at the University of Iowa; and B's appointment gets through at the next meeting of A.P.C. In the face of the needs of the Mathematics Department, and in the absence of a candidate of its own, the anti-Yoruba faction is not in a position of opposing the appointment of an obviously qualified Nigerian without making its "tribalism" obvious and undermining its position in the forthcoming and more important battle for the professorship of Botany.

Clearly, any simple normative model does not go very far in accounting for this kind of situation. Yet, equally clearly, the behavior of the actors is far from random and unpredictable. The simplest possible model would be to accept at face value the universalistic norms as officially stated in the regulations and procedures for the filling of staff vacancies, to believe that the members of A.P.C. accept the legitimacy of these norms, and to conclude that, to the best of their ability, they implement these norms and choose the best qualified applicant for a given job. An equally simplistic counter-model is the cynical view that, in fact, these universalistic norms are nothing but a smokescreen for the operation of blatant nepotism, favoritism and "tribalism." The ethnic variant of the cynical model is perhaps the most widespread, holding that staff appointments are first and foremost an arena for ethnic conflicts.

At a slightly higher level of theoretical sophistication would be the normative model used by a number of sociologists in dealing with "complex organizations" in industrial societies. They contrast a "formal" and an "informal" organization, each with its set of norms. Thus, in a factory for example, the formal organization (as represented by management) is interested in maximizing profit and labor productivity, while the informal organization (as represented by the rank and file workers) is interested in getting a production norm established which is considerably below maximum efficiency. Consequently, powerful sanctions are exercised against "rate busting," and workers generally oppose piece-work as an attempt by management to encourage rate busting. Management would like the workers to compete against each other in the interests of profit maximization; the workers' main interest on the other hand is in the non-competitive class solidarity for the sake of collective bargaining and security of employment. We might term this model the "simple normative conflict model."

For some purposes, this model is useful. For example, at U.I., the Junior Staff operates well below peak efficiency, because it is collectively interested in maintaining a vast amount of redundancy on the payroll. It would be easy, with some capital investment and a more efficient use of labor, to reduce the Junior Staff of the University by at least one-third. However, it is doubtful that labor efficiency would be in anybody's interest. Some savings in running the University might result, but, on the other hand, in "developing" countries, labor is abundant and cheap while capital is scarce. Thus the incentive to save on the one plentiful resource is minimal. It is true that this perpetuates the vicious circle of low wages and low productivity, but in an economy still largely based on subsistence agriculture, the results of a high-productivity and mechanization drive would be to reduce the wage sector of the labor force from, say, ten to five per cent, to double or treble the rate of urban unemployment, and to squander scarce capital in order to save on cheap, superabundant labor.

At University, since "management" is not interested in profits, and since there is not way of balancing cost against quality of the finished product, the Senior Staff is in connivance with the Junior Staff in not enforcing high-productivity norms, and there is no class conflict on this dimension. During the Civil War, when budget cuts imposed an austerity drive, there was some retrenchment of labor and a slightly greater emphasis on efficiency, but even the Government would be very reluctant to enforce high efficiency standards at the certain cost of even more catastrophic unemployment rates than already prevail, and, hence, at the probable risk of mounting social unrest. Therefore, official pronouncements by the University administration that the operating budget had been cut to bare bones did not prevent in practice the continuance of some labor redundancy; nor did the Government dare scrutinize too closely the accuracy of the claims, despite the pinch imposed by the war on the civilian budget. Economies were achieved by curtailing capital expenditures on buildings and by leaving some Senior Staff vacancies unfilled, but not by substantially reducing the Subordinate Staff where redundancy was greatest.

In the case of an appointment to the Senior Staff described above, the normative situation is more complicated yet than a "simple conflict model" would suggest. The same group of actors operates within multiple sets of norms which are partially conflicting and partially complementary. First, there are the official universalistic norms that the most academically qualified applicant should be hired in a process of open competition through advertisement of posts in the press and well-defined procedures of evaluation.

Overt verbal behavior tends to conform rather closely to these norms, and, in that sense, they can be said to be "legitimated." It is bad tactics not to pay "lip service" to these norms.

However, both the cynical view that these norms are irrelevant to the outcome of the decisions, and the naive view that they are the main determinant thereof are equally inaccurate. The universalistic norms are important in at least three different ways. First, they impose limits on the operation of other norms. Candidates must possess the minimal paper qualifications to be considered. Second, the political effectiveness of a member of A.P.C. depends to a large degree on the extent of his knowledge of the "proper procedure," because an opponent's procedural mistakes are the most potent weapons to be used against him. Thirdly, one's own position, whatever one's actual motivations might be, must be overtly presented in terms of these norms. The essential question, then, is not whether consensus is present. Some members do accept the validity of these norms and behave accordingly; others, more numerous perhaps, accept the norms in theory but frequently behave in violation of their spirit; others yet are thoroughly cynical and consciously manipulative. However, whether the actors accept or "internalize" the norms or not, they are *cognitively aware* of them, and, unless they are extraordinarily inept, their behavior is partially determined by them, even when they use procedural legalism to violate the spirit of these norms.

A second basic norm concerns Nigerianization of the staff. The interesting fact about this norm is that, while logically incompatible with the first set of norms, it is also regarded as legitimate by the majority of both Nigerians and expatriates, the former for obvious reasons of self-interest and the latter as guilt-atonement for past colonial sins. Of all the "official" norms, this one comes perhaps closest to commanding consensus, although some more conservative expatriates still do not accept it. When I say that Nigerianization and universalism are incompatible norms, I am not suggesting that Nigerians are less qualified for posts than expatriates; in fact, the reverse is often true because Nigerian academic salaries are too low to attract many high-quality expatriate applicants. The point is simply, that, assuming a random distribution of qualifications between nationalities, the norm of preferential hiring of Nigerians conflicts *in principle* (though not necessarily in practice) with the norm of universalism. Thus, a particularistic norm is also granted legitimacy, and this facilitates the intrusion of other unstated and unstatable particularistic criteria.

An attempt is made at the overt level to reconcile this contradiction, namely by stating that the Nigerianization norm is subordinate to the universalistic one, i.e. that given several *equally well qualified* candidates, preference should be given to the Nigerian. Such a situation is, of course, relatively rare. In actual practice, where "all other things" are typically *not* equal, expatriates are hired mostly in cases where they are either clearly better qualified than *any* Nigerian applicant, or indeed where they are the sole minimally qualified candidates. In effect, if there is a well-qualified Nigerian candidate, there is fairly wide consensus that he should get the job, especially if his prospective department falls below the University average in degree of Nigerianization. Thus, the universalistic norms simply set limits within which the Nigerianization norm applies.

So much for the "official" or "legitimate" norms, i.e. those which can be and are overtly referred to in order to argue cases. Whether these norms are "believed in" or not, actors behave as if they accepted them, and there are powerful sanctions against either overtly introducing irrelevant or illegitimate considerations, or openly expressing cynicism. Nearly everybody *expects* his colleagues to be motivated by "illegitimate" considerations, but it is considered in extremely bad taste *openly* to question the integrity of one's peers. The core of the game thus consists in achieving one's aims, whether legitimate or not, by invoking and manipulating the "proper procedure," and in tripping up one's opponents on similarly legalistic grounds while giving vent to one's pet prejudices. These, as suggested in our hypothetical example, are numerous, but in any given case, at least three or four of the following factors can be expected to intrude with predictable regularity: sex (taking the form of anti-feminism since A.P.C. is an all- or nearly-all male body), kinship, locality, ethnicity, nationality, school ties, tradition of university training, academic discipline and faculty, clientage ties, and personal enmities. Some of these are independent (e.g. ethnicity and place of training), while others (such as kinship and ethnicity) are so closely linked that one cannot always ascertain which is at work.

These particularistic criteria are normative in the sense that actors are able partially to predict each other's behavior, even though there is neither consensus as to the validity of these norms, nor even any legitimate recourse to them within A.P.C. Everybody expects those norms to be operative, but everybody also recognizes that, to the extent that they conflict with the official norms, it would be disruptive to do anything except pretend that everybody's behavior is determined by the objective merits of the case. The charade consists in clearly recognizing the game as a political one (to the extent of caucusing and planning strategy ahead of meetings), yet officially denying that this is so, and pretending that one plays it "by the book." The intent is not deceit, because hardly anybody is a dupe, but rather the containment of political conflicts within limits which do not seriously jeopardize the entire system and hence threaten everybody's interests. When imputations of motives are made outside the confines of the A.P.C., they are usually easy to refute because they are so often phrased in the simplistic form of a single factor theory (e.g. "tribalism") which does not come close to a satisfactory account of the facts.

It is true, of course, that a norm which may be illegitimate in one context might be strongly legitimate in another. Thus, powerful traditional norms of mutual aid between kinsmen are interpreted as "nepotism" in the University situation; solidarity between fellow townsmen becomes "tribalism"; loyalty to a client becomes "favoritism"; devotion to a patron may be viewed as "sycophancy"; returning favors might be called "bribery" and accepting them, "corruption." But the picture of the individual as torn between two conflicting systems of values and squirming on the horns of an ethical dilemma is probably much less common than some social scientists would assume. The basic conflict is not between value systems inside individuals, but one of interests between individuals and groups. For example, few people seem to be facing the moral dilemma of choosing between universalistic and familistic norms, because in most cases that dilemma has already been resolved. The problem rather, for the universalistically oriented academic, is how to shake off the importunities of less fortunate kinsmen; for the familistically oriented person, the problem consists in how to get his cousin or nephew in, while posing as a champion of academic excellence.

Finally, we come to a fourth set of norms, probably the crucial ones in preventing an anarchic war of all against all in the ruthless pursuit of self-interest. These norms are both largely consensual and dictated by collective interests, but they do not imply agreement about basic values. The members of the A.P.C. have a "gentlemen's agreement" to "fight clean," i.e. not to use tactics which threaten the collective interest of their group. Outside interests such as the press are not to be brought in; the integrity of colleagues is not to be publicly assailed; and one must pretend to follow the official rules and to accept the pretense of others as genuine. One of the reasons why that normative agreement on the rules of the game has been so relatively effective is that, with the expansion of the entire Senior Staff, the acceleration of promotions and the creation of multiple chairs, the game is one in which nearly everybody wins, though some win more than others. Gains are largely made at the expense of the taxpayers rather than of any of the contending parties; conflicts and deadlocks between factions of the Senior Staff are often resolved by appointing or promoting both of the opposing candidates, or by loose, informal *quid pro quo* exchanges in which each contending faction makes some gain. The game of academic politics is thus, at one level, one of collusion of the elite against the public weal; at another level, it is a case of competition between the academic elite and other segments of the elite; at another level yet, it is an aspect of ethnic rivalries in the larger society; and finally it is the expression of micro-factionalism within the academic Senior Staff itself. Underlying all these conflicts is the clear perception that the University is the goose that lays the golden eggs; therefore, there are very strong protective mechanisms against killing it. Only during the Nwanneh-Babalola crisis and its numerous ethnic and other political ramifications did the conventions about the rules of the game break down seriously, notably when outside political forces were brought to bear on the resolution of internal University conflicts.

While the behavior of actors at the University is clearly regulated by norms, any attempt to explain the continuance of that social system by reference to normative consensus and mutuality of expectations is at best unconvincing. To be sure, there exists some measure of agreement at least on instrumental norms if not on ultimate goals; but there is also plenty of conflict between a multiplicity of individuals and groups. If anything, the University resembles more the proverbial French "basketful of crabs" than the mythical "big happy family" that a number of large-scale organizations are held by their ruling oligarchies to approximate. At the same time, however, U.I. is not primarily held together by coercion, the main alternative to consensus suggested by some conflict theorists as a basis for social integration. Nearly everybody, from Junior Staff to Vice-Chancellor, is at U.I. by choice rather than force. Disciplinary sanctions are remarkably weak, a fact deplored by some members of the Council and some senior administrators; even more remarkable is the fact that no very convincing case can be made for the need for more severe sanctions. The few persons who are convinced are non-academics with little understanding of how a university operates.

The Problem of Order

Perhaps we are now in a better position to answer the Hobbesian problem of order with which we started this chapter. The problem can be broken down into two components, a "passive" and an "active" one. On the "passive" side, U.I. may be said to be held together by crisscrossing lines of cleavage. The notion that conflict can be a binding force has a long history in anthropological and sociological conflict theory. Evans-Pritchard (1940), in dealing with a homogeneous segmentary lineage society, the Nuer of the southern Sudan, describes the process as "fission and fusion." Conflict divides, to be sure, but it also unites, and, if the alignments keep shifting depending on a variety of circumstances, as is the case among the Nuer, the integrity of the whole is not threatened. Everybody knows that today's opponent may be tomorrow's ally when the issue will be different. More recently, this theme has been generalized to more differentiated industrial societies by such theorists as Coser (1956) and Dahrendorf (1959).

U.I. is a good example of the general applicability of the principle. The stormiest period in the history of the University occurred when its politics came closest to being polarized along ethnic lines in the overriding Ibo-Yoruba conflict. Each group was large enough to do serious damage to the University in acting out its conflicts with the other; and other bases of factionalism, while never completely absent, paled into relative insignificance, both at U.I. and in the country at large. The very survival of Nigeria as a unitary state hung in the balance.

During the period of my field work, the departure of most Ibo Senior Staff had resolved by default this threatening cleavage within the University, and radically changed the political structure of U.I. Conflicts did not diminish in number or intensity, but the entire structure of political alignments became much more diffuse and complex. Ever shifting Yoruba factionalism emerged as a much more important factor than had hitherto been the case. Other factors which cut across ethnicity gained in relative importance, such as religion, social status, and departmental or faculty membership. Paradoxical as it appears at first glance, the very fluidity and instability of internal alignments contributed to the stability of the whole. *Plus cela change, plus cela reste la même chose.* Differently based groups oppose each other on a wide variety of issues. Most of the conflicts only involve a small segment of the University, e.g. a department or a faculty. From one crisis to the next, alignments change. The University thrives from controversy to controversy, though of course individuals may end up the losers, if only in relative terms.

The sheer fact that lines of cleavage are shifting with issues prevents polarization, but is not sufficient by itself to account for the integration of the University, and indeed for its relative stability. It merely constitutes the "passive" side of the problem. On the active side, U.I. is held together by the fact that the vast majority of its members have a strong interest in keeping it going. This interest transcends, in the vast majority of cases, any conflicts persons might have with other members of the University, so that there are powerful restraints against letting internal conflicts turn into an attack against the University itself. *Vis à vis* the larger society, the University is a solidary group; on the other hand, envious and antagonistic though many persons outside U.I. are toward it, the society at large, and particularly its ruling stratum, have too large a stake in the University to want to threaten its existence. The University simply plays too important a role in training the elite that runs the country for the ruling stratum to want to destroy it. There are periodic press campaigns urging reforms within U.I., but their effect is always limited, not to say nil.

Safe from the outside, the University need fear no subversion from the inside either. The Senior Staff collectively run the University for their own benefit, and enjoy conditions of work, salaries, fringe benefits, freedom and leisure on a scale undreamt of in any other occupation in Nigeria. Even the expatriates enjoy working conditions which are in many ways far superior to those prevailing in their home countries. The students see their three years at U.I. as an educational investment which will open their way to elite status and a secure life-long salary of at least 25 times the average per capita income. Their entire future would be disastrously affected by the closure of the University, as indeed students at the University of Nigeria in the East discovered during the Civil War when that University had to close its doors for three years. The Junior Staff, though far less well off than the Senior Staff and deeply resentful of that wide gulf between the two estates, see in the University a source of employment in a country where job opportunities are exceedingly scarce relative to supply of qualified work seekers. Furthermore, their salaries, though low compared to those of the Senior Staff, are often twice as high as what they could earn off campus, assuming that they would be lucky enough to find a job at all. Even the many thousands of Ilosho townspeople who are not employed by U.I., but who derive part of their livelihood from it want to see it thrive, however much they might envy its staff and students. In short, what is good for the University is good for nearly everybody, though by no means equally so.

Social Change

Having attempted to answer how a heterogeneous social system achieves a measure of order and stability, we must also examine how it changes. Any social system is a balance of cooperation and conflict, of continuity and change. In the past chapters, numerous references to specific changes were made, but so far we have not tried to deal with change as an analytical problem. Viewing the University as a partially autonomous system within a larger society, change may be classified as endogenous (i.e. originating from within the University) or exogenous (i.e. emanating from the larger setting), although it is clear that these two categories are not independent of each other.

The main exogenous changes have been precipitated by Nigerian political events, especially since 1960. Independence marked the implementation of a policy of Nigerianization of the Senior Staff, and most symbolically of the Vice-Chancellorship. The University lagged behind the government in transferring power from expatriates to Nigerians, and the process at U.I. is not yet completed, but by the late 1960's, Nigerians had certainly gained majority control. It is interesting to note here that both at the "national" and at the University levels, "independence" has been characterized primarily by a change of citizenship in the top echelon personnel rather than by fundamental changes in the structure of institutions. Independence in Nigeria, as in most of post-colonial Africa, has resulted in little more than "circulation of elites." To be sure, there have been some changes: racial discrimination has been largely abolished; external control of the country has diminished; rituals of mass participation in politics have been instituted for a few years; corruption became generalized; and conflicting ethnic nationalisms became exacerbated in the process of competition for the capture of the power apparatus between various sectors of the elite.

However, the basic political and economic structure of the country was not fundamentally affected. The exercise of power remained as oligarchical as ever. Except for growth in size and increasing parasitism, the bureaucracy retained its colonial structure nearly intact. The educational system also grew, literacy increased and the curriculum was superficially "africanized," but schools continue to be extremely alien in organization, values and content of the skills taught. The enormous regional, ethnic, religious, and class disparities in levels of income, living standards, economic development, literacy, and health remain substantially unchanged, except for the emergence of a tiny indigenous elite who were the main beneficiaries, not to say profiteers of independence. Nigeria exhibits the tragic paradox of underdevelopment that the less developed a country is economically, the *greater* the internal disparities in the distribution of what little wealth there is.

U.I. too remained basically a European, indeed a British, type of University. Curriculum changes have been relatively superficial except perhaps in history and some of the social sciences. The recruitment of students and Senior Staff remains highly selective on the basis of ascriptive criteria such as sex and ethnicity. The philosophy of education continues to be very elitist: the University is training a ruling mandarinate. The structure of privilege within the University maintains the steeply pyramidal character of a colonial society without any appreciable signs of change towards a more egalitarian distribution of resources, except in the very limited sense that the proliferation of professorships has made the University more top-heavy, and hence a greater drain on the public weal. The definition of academic excellence is determined by Western standards and values, and tied to recognition of the University's "international reputation." In short, the University is African only by geographical location and origin of its personnel. It is far more alien to a Yoruba diviner or a Hauso *mallam,* than to an Anglican clergyman or an Oxford don.

The second major exogenous source of change at U.I. has come from the complicated sequence of political events since independence which resulted in increasing ethnic polarization, and two and a half years of civil war. At University these changes took the form of a growing Ibo-Yoruba conflict, the massive departure of Ibo Senior Staff, and thereafter, a more diffuse form of conflict with intra-ethnic Yoruba factionalism. For both the country and the University, the Civil War resulted in a weakening of the already fragile fabric of inter-ethnic ties at the elite level; more ethnic homogeneity within regions as groups that felt threatened sought the safety of home; and, hence, a "regionalization" of the personnel in the bureaucratized sector including government and the universities. U.I. emerged from these events a much more Yoruba university than it entered them. The trend will probably be partially reversed in the coming years, but it will take a long tie to re-establish the *status quo ante bellum,* if indeed this is ever achieved.

The major endogenous change at U.I. has been sheer growth in size to meet the rising demand for graduates in the expanding state and private bureaucracies and in the secondary school system. There are now signs that Nigeria may be reaching a saturation point in its capacity to absorb university graduates at the level of privilege which they have come to expect, but it seems probable that U.I. and the other Nigerian universities will continue to grow, especially in the technical fields. The numerical growth of U.I. has been accompanied by a growth in organizational complexity: administrative offices, especially the Registry, split up into increasingly specialized sub-units; the committee structure of the Senate and the Council became elaborate; in short, the bureaucratic structure of the University grew not only in size but also in functional specialization. Despite this growth, U.I. still is a relatively small university and exhibits none of the qualitative changes which characterize the American "multiversity." Essentially, Ilosho has grown from an unviably small institution to one which has achieved the minimum size necessary to offer a wide spectrum of academic specialties and adequate research and study facilities.

Except for sheer growth, Ilosho has not been characterized by much endogenous change. The endemic conflicts within the University have resulted in individual and factional power struggles and in personnel changes, but they have not generated any appreciable structural changes, such as major shifts in the distribution of power, wealth and prestige. The creation of multiple professorships and rotating headships has reduced the status and power of some Heads of academic departments. The University has expressed concern in recent years about the living conditions of its Junior Staff, and the elitist character of its primary and secondary school, but aside from investigating committees, soul-searching, the construction of a few more cottages and classrooms, the promotion of a few Intermediate Staff employees to newly created "super-scale" categories, and some timid attempts at diminishing the visibility of invidious distinctions between Junior and Senior Staff, the gap between the estates is practically unchanged. Neither Junior Staff nor students have anything more than a barely audible consultative voice in the affairs of the University. The U.I. Workers Union has, if anything, lost effectiveness as a bargaining agent in the last few years. Student participation in the governance of the University remains a vague promise and such student government as exists is a misnomer offering little more than opportunities for petty venality.

Curriculum reform, or indeed any change in admission policy, examination procedures or any such academic subject is agonizingly slow as departmental autonomy is minimal and as the Senate is heavily loaded with more senior and conservative people. Furthermore, the British Common Law model of the Senate, which operates essentially on the basis of precedents, is heavily stacked against change. The clinching argument against reform is typically that the implications of proposed changes must be carefully examined; that, since things have not been done that way before, there is is really no reliable way of doing that; and that, therefore, all kinds of adverse consequences might very well result from change. In one year of field work, I only witnessed one appreciable change voted by the Senate, namely the elimination of the annual Graduation ceremony in June, and its consolidation with the November ritual of Foundation Day.

The centralization of power within the University has shifted somewhat depending on the personality of the Vice-Chancellor, but the inertia of the University has severely limited the ability of even autocratically inclined Vice-Chancellors to arrogate power to themselves. The one major attempt by a Vice-Chancellor to change markedly the relative status of University officials (by downgrading the Registrar) ended in failure. The administration has remained generally subordinate to the academic staff despite an attempt to change this relationship during the autocratic Simpson era. Within the academic staff, power is wielded by an oligarchy of its more senior members, namely the elected deans, the department heads, and a few "committee professors." The power structure, then, has been fairly consistently oligarchical, but at the same time diffuse and decentralized because of factional conflicts within the ruling group.

One significant conclusion from our study of U.I. is that conflict does not necessarily generate basic structural change. U.I. has been characterized by a relatively high level of both internal conflict and inertia. Of course, the very existence of the University, and the effects the University has had in creating the country's new ruling class are themselves the result of a process of change initiated during the colonial period. To the extent that Ilosho is an exotic product, its effects in changing the larger society can be regarded as exogenous in relation to Nigeria. The relative lack of adaptability of the University to the country has been coupled by a considerable adaptation of the country to the kind of social system that the University helped create. This is what Westerners ethnocentrically call "modernization," or, even worse, "westernization." The end product, however, is not a "modern" society or a "western" society, but a colonial society externally dependent and internally rent by conflict and disequilibrium.

The dynamics of Nigeria, after a decade of political independence, are still basically the dynamics of a colonial society. U.I. as a late colonial creation, fulfilled its intended historical role in producing the successor elite to the British colonial bureaucracy. Steeped in the Western tradition, the neo-colonial mandarinate is, not surprisingly, a creditable intellectual replica of its mentors. In the political and economic context of Nigeria, however, the University became an island of privilege and a hotbed of ethnic and other political conflicts wrapped in the deceptively serene-looking shell of a palm-shaded Oxbridge. So far, the greatest discontinuity in Nigerian, and more broadly in tropical African history, has been the inception of European rule, not its formal political demise.

NOTES

[1] Once more, I am not suggesting that Nigerian universities and academics are any more perverse than their counterparts in other countries. C. P. Snow's well-known novels about British academia are, in fact, accurate sociological portrayals of university politics in the United Kingdom. My own book, *Academic Gamesmanship* (1970a), which deals with the United States, will, I think, absolve me of the accusation that I am any more critical of Nigeria than of the country where I established my permanent academic domicile.

Bibliography

Note: To preserve a measure of anonymity, all references to books, journals and articles which mention the real name of the University of Ilosho, as well as works by prominent members of the University have been deliberately omitted from the bibliography. While I regret not being able to mention most of my primary written sources, I disguised the name of the University at the request of several colleagues there. The specialist, however, will experience no difficulty in finding the sources.

Adelabu, Adedeji
    1971   "Studies in Trends in Nigeria's Educational Development," *African Studies Review*, 14, n⁰ 1, 1971, pp. 101–112.

Andreski, Stanislav
    1968   *The African Predicament*, London, Michael Joseph.

Ashby, Eric
    1962a *Investment in Education*, Lagos, Federal Ministry of Information.
    1962b "Mission and Challenge of West African Universities," *Teachers College Record*, 64, pp. 227–232.
    1964   *African Universities and Western Tradition*, London, Oxford University Press.
    1966   *Universities, British, Indian and African*, Cambridge, Harvard University Press.

Asquith, C.
    1945   *Report of the Commission on Higher Education in West Africa*, London, His Majesty's Stationery Office.

Balandier, Georges
    1965   "Problématique des Classes Sociales en Afrique Noire," *Cahiers Internationaux de Sociologie*, 38, pp. 131–142.

Banton, Michael
    1965   "Social Alignment and Identity in a West African City," in Hilda Kuper, ed., *Urbanization and Migration in West Africa*, Berkeley, University of California Press.

269

Bascom, William
  1969   *The Yoruba of Southwestern Nigeria*, New York, Holt, Rinehart and Winston.
Biobaku, S. O.
  1963   "Africa's Needs and Africa's Universities," *West African Journal of Education*, 7, pp. 61–63.
Bottomore, T. B.
  1966   *Elites and Society*, Baltimore, Penguin.
Carr-Saunders, Alexander M.
  1961   *New Universities Overseas*, London, Allen and Unwin.
  1963   *Staffing African Universities*, London, Overseas Development Institute.
Clignet, Rémi and Philip Foster
  1966   *The Fortunate Few, A Study of Secondary Schools and Students in the Ivory Coast*, Evanston, Northwestern University Press.
Coleman, J. S. ed.
  1965   *Education and Political Development*, Princeton, Princeton University Press.
Coser, Lewis A.
  1956   *The Functions of Social Conflict*, New York, The Free Press.
Couch, Margaret
  1962   *Education in Africa: A Select Bibliography*, London, Institute of Education, University of London.
Curle, Adam
  1961   *The Role of Education in Developing Societies*, Legon, Ghana University Press.
Cowan, L. Gray, James O'Connell and David G. Scanlon, eds.
  1965   *Education and Nation-Building in Africa*, New York, Praeger.
Dahrendorf, Ralf
  1959   *Class and Class Conflict in Industrial Society*, Stanford, Stanford University Press.
Dalan, Eleanor F.
  1961   *Higher Education in Africa South of the Sahara, Selected Bibliography*, Washington, American Association of University Women.
Dillon, Wilton S.
  1963   "Universities and Nation-building in Africa," *Journal of Modern African Studies*, 1, pp. 75–89.
Dumont, René
  1966   *False Start in Africa*, New York, Praeger.
Emmerson, Donald, ed.
  1968   *Students and Politics in Developing Nations*, New York, Praeger.
Evans-Pritchard, E. E.
  1940   *The Nuer*, London, Oxford University Press.
Fanon, Frantz
  1963   *The Wretched of the Earth*, New York, Grove Press.

Foster, Philip
  1965 *Education and Social Change in Ghana*, London, Routledge and Kegan
        Paul.
  1970 "The Nigerian Tragedy," *History of Education Quarterly*, 10, n° 2,
        pp. 255–265.
Goldthorpe, J. E.
  1965 *An African Elite*, Nairobi, Oxford University Press.
Hannah, A. W. and Robert R. Caughey
  1967 *The Legal Basis for Universities in Developing Countries*, Urbana,
        University of Illinois Press.
Hanson, John W.
  1968 *Education, Nsukka*, East Lansing, Michigan State University.
Harbison, Frederick, and Charles A. Myers
  1964 *Education, Manpower and Economic Growth*, New York, McGraw
        Hill.
Hilliard, Frederick H.
  1957 *A Short History of Education in West Africa*, Edinburgh, Thomas
        Nelson.
Ikejiani, Okechukwu, ed.
  1965 *Education in Nigeria*, New York, Praeger.
Kaunda, Kenneth
  1967 "Africa's March to Unity: The Role of the University," *Mawazo*,
        1, n° 1, pp. 3–5.
Kenyatta, Jomo
  1962 *Facing Mount Kenya*, New York, Vintage.
Klineberg, Otto and Marisa Zavalloni
  1969 *Nationalism and Tribalism Among African Students*, The Hague,
        Mouton.
Kuper, Adam
  1969 "The Troubles of Prospero: The Expatriate Academic," *East Africa
        Journal*, December.
  1971 "The New Men and the Universities in East Africa," *Bulletin, Institute
        of Development Studies*, 3, n° 3, pp. 18–26.
LeVine, Robert A.
  1966 *Dreams and Deeds, Achievement Motivation in Nigeria*, Chicago,
        University of Chicago Press.
Lewis, L. J.
  1965 *Society, Schools and Progress in Nigeria*, Oxford, Pergamon Press.
Lipset, Seymour Martin
  1966 "University Students and Politics in Underdeveloped Countries," *Com-
        parative Education Review*, 10, pp. 132–162.
Lloyd, P. C.
  1967 *Africa in Social Change*, Harmondsworth, Penguin.
Lloyd, P. C., ed.
  1966 *The New Elites of Tropical Africa*, London, Oxford University Press.

Marris, Peter
    1967   "What are Universities For?" *Mawazo*, 1, n⁰ 1, pp. 6–11.

Mason, Reginald J.
    1959   *British Education in Africa,* London, Oxford University Press.

Mercier, Paul
    1965   "Les Classes Sociales et les Changements Politiques Récents en Afrique
            Noire," *Cahiers Internationaux de Sociologie,* 38, pp. 143–154.

Michels, Robert
    1949   *Political Parties,* Glencoe, Ill., The Free Press.

Mosca, Gaetano
    1939   *The Ruling Class,* New York, McGraw Hill.

Nadel, S. F.
    1942   *A Black Byzantium,* London, Oxford University Press.
    1956   "The Concept of Social Elites," *International Social Science Bulletin,*
            8, pp. 413–424.

Nicol, Davidson
    1963   "Politics Nationalism and Universities in Africa," *African Affairs,* 62,
            pp. 20–27.

Nigerian Universities Authority
    1967   *A Plan for the Operation of the Nigerian University System Within
            the Framework of Twelve States,* Lagos, December.

Nimrod, R.
    1966   "Education and Political Development in Southern Nigeria," *Civilisa-
            tions,* 16, pp. 67–80.

Nyerere, Julius
    1967   "Education for Self-Reliance," *Africa Report,* 12, n⁰ 6, pp. 72–79.

Okafor, Nduka
    1971   *The Development of Universities in Nigeria,* London, Longman.

Pareto, Vilfredo
    1935   *The Mind and Society,* New York, Harcourt.

Peshkin, Alan
    1966   "Education in the Developing Nations: Dimensions of Change," *Com-
            parative Education Review,* 10, pp. 53–66.

Porter, Arthur T.
    1969   "African Universities: Our Needs and Our Priorities," *African
            Studies Bulletin,* 12, n⁰ 3, pp. 247–253.

Rimmington, Gerald T.
    1965   "The Development of Universities in Africa," *Comparative Education,*
            1, pp. 105–112.

Shils, Edward
    1961   "The Intellectual between Tradition and Modernity," *Comparative
            Studies in Society and History,* Supplement 1.

Smythe, H. H., and M. M. Smythe
    1960   *The New Nigerian Elite,* Stanford, Stanford University Press.

Sofola, J. A.
   1969   "Social Adjustment of Nigerian Students," *Ghana Journal of Sociology*, 5, n° 1, pp. 15–32.
Southall, Aidan
   1961   *Social Change in Modern Africa*, London, Oxford University Press.
van den Berghe, Pierre L.
   1965   *Africa, Social Problems of Change and Conflict*. San Francisco, Chandler.
   1967a *South Africa, A Study in Conflict*, Berkeley, University of California Press.
   1967b *Race and Racism*, New York, John Wiley.
   1968a "European Languages and Black Mandarins," *Transition*, 7, n° 34, pp. 19–23.
   1968b "An African Elite Revisited," *Mawazo*, 1, n° 4, pp. 57–71.
   1970a *Academic Gamesmanship*, New York, Abelard-Schuman.
   1970b *Race and Ethnicity*, New York, Basic Books.
Weiler, Hans N., ed.
   1965   *Education and Politics in Nigeria*, Freiburg, Rombach.
Wilson, John
   1963   *Education and Changing West African Culture*, New York, Teachers College, Columbia University.
Wise, Colin
   1956   *History of Education in British West Africa*, London, Longmans, Green.